THE GREAT DEPRESSIO

St. Louis Community College
at Meramec
Library

THE GREAT DEPRESSION IN EUROPE, 1929–1939

Patricia Clavin

THE GREAT DEPRESSION IN EUROPE, 1929–1939

© Patricia Clavin 2000

All rights reserved. No part of this book may be reproduced in any manner whatsoever without written permission except in the case of brief quotations embodied in critical articles or reviews. For information, address:

St. Martin's Press, Scholarly and Reference Division,
175 Fifth Avenue, New York, N.Y. 10010

First published in the United States of America in 2000

This book is printed on paper suitable for recycling and made from fully managed and sustained forest resources.

Copy edited and typeset in *New Baskerville* by Password, Norwich, UK
Printed in China

ISBN 0–312–23734–0 clothbound
ISBN 0–312–23735–9 paperback

Library of Congress Cataloging-in-Publication Data

Clavin, Patricia.
  The great depression in Europe, 1929–1939 / Patricia Clavin.
     p. cm.
  Includes bibliographical reverences and index.
  ISBN 0–312–23734–0 (cloth) – ISBN 0–312–23735–9 (pbk.)
     1. Europe–Economic conditions–1918–1945. 2. Depression–1929–Europe.
     I. Title.

HC240 .C518 2000
338.5'42–dc21

                                                                    00–030887

CONTENTS

TABLES

ACKNOWLEDGEMENTS

In the course of writing this book, I have accumulated a variety of financial, scholarly and personal debts. Financial support for the book came from a Keele University Research Award which gave me time free of teaching to begin work on the first draft. Research awards from the small grant schemes of the British Academy and the Nuffield Foundation, although made for an allied project, must be acknowledged as this archival research support inevitably fed into the content of this book too. Special thanks go to my colleagues at Keele, Malcolm Crook, an entirely selfless Head of Department, and Ann Hughes who read the entire manuscript as representatives of the intended undergraduate readership. Mark Roseman's contribution was a reliable, if not reliably funny, supply of jokes that lifted my spirits when studying the history of Europe in depression threatened to depress me too. Richard Overy gave a detailed and insightful commentary on the text. He did his best to save me from errors and some very convoluted prose. His scholarly and personal support have been invaluable. I have also benefited from discussing some of the issues raised herein with Susan Brewer, Larry Butler and Harold James who, with characteristic kindness, invited me to participate in a fascinating conference, 'The Interwar Depression in International Context', hosted by the Bavarian Historical Academy in May 1999. My thanks also go to Conan Fischer who generously shared with me some of his new research into the Ruhr occupation. Jeremy Black and Terka Bagley provided important editorial assistance and successfully shepherded the book to production. My final and greatest debt is to my husband Andrew for his unfailing patience, encouragement and good humour. This book is dedicated to him.

INTRODUCTION

The Crisis has caused national measures to breed virtual economic warfare. Failure to resolve this conflict of national economies will shake the system of international finance to its foundations, standards of living will be lowered, and the social system as we know it can hardly survive.
Report of the Preparatory Commission for the World Economic Conference, November 1932[1]

When this report was published in 1932, the European economy had been in the grip of an unprecedented crisis for three long years. The scale of economic and social disruption was remarkable. In the worst affected European countries – Poland, Germany and Austria – one in five of the adult population was unemployed, and industrial output had fallen by 40 per cent in three years. Although there were national variations, no part or Europe was left untouched. At its lowest point, the economic collapse saw levels of European trade fall to one-third of its value in 1929, while many of Europe's most respected banking houses and currencies teetered on the brink of collapse. Although by the late 1930s, some semblance of recovery was achieved, it was neither complete nor sustained. If it had not been for the outbreak of the Second World War, it is very likely the world economy would have entered a new 'Great Depression' after 1937.

The Great Depression had profound consequences for domestic politics and international relations. When politicians from moderate, centrist political parties (Liberals, Conservatives, reformist Socialists) failed to implement policies to ease the crisis, they lost out to extremist parties to the Right and the Left of the political spectrum. European diplomatic relations were also altered by the impact of the depression. The severity of the crisis pushed countries to protect their national interest above all else. By November 1932, every country in Europe

1

had adopted, or enhanced existing, measures to protect the national economy. The world was now divided into competing monetary and trading blocs, and this development, coupled with the new National Socialist government in Germany and Japan's descent into militarism, had profound implications for international peace. For Germany and Italy, economic nationalism was the first step on the road to the creation of empire. By 1935 it had become clear their nationalism was not confined to economics as Mussolini and Hitler began to assert territorial claims in the Mediterranean and Africa, although German ambitions were soon to be directed at eastern Europe. It was also clear that the depression had undermined diplomatic cooperation and the ability of other countries to resist the aggressors' demands. Indeed, the atmosphere of intense economic competition soured relations between countries who shared common diplomatic and strategic interests, notably Britain, France and the United States.

This book offers a concise narrative and analytical account of this unprecedented 'Slump', the term Europeans used in the 1930s for what the Americans called the 'Great Depression' – a name usually applied to the period 1873–96 in Europe. The phrase 'Great Depression' has been adopted in the title of this book to underline the commonality of the European and American experience in the depression and to reflect the fact that the Great Depression was a global economic crisis. The book does not attempt to give a comprehensive account of the economy of interwar Europe, but, instead, to answer four central questions: what were the origins of the depression? Why was it so severe? How was recovery effected and was it sustainable? And what were the implications of that recovery for political relations in, and between, nation-states?

One consequence of this focused and concise approach is that the discussion pays greater attention to the economic history of some countries than others. This asymmetry reflects the nature of the international economy, where the actions of large nations can have a huge impact on smaller ones. Countries with open and powerful economies, like those of Britain, France, Germany and America, inevitably played a bigger role in the history of the depression than lesser economies, or those that were isolated from the international economy, like that of Spain, by their choice of economic and/or foreign policy. None the less, the discussion does attempt to draw in all the regions, if not all the nations, of Europe. At the same time, it pays attention to national case studies and events, like Britain's

departure from the gold standard in 1931, which play a particularly
significant role in the history of the Great Depression.[2] Key policies
are also treated in greater depth in order to explain the economics
and/or to relate economic developments to the political and
diplomatic history of the period. The tables that accompany the text,
too, are intended to be illustrative, not comprehensive.

The book is written explicitly with non-economists in mind. The
troubled economic history of Europe in the interwar period is an
essential component in the political, social and cultural history of
the period. Yet thanks, in part, to the increasingly cultural bent of
political history and the impact of econometrics on economic history,
the political and economic developments of the period are often
treated entirely separately. The purpose of this book is to introduce
students of interwar Europe to recent research on the history of the
depression and help to reintegrate it into our understanding of the
political, domestic and international history of the period. The
explanations of the few technical terms used are not confined to a
glossary because it is easier to understand economic developments
and policies in their historical context. The page references in
parenthesis, which appear from Chapter 1 onwards, are intended as
a short cross-reference to the first time an important economic process
is discussed.

The material in the book is organized around central themes
(identified by chapter titles and subheadings), however the structure
remains chronological. This is because chronology is important in
understanding the origins of the Great Depression. In the 1920s it
was the perceived lessons of the history of the nineteenth century, as
an era of unprecedented economic growth and European dominance
in international trade, that shaped the policies adopted by statesmen
and economic advisors when it came to the task of European
reconstruction after 1918, sometimes with disastrous results. As
Chapters 1 and 2 demonstrate, the impact of the war and the postwar
inflation that spiralled into hyperinflation in much of central and
eastern Europe played a crucial role in shaping the public's
expectations of government and economic policy after 1924.
Thereafter, currency stabilization became the dominant, sometimes
the sole, preoccupation of government policy, while the rules
governing the behaviour of central banks were changed with
important consequences for events in the Great Depression. After
1929, the lessons of history, although sometimes redefined, continued

to play a central role in the evolution of economic policy. The strong determination to avoid inflation (currency chaos) remained, although the fear made little sense in the current context.[3] Nor could governments shake the habit of interpreting almost all problems as financial ones.[4]

Inevitably, the need to organize the discussion under neat subheadings also gives the misleading impression of order, when so much of the history of the Great Depression was about disorder. The origins of the Great Depression were political and social, as well as economic, in origin. They traversed national and regional frontiers. Nor did they respect the boundaries of 'time' delineated by historians. To give one important example: while the Wall Street Crash of October 1929 continues to mark the onset of the economic collapse, historians have long agreed that, for central and eastern Europe, at least, the Great Depression began in 1928 (some have even argued for 1927). They also accede that it was not the Wall Street Crash, but the policy response to it, which caused the depression to become 'Great'. Even within Europe, countries entered the Great Depression at different times: Britain was one of the first nations affected, France was one of the last.

The need for brevity has helped to shape this book's preoccupation with the relationship between politics and economics. There is much more that could have been said about the impact of the Great Depression on European society, although this remains a comparatively under-researched topic when set against what we know about the social history of the two world wars. The preoccupation with financial policy also reflects the present state of scholarship on the Great Depression. Some of the weaknesses which rendered the European economy increasingly vulnerable to the economic and financial shocks experienced after 1929, were the 'natural' consequence of agricultural and industrial changes already under way in the nineteenth century. The process of 'Americanization' also played a role. But in the past ten years or so, a new scholarly consensus has emerged regarding the causes of the Great Depression. The most important contribution has been a new appreciation of the role of the international gold standard. The discussion here has moved on from technical explorations of how this fixed exchange mechanism failed to operate as predicted, to examine the policy regime and assumptions underpinning the impact of the gold standard on distinct national economies as well as the international economy as a whole.[5]

New studies have underlined the degree to which the policy regime that accompanied the gold standard helps to make sense of many of the wrong decisions taken by governments in their first efforts to deal with the economic downturn.

Although the history of the depression has become a monetary history with the gold standard as a unifying theme, those who favour monetary explanations have not had it all their own way. The nature and extent of countries' commitment to the gold standard underlines the importance of policy (not markets) to the history of the interwar economy and to the power of domestic political priorities in shaping economic policy. Research into what has become known as the 'historical political economy' has been especially fruitful, although much remains to be done. This explores the political behaviour of different interest groups – landowners, tenant farmers, small businessmen, bankers, trade unions and so on – and their impact on the evolution of economic policy. Their behaviour helps to explain why one policy is chosen over another. These studies also draw out how the political, constitutional and social context of each country played a vital role in shaping each nation's distinct approach to the crisis.

In the Great Depression, European countries faced very similar problems and dilemmas, but opted to tackle them on their own. In the 1930s there was much talk of the need for international cooperation – now believed to be the most effective step to curing the depression – but very little action. The international system grew only more fragmented as the decade went on. The book's original contribution to current scholarship on the Great Depression is its attention to the international dimensions of the crisis. It explores what European countries understood by, and expected from, international economic cooperation. Here the discussion steps beyond the boundaries of Europe to ask how far the absence of American leadership in the international economy can explain the failure of international cooperation. The book draws on archival materials to illuminate how measures adopted to fight the depression affected countries' ability to prepare for the Second World War, as well as their impact on diplomacy more generally after 1931.

For much of the 1930s, the economic causes of war was a hot topic in intellectual circles. Papers were written, conferences organized and ideas exchanged in fervent debate. But the deliberations of 'experts' on the need for international cooperation to effect a thoroughgoing reform of national and international economic relations came to naught in the absence of genuine political support. As the book's conclusion demonstrates, the Second World War, and its aftermath, led to a revolution in the way countries interacted in the international economy. However, the origins of the Great Depression begin with the impact of the First World War on the European economy and it is to this history that we must first turn.

1

FRUSTRATED EXPECTATIONS, 1919–24

Almost all histories of the Great Depression dedicate their opening chapter to an assessment of the impact of the First World War on the world economy. This book will be no different. During the depression the causal link between the two events seemed obvious to most Europeans: 'Thirteen years after the war we seem to be back in the chaos that immediately followed it', as one best-selling British author put it in 1932.[1] In fact, the character of the Great Depression was quite different to the economic chaos after the First World War. The relationship between the two events had as much to do with how Europeans perceived the impact of the war, as with modifications wrought to the European economy by the war itself. Moreover, the most significant changes triggered by the war were the least visible – most dramatic was the redistribution of wealth in the international economy with the emergence of the United States as the leading financial power. A central question, that has preoccupied scholars examining the financial changes brought about by the war, was how far the United States recognized its responsibilities as the world's premier financial power and this theme will resurface in subsequent chapters. The war also unleashed inflation in the European economy. Europe's ensuing slide into 'serious' inflation, and in some cases hyperinflation, became one of the most important by-products of the war as governments became determined to 'learn the lessons of history' to secure and to maintain currency stability above all else. The conviction had critical consequences for European economic prospects in the interwar period.

Political changes caused or accelerated by the war were also an important, though until comparatively recently neglected, influence on economic and financial policy of interwar Europe. Domestic political change altered the context for, and expectations of, economic policy. So, too, did territorial modifications, notably in central and eastern Europe, brought about by the postwar peace settlements. These political developments, alongside bitter divisions over reparations and war debts, and the failure of the Paris Peace Conference to create an institutional framework to facilitate international economic cooperation, provided the ideal climate for economic nationalism to flourish.

The Visible Costs of the War

In 1919, managing the peace was the most immediate problem that faced the political leaders of a war-weary Europe. The situation was different from that after the Second World War, for few plans for postwar Europe had been drafted by the Allies during the First World War, yet the damage caused by the war to Europe's economy was substantial. The loss of life and monies were amongst the most easily quantifiable of its costs. The number of deaths and casualties was unprecedented and at the time many believed this would be a serious impediment to Europe's economic recovery, particularly as fighting continued in Russia, Poland, Hungary, the Balkans and Turkey long after the armistice was signed on 11 November 1918. Estimates as to how many men were killed or wounded in battle vary. Historians calculate total losses of between 9.4 and 11 million people, a figure which amounted to over one per cent of Europe's population in 1913. Expressed nationally, Germany lost 2 037 000 men, Russia 1 811 000, France 1 398 000, Austria-Hungary 1 100 000 and Britain 723 000. Only American casualties were substantially less, with 114 000 killed in action.[2] These military losses posed a greater challenge to the postwar economic order when expressed in relation to the labour supply: France and Germany lost around 10 per cent of their male workforce; Austria-Hungary and Italy over 6 per cent; and Britain around 5 per cent. Civilian deaths and injuries, the majority through malnourishment and disease (particularly in the wake of the 1918 influenza epidemic which killed more people than the war proper), were more severe and more difficult to calculate, although all were agreed that the figures for the casualties of war were much higher than ever before.

Amongst the victorious nations, the sacrifices made by France in pursuit of victory have drawn the most attention from economic historians. Its demographic costs were disproportionately high, as was the damage to its infrastructure and industry. In all, some 15 000 km^2 of France were laid waste, and damage to French municipal, private and industrial buildings amounted to $17 000 million, the lion's share of a world loss of $29 960 million. Much of the remaining physical damage wrought by the war was concentrated in western Russia, Poland and Belgium. In Belgium no aspect of life was untouched by war. Four years of occupation and warfare on Belgian soil had brought industry to its knees. Here the Germans had gone as far as to partially dismantle Belgian factories and transfer their equipment to Germany.

None the less, Europe's population and infrastructure was to recover comparatively quickly. In the west of Europe the population rose from 170.2 million in 1920 to 189.9 million in 1940, although there was only slight growth in France and Austria, and a static population level in Ireland. In the east and south the statistics were more impressive. In eastern Europe the population rose from 84.4 million to 102.4 million between 1920 and 1940, and in the south it increased from 68.6 million to 84.9 million over the same period. The impetus for the rise came from the continued popularity of marriage at an early age and improvements in health-care. Although it may seem heartless to say, the slaughter of the trenches was not a serious impediment to Europe's economic recovery, particularly as the character of European population migration had also begun to change. Scots, Germans and Russians, for instance, no longer migrated in large numbers to the United States as the open door of New York gradually edged shut. The end of large-scale emigration, however, had important implications for structural adjustment in Europe since it was no longer possible to export regional or national unemployment problems to the United States and Australasia, for example, as it had been in the nineteenth century.

It proved easier for European governments to recover from the loss of life than the loss of important markets for trade, newly distorted patterns of industrial production and the financial costs of the war. The disruption to established patterns of trade was the most damaging, for it was hard to reverse the changes and poor trade performance made it all the more difficult for Europe to recover the financial costs of the war. Most dramatic was the arrival of new competitors outside Europe, notably the United States and Japan. Both countries had demonstrated strong domestic, and some export, growth before 1914. However, the preoccupation of Europe in supplying and waging the First World War, coupled with the limited involvement of the United States and Japan in the conflict, presented American and Japanese manufacturers with an unrivalled opportunity to supply belligerent Europe. Both the newcomers experienced a trebling in their export levels, although this was not sustained in the 1920s. More importantly, the United States and Japan penetrated markets overseas previously dominated by Europe's leading powers. American exports to Latin America rose by more than 75 per cent in 1916. In Asia, Japan built on its expertise in silk manufacture to considerably expand its textile exports to the United States and China and, for the first time, to export textiles to Britain (this was particularly bad news for the textile manufacturers of Lancashire). During and after the war, Japan also expanded its capacity to produce its own iron and ships – developments which hit Britain in particular – chemicals and machinery.

On the whole, countries which had industrialized to some degree, including European neutrals like Denmark, were better placed to take advantage of the temporary indisposition of the industrialized European belligerents than the developing world: manufacturing production in Latin America and the British Empire, with a few exceptions, grew at modest levels throughout the war. But it was not all good news for Japanese and American manufacturers. The expansion of their heavy industries only served to contribute to a global problem which had already begun to plague Europe before the outbreak of war, and was exacerbated by its prosecution and the short-lived postwar boom of 1919–21: global overcapacity in the production of ships, iron and steel, and coal. The character of Europe's domination of the world economy in the nineteenth century contained within it the seeds of problems which were to germinate in the 1920s with, for example, the reliance on heavy industrial output. Many European plants became increasingly uncompetitive, notably in Italy where, from the beginning, industrialization was tightly bound up with the state's determination to establish a heavy industrial base for strategic purposes.

Writing in 1949, Arthur Lewis calculated the delay to Europe's long-term expansion caused by the war by comparing the increase in output between 1913 and 1929 with what it would have been if pre-1913 trends had continued without a break. In the period 1881 to 1913, European output of manufacturing industry rose, on average, by some 3.25 per cent a year. If the rate of increase had been maintained throughout the war, the level attained in 1929 would have been reached as early as 1921. So, following this reasoning, one might argue that Europe's industrial development was set back some eight years as a result of the war. Of course, such an approach is a simplistic one as there is no place in this model for variables, other than world war, which might have accelerated or interrupted economic growth. One such variable was the changing composition of trade. Even without the war, European manufacturers would have faced the challenge of adapting production to supply the growing demand for consumer products which pointed the way to future economic growth.

The arrival of American technology, products and methods of industrial organization underlined the fact that the century of European economic dominance had closed, to be succeeded by the 'American century' – a development which generated both attraction and resistance across the Atlantic. By the 1960s and 1970s, historians made greater play in their accounts of the structural difficulties (the decline of the so-called heavy industries) which plagued the European, and most notably, the British economy. In most of central and eastern Europe, moreover, there was a pronounced recession in consumer goods for most of the 1920s – economists call it a transition crisis – as investment and demand remained concentrated on producer goods, despite the fact that before 1914 factories making consumer goods enjoyed higher levels of investment and productivity than heavy industries. But more recent research argues that changes in the structure of the world economy were not especially rapid in this period, particularly when compared to the rapid pace of economic change after the Second World War, and that a considerable upturn in consumer goods production would not necessarily have helped the European economy. Rather, the western European and, especially, American economies grew more vulnerable to depression because of the direction rather than the pace of change. Consumer industries, like the motor car, pointed the way to the future, but politicians and economists had yet to learn that the consumer market is notoriously fickle. In times of economic uncertainty people were, and are, unlikely to spend. This was especially so in the interwar period when most consumer goods were bought on hire purchase. So the new consumer industries (sometimes called 'sunrise' industries to contrast with the 'sunset' industries like shipbuilding) made western Europe and the United States more, not less, vulnerable to depression.

There was also the interdependence of the European economy, which was a source of potential weakness as well as strength. Before the war, half the total recorded trade of the world was made up of exports and imports into and out of seven European countries. Germany was Britain's main industrial rival inside Europe, surpassing its production of coal, pig iron and steel, but Britain was also Germany's best customer, and Germany came second only to India as a customer for British goods. British coal was being burnt in Berlin when war broke out, at the same time as blast furnaces were being built in France with the help of German capital and the Germans were making chemicals in Russia. Just as this interdependence was an important element in securing unprecedented rates of economic growth in Europe before the First World War (and after the Second World War), it also meant that each country's economic and financial vulnerabilities were burdens shared by all European powers.

For many in Europe, notably in central, southern and eastern Europe, wartime changes in primary production were more important than the challenges faced by industry. Again, some of these changes were under way before war broke out. The introduction of refrigerated ships meant that cheap meat, from Argentina for example, could now be exported to European dinner tables. Primary producers in India and Latin America all saw the levels of their primary exports rise. To the north, the opening up of vast acreage in Canada, the United States and Russia to wheat production, ever more sophisticated methods of intensive farming, and a decline in the demand for cereal products in preference to dairy ones, all meant that European farmers, many if not most of whom were smallholders, became increasingly un-competitive. Indeed, the disruption to Russian and eastern European cereal production during the mobile war on the Eastern Front prompted producers elsewhere to increase production: Canadian acreage was increased 80 per cent during the war, Argentine meat exports grew by 75 per cent, while, most spectacularly, the value of American exports of wheat and flour more than tripled and meat exports rose tenfold between 1913 and 1918.

The new pattern of industrial and agricultural trade was not an insuperable problem to western European governments after 1918 provided they could export enough manufactures to pay for the higher level of agricultural imports and provided they could appease their own agricultural communities. That they failed to do so reflected both the growth of non-European manufacturing competition and the considerable fiscal and monetary problems confronting Europe in the postwar period. In eastern and southern Europe the problem was even more acute with over 70 per cent of the population earning a living from farming. At the time, many argued that these changes in world agriculture production were temporary. Diagnosing the problem is at least half the battle in formulating effective economic and monetary policy. Only as time wore on did it become clear that the war had helped to shunt industry and agriculture onto a new track.

Many of the war-induced, or exacerbated, changes to the European economy were obscured by the short-lived postwar boom between 1919 and 1921 which sent out misleading signals to policy-makers. The boom depended both on pent-up consumer demand – products which had been unavailable during the course of the war could once again be bought now that rationing was removed and production resumed – and spending on government orders to replace war-damaged goods like ships and railways. Smaller firms, less well placed to maintain their stocks than their larger rivals during wartime, also took the opportunity to restock their inventories. The speed and vigour of the postwar boom took many commentators by surprise as they had anticipated a serious recession after the war when military expenditure was curtailed and servicemen demobilized. European policy-makers were temporarily blinded to many of the difficulties confronting them by the spending boom, but most were troubled profoundly when, in the summer of 1919, inflation in all European countries began to rise steadily.

The 'Invisible Price': The Financial Costs of the War

From war's end to the beginning of 1921, Europe experienced the helter-skelter of deflation and stagnation, followed by inflation and boom, before the collapse of prices and production. Between 1871 and 1900 many of the world's leading powers joined the gold standard. It was a fixed exchange mechanism (currencies were convertible into gold at a fixed rate) that helped to regulate currency movements and to facilitate the exchange of currency and goods between countries (p. 41). However, at the outbreak of war, European powers (and later the United States) had acted to constrain the effects of gold convertibility on their national currencies. In other words, although countries like Britain and France theoretically remained on the gold standard to control inflation and to maintain confidence in the currency, limits were placed on the export of gold and extensive controls were introduced to prevent prices from rising. The moves were essential to managing the war economy.

In 1919 most governments, in their anxiety to return national economies to their comparatively prosperous peacetime footing, quickly removed most, if not all, price controls without restoring the gold standard. Indeed, some countries, like Britain and Germany, first officially abandoned the gold standard in 1919. The growth of inflation was inevitable without constraints to control it in the climate of want and dislocation which accompanied war's end across Europe. The fact that many goods were in short supply also encouraged prices to go up. From the spring of 1919 until the spring of 1922 prices rose by 50 per cent before falling again. Some historians see the increase in inflation as a major contributing element in the postwar boom and bust, while others regard the upsurge in inflation as purely incidental. More important than determining the contribution of the monetary expansion in 1919–20 to the postwar boom, however, was the revelation to working- and middle-class men and women across Europe that their governments faced profound problems managing their national currency, regardless of whether it was the world-renowned pound sterling or the newly established Yugoslavian dinar.

The impact of the postwar inflation – its origins, its myriad impact on different European societies, particularly those of continental Europe, and lessons drawn by leading politicians, economists and the electorate – was very important in helping to shape economic and monetary policies during the subsequent decade. Eichengreen, the leading economic historian of the depression, has placed monetary elements at the centre of his account of the Great Depression. These factors are complex, and sometimes unnecessarily forbidding to the non-economist. Yet they are fundamental to the breakdown of the world economy ten years after the war ended and their origins lie in an obvious place: the cost of financing an unprecedented war waged between industrialized powers.

In the First World War, a 'war of attrition' which came to be a 'war of exhaustion', each government was forced to borrow money and to tax its subjects more than ever before. Prior to 1914 governments made few plans for financing the war, and those plans which were laid sometimes had unfortunate side-effects. Most notably, as international tension mounted in the wake of the 1908–12 Balkan Wars, the German Reich, France and Russia all accumulated reserves of gold as a war chest. In the 18 months preceding the declaration of war, these three countries increased their stocks of gold by $360 million, largely at the expense of the United States. Until the First World War the United States was a debtor, and so was vulnerable to outflows of capital and gold overseas when its foreign investors, mostly Europeans, chose to sell their American investments. Therefore, throughout 1914–15, as both the Entente and Central powers competed for the sympathy of the American public and the support of the United States government, the exchange rate of the US dollar took a battering as European governments and investors sold their US assets in exchange for gold. So much for economists' claims for the 'efficiency of markets', the spectre of war in Europe had caused the value of the US dollar to fall! This did not endear Europe to the United States, although the situation soon changed dramatically as the prerogatives of the war economy determined that Europe's creditor nations sacrifice assets to win the war, and the United States became the world's leading creditor. By the end of the war, European countries were vulnerable to American investors selling assets in, for example, sterling, the German mark and the French franc. Moreover, many of Europe's investments overseas were not recovered. Amongst the most famous were French loans extended to its ally Imperial Russia, which by 1914 totalled 9 000 million francs. An investment lost, not at war's outbreak, but in the wake of the Bolshevik Revolution in 1917; the sum amounted to over one-quarter of all French investment overseas.

An essential corollary of the need for Europe to raise capital overseas to finance the war effort, was the difficulty all governments faced in raising sufficient money at home to pay for domestic expenditure and imports. The issue of raising taxation was a sensitive and complex one in all European countries. The political question of how the taxation burden should be distributed across society was especially difficult – the origins of the French and American revolutions were potent testimony as to the risks to political stability if the imposition of taxation was mismanaged. The fact that no belligerent foresaw, let alone planned for, the financial consequences of war, and the fact that it was to last until Christmas 1918, not Christmas 1914 as had been widely predicted in 1914, helped to wrong foot efforts at financial management completely during the first three years of the conflict. French attempts to increase revenue from taxation were particularly poor. The level of income from taxation actually fell (by 60 per cent in 1914) from its prewar levels until June 1917, when the law introducing income tax, passed in 1914, finally came into effect. In the meantime, indirect taxation became very important to financing the French war effort. Matters were little better in Germany where there was the widespread expectation, as in France, that the enemy would be made to pay for the war as they had in 1871. In August 1915, in words which were later to haunt him, the German Finance Minister, Karl Helfferich, claimed, 'the instigators of this war have earned this dead weight of billions'.[3] The issue of taxation was also problematic because the two-tier structure of Reich government prevented the Kaiser's war cabinet from levying direct taxes. The *Länder* (states) did increase rates of direct taxation – they doubled during the war – but their contribution to the overall finance of the war remained small. Instead, the state had to rely heavily on indirect taxation. In 1915 Helfferich agreed to levy taxes on tobacco, beers and spirits, rail fares and postage, but strongly resisted Socialist demands for taxation to be extended to more lucrative areas like war profits or mortgages. By 1917, however, German profit tax was fixed at 60 per cent.

Britain seemed better placed than the remainder of Europe to pay for the war. The principle and practice of levying income and direct taxation was well established, and in November 1914 Chancellor of the Exchequer David Lloyd George doubled income tax and supertax rates (by 1918/19 British income tax was fourfold its 1913/14 rate). There were also considerable hikes in indirect taxation, too, with duties up on beer and tea, and, in a historic departure from Britain's cherished free trade, custom duties were extended to most imports except desperately needed supplies of food.

In many instances, however, government preferred to shy away from the practical and political problems of taxation by raising loans at home and abroad. Britain and, later, the United States were able to finance their wartime budget deficits with long-term loans. They, like all the belligerents, also issued government bonds – war bonds (in Britain) and Liberty Loans (in the USA) to the public. France, too, slid into further debt at home and overseas. The volume of French national debt appeared to grow more slowly than that of Britain and Germany, but this was only because the French state, like its Russian ally, was heavily in debt before the war broke out. (The overall level of French national debt was high because of the reparations imposed by Germany as a consequence of the Franco-Prussian war.)

In Europe the growth of the German domestic public debt surpassed all others. By 1918 it had grown tenfold from its 1914 figure. The government's inability to raise sufficient capital from taxation and its inability to secure credit overseas to buy essential imports (aside from a mutually beneficial financial and trading relationship with Sweden), threw the government on the mercy of the bond-buying German public and the domestic banks. By 1918 the German imperial debt was 156.1 billion marks; it had been 5.4 billion in 1914. Moreover, the German government was not the only one in search of credit: German merchants, industrialists and small businessmen needed it too. As a consequence the Reichsbank discounted a growing quantity of Treasury bills, and the volume of currency in circulation grew at an alarming pace. All European belligerents printed money with insufficient reserves in order to pay for the war effort, although most deployed controls, like the rent and debt moratorium introduced in France in August 1914, to prevent price rises. Even so, during the war countries experienced considerable inflation – in France the wholesale price index rose from 100 in 1913 to 340 in 1918 (over the same period the British price index rose to 227, Italy's to 409, Germany's to 415 and Hungary's to the spectacular figure of 2287); in Russia (between 1914 and 1918) wages only doubled, while prices rose by around 500 per cent, causing serious hardship.

In 1918, despite these indicators, most politicians and financiers in Europe (aside from those in civil war wrecked Russia) believed that the tide of inflation and exchange rate depreciation could and would be reversed at war's end. So long as the political climate fostered this optimistic view, bond holders across Europe, whether citizens or subjects, were prepared to hold onto their government bonds and roll over the state debt (buy new bonds) when their existing bonds matured. However, if and when confidence was disturbed, the consequences were dramatic: members of the public acted quickly to sell their bonds, forcing the state to transfer some its scant cash reserves to the Treasury from the central bank, thereby boosting inflation, and, at the same time, limiting the power of the government and central bank to control it.

Even more important to the transformation of postwar financial relations than the growth of taxes and monies loaned by citizens and subjects to their governments was the wholesale liquidation of foreign assets and the accumulation of foreign liabilities. All the European belligerents had lost loans and bonds invested overseas when war broke out, and the Entente powers accumulated large debts to the United States during the course of the war. Britain and France, in particular, borrowed heavily in America to fund their victory in Europe and they, in turn, lent some of their resources to subsidiary allies. Britain, for example, lent heavily to members of the British Empire; France lent money to Italy. In much the same way that imperial rivalries had paved the road to war, imperial alliances helped to extend the financial consequences of the war around the globe. Although some recent accounts argue that the levels of European indebtedness triggered by the war have been overestimated, the levels remain considerable. France borrowed heavily from Britain (around $3 billion dollars) and the United States ($2.9 billion dollars), and Britain borrowed from the United States ($4.3 billion dollars), while imperial allies, as well as European ones like Russia, Italy, Belgium and Serbia, borrowed from Britain and France. Bereft of empire and without powerful and wealthy 'friends' overseas, Germany and Austria-Hungary relied less on international credit and, as we have seen, had little choice but to extend the tax burden, particularly to war profits.

Who Will Be the World's Banker?

By 1919 it was clear that the emergent manufacturing strength of the United States was dwarfed by its new found financial supremacy. Before the First World War, Britain had been the world's banker – it was the primary source of overseas investment capital. In the second half of the nineteenth century, sterling's pre-eminence as a trading and reserve currency, alongside Britain's promotion of free trade, had helped to foster stability and growth in the international economy. In 1914, regardless of new rivals on the international stage, Britain was the only European country that was selling more outside Europe than inside it. British purchases of European manufactures and other products were paid for in cash, and with overseas produce. Britain exported capital to the rest of the world as well as manufactures. In 1914, 43 per cent of the world's foreign investment in 1914 was British, with Germany providing 13 per cent and the United States only 8 per cent. British financial strength was reinforced by other features of its economy. It was Britain's role as a free-trading country with a dominating interest in the world's commodity markets and a highly flexible money market that appeared to allow the gold standard to operate as automatically as possible. On the eve of war, the 'automatic nature' of the economic system contrasted with the contrivance of the political and, especially, the diplomatic system with its alliances and secret pacts.

After the First World War, the United States replaced Britain as the world's greatest creditor nation, with an important, though different, role from that of Britain in supporting the world economy. The emergence of the United States as the 'world's banker' and the dramatic redistribution of assets and liabilities which provoked this change, had profound consequences for the world economy as a whole, and the operation of the international monetary system in particular. While American foreign liabilities (debts) stood at $7 billion in July 1914, by 1919 they had fallen to $4 billion. At the same time, America's portfolio of foreign securities grew from $1 billion to $3 billion, and the US government held foreign public obligations (bonds) worth around $12 billion. The change is still best illustrated by Alfred Sauvy's 1965 table.

Inter-Allied Debts at the End of the First World War (in billions)

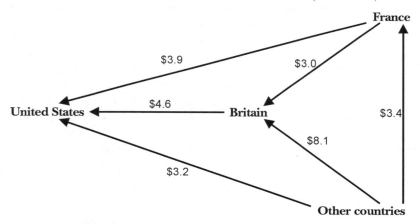

Schematic taken from Alfred Sauvy, *Histoire économique de la France entre les deux guerres*, vol. 1: 1918–31, 1965, p. 169.[4]

It was not just this changing balance of monetary power that was to be important to the history of interwar Europe. So, too, was the differing character and mission of the central banks. Unlike the traditions and employees of the Bank of England, the Federal Reserve System, bankers employed by the new American 'central bank' set up in 1913, lacked experience and was much more influenced by domestic considerations than the questions of international finance that dominated the policies of the cosmopolitan Bank of England. Equally significant was the huge growth in the volume of short-term, as opposed to long-term, credit which the exigencies of financing wartime trade demanded – a trend which strengthened New York's claim as the leading centre of financial transactions and undermined that of London. The need to finance the payment and transportation of imports from the United States to Europe increased the amount Europe owed to the United States and made global capital movements, and therefore the economy as a whole, more vulnerable to any monetary and economic shocks.

In the scramble to secure resources to pay for essential war and postwar imports, governments were also forced, albeit reluctantly, to part with some of the gold reserves kept in their central banks for the peacetime management of currency; much of the gold found its way across the Atlantic. Here Britain was a notable exception. The Bank of England's gold reserves actually went up during the war, boosted by the patriotic donations of gold from its citizens and newly mined gold from the Empire. Of the main European belligerents, France, Belgium, Germany and Italy lost gold during the war, a trend partly offset by the accumulation of foreign reserves in place of gold, to finance trade. The 'invisible' costs of the war – indebtedness and the changing balance of monetary power – were to be exaggerated by further intra-European indebtedness generated by the peace treaties signed at the Paris Peace Conference. Both wartime and peacetime debts were to have important consequences for international monetary stability and diplomatic relations between the world's leading economic actors in the interwar period.

The Peace Settlements

The peace treaties, negotiated for the most part at the Paris Peace Conference in 1919, had a number of important consequences on an international and national level for the future health and stability of the European economy. The first blow to the prospects of international cooperation on every level, including economic, came with the American Senate's failure to ratify the Covenant of the League of Nations and the Treaty of Versailles. As is well known, the American President, Woodrow Wilson, worked hard to foster European support for his, at first vague, plan for an organization which would safeguard international peace and serve as a forum for a more orderly management of the world's political, economic, financial and cultural affairs. But enthusiasm in the United States for such an international commitment soon began to wane as Congress and public opinion grew increasingly fearful of repeated involvement in European squabbles, and suspicious that the League would cripple America's cherished freedom to take independent action whenever, and however, it pleased. The American rejection of the League had a profound impact on European-American relations. Thereafter, regardless of whether economic or diplomatic issues were under discussion, the European powers claimed that American 'irresponsibility' in November 1919 gave them ample reason to distrust the United States. The League now fell under Anglo-French domination and the failure of collective security prompted a knee-jerk reaction from France, who, throughout the 1920s, resolutely maintained that the Paris treaties could not be revised. Aside from the lingering distrust of American 'words', French determination to constrain German economic restoration, and the absence, until the completion of the Treaty of Locarno in 1925, of a stabilizing security umbrella beneath which the European economy could recover created a poor context for European economic relations.

There were other limitations to the postwar order, some directly related to economic provisions of the peace settlements, others born of the political change triggered by the war or political arrangements fostered by the conference. Most striking was the talk of returning to prewar 'normalcy' when it came to economics. It contrasted sharply with the widespread desire to move away from the 'international anarchy' of the prewar period in diplomatic relations. The freedom of nineteenth-century, unregulated business transactions was hailed as the economic ideal. The rush of governments to remove wartime monetary and trading restrictions to return to 'business as usual' was evident across Europe. The immediate consequence, as we have seen, was to fuel the postwar boom. Moreover, as all Europe soon discovered, the interdependence of the world economy in the nineteenth century, founded on a system of economic specialization designed to meet European interests, was not the same in the postwar period. New industrial competitors outside Europe, coupled with the European dependence on non-European parts of the world for food, as well as the raw materials of industry, underlined both the relative 'decline' of European power and the growing interdependence of the world economy. So, too, did the expansion of new networks of loans and debts.

Yet despite the growing interdependence of the world economy progressing apace before the outbreak of war, there was little attempt to enshrine notions of economic interdependence, for times of disaster as well as for times of growth, into the Paris Peace Settlement. True, the League of Nations established an Economic and Social Council to collect data on the performance of national economies, as well as on the world economy as a whole. But there were no organizations dedicated to promoting international economic and monetary cooperation at the highest level and to act as a brake on economic competition between nations. As Keynes admonished, there was a 'failure' on the part of all the peacemakers, notably 'Britain and the United States to apprehend that the most serious of the problems which claimed their attention were not political or territorial but financial and economic'.[5]

The League's lack of economic muscle was apparent as early as 1919 when it carried insufficient clout to provide economic aid to the emerging nations of central and eastern Europe, and it was the Americans who stepped in. Flexing its new economic muscles, the American government created the American Relief Administration which supplied food to the value of $1145 million, spearheaded by Herbert Hoover, the United States Food Administrator and a future President of the United States. As 'Food Regulator of the world', Hoover was enthusiastic in his duties, but he was never above giving a political twist to American aid. Thus, he offered the carrot of food to capitalist Austria, while granting none to a Hungary which stood under threat of communist domination and he arranged deals which cut across wartime divisions: Austrian machines for Polish eggs and ham; Yugoslav wheat for Polish gasoline; and German coal for Polish potatoes. The strong political dimension to American economic relations with Europe persisted throughout the interwar period, further complicating American troubled efforts at international cooperation.

The priority of securing national economic recovery, popularly perceived as distinct and separate to the health of the international economy as a whole, received an important boost from political changes during and immediately after the war. From Ireland in the west to the Baltic Republics in the east, a far greater proportion of Europe's population had the right to vote than ever before. In some countries, the extension of democracy was an obvious consequence of the war as the empires of central and eastern Europe gave way to new nations and new democracies. The new countries were broadly defined as both nation-states and parliamentary democracies. Dedicated, as far as practicable, to the notion of self-determination, the Paris Peace treaties marked the triumph of nineteenth-century notions of nationalism. This had a number of consequences. As the Italian Prime Minister, Francisco Nitti, put it: the 'keen contest of nationalism, land-grabbing and cornering of raw materials renders friendly relations between the thirty states of Europe extremely difficult.'[6] Some countries, like Hungary, Austria and Germany were even prohibited from cooperating with one another. This was important because the national boundaries of the new nation-states of eastern Europe divided economically integrated regions of the former Austro-Hungarian Empire. Economies already struggling with an altered resource base and the costs of establishing new currencies – in the case of Yugoslavia a transportation system also had to be built from scratch – were prohibited from, or chose to reject, economic cooperation with their neighbours.

The new nation states of Austria and Hungary were obvious losers in the peace settlement. The punitive Treaty of Trianon, for example, left Hungary with only 32.7 per cent of its prewar territory and 41.6 per cent of its prewar population. It also had to pay reparations. With the loss of its domestic market and access to large quantities of domestically produced cereals, the Hungarian food processing industry (dominated by flour milling) struggled to regain its pre-1914 dominance that had seen it lead the world's agriculture exporters – it had even exported milling technology to the United States. Hungary needed to cooperate with its neighbours to make the most of its remaining economic assets. The fact that central and eastern European countries took a national rather than a regional approach to their economic difficulties was the second way the nationalism embedded in, and fostered by, the peace treaties damaged economic prospects. Indeed, the emphasis on self-determination served to legitimate all sorts of nationalist demands that threatened the prospects for peace and economic growth in postwar Europe. It was even more harmful than the dislocation to trading routes and the disruption to established links between producers and consumers. In countries that perceived themselves to have been on the losing side of the peace settlement, there was also a persistent pessimism, damaging the psychological backdrop to economic recovery, and a growing determination to revise the peace treaties.

A third feature of the Paris Peace settlements which influenced policy formulation, both prior to and during the depression, stemmed from the constitutional consequences of self-determination. In an effort to protect the rights of the around 30 million Europeans who became members of new nation states, but who were not members of the ethnic majority, most new, and some established, democracies in Europe opted for constitutions based on proportional representation: Germany, France, Belgium, Italy, Norway, Finland, Poland, Latvia, Estonia and Czechoslovakia. These constitutions were modelled on the third French Republic with its dominant legislature and weak executive. The move offered a limp guarantee of political representation to ethnic minorities and to established political elites, notably the landowning class who feared the advent of the working classes in political life, but it also had important consequences for party politics (and consequently policy) in a time of economic crisis.

In the 1920s proportional representation made it easier for smaller political groups to compete against larger and more established rivals, encouraging a proliferation of political parties, and spawning minority and coalition governments across Europe. Today's political scientists offer conflicting interpretations of the impact of proportional representation for economic policy: its supporters argue that proportional represent-ation enhances political stability by encouraging compromise by parties who wish to avoid toppling the government; its critics argue that proportional representation increases the likelihood of political instability and policy deadlock by investing a large number of interest groups with the power to bring down a coalition or minority government if it attempts to pursue a policy inconsistent with the group's interests. The history of interwar Europe demonstrates that there is an element of truth to both claims. Put simply, the most important factor in determining whether a coalition or minority government survived was the importance of the topic under dispute. If trouble blew up over a minor issue, it was in the interests of the coalition partners to cooperate, for the costs of bringing down the government and the subsequent political instability were likely to be much higher than any political gain. But for most of the 1920s, many European governments were in dispute over fundamental questions like the level and distribution of taxes, and the extent and character of government welfare provision (particularly when governments were preparing for a return to the gold standard). Germany, Belgium, Italy, France, Poland and Hungary all struggled to form stable governments in the face of disputes over who should pay for, or benefit from, government spending.

In 1922 Italian democracy's failure to survive distributional conflict resulted in a fascist government led by Benito Mussolini, who claimed that such distributional friction was damaging to 'national vitality' and that there was a 'best way' to organize political and economic life. For most of the 1920s, the political systems of Germany, Belgium and France survived because the postwar inflationary crisis (coupled with exaggerated fears of a communist coup), both compelled and facilitated political cooperation amongst leading coalition members. This was to change after 1929. Moreover, conflict over economic policy was heightened in Germany and France, in comparison to countries like Czechoslovakia and the Netherlands, because of the magnitude of the task of reconstruction and because social groups were defined predominantly on economic lines (particularly given the contribution of economic success to the legitimization of the nation-state forged by Bismarck). In Dutch and Czechoslovak politics, by contrast, religious and ethnic questions were every bit as pressing as economic ones, which meant that in times of crisis, economic issues could be traded against religious or ethnic issues to preserve the power of the governing coalition.

In 1919 it was not just the structure of the many European political systems that had changed, the extension of the franchise was equally important. Even in established parliamentary systems like Britain, the voting age was lowered and extended to women for the first time. This peacetime concession was preceded during the First World War by the absorption of the working-class representatives into government. After the war there were, for the first time, European governments dominated by members of working-class or peasant parties. The changing composition of governments also altered society's expectations about what politics could achieve. As the war had forced the nation state to demand new sacrifices of all its citizens in the name of loyalty, governments, in return, were prompted to extend obligations to their peoples and make changes to the political system which such promises implied. The new political legitimacy accorded to members of the non-revolutionary working class underlined a comparatively new feature of political life: government was assigned responsibility for maintaining a continuing level of economic activity and political legitimacy was increasing dependent on its ability to manage the domestic economy to the collective advantage of its electorate (or at least its participating majority).

The new responsibilities carried by the state were reflected in the growth of modern bureaucracies across Europe advancing, amongst other things, modern notions of education, policing and communications. In Germany, for instance, the number of state employees in all levels of administration rose 66 per cent between 1907 and 1925. It is irrelevant here to consider how far these changes were sponsored by prewar or wartime developments, what is important, however, is that they cost money and that the extension of political representation, coupled with the growing link between political legitimacy and economic success, served to strengthen the primacy of national economic solutions over (as opposed to in conjunction with) international economic consideration. When the tension between national and international economic obligations defied an apparent solution, as in the Great Depression, then national remedies quickly took priority.

The peace treaties concluded in Paris also worked to underline divisions between European powers which ill-served their economic interests. Although the nineteenth-century 'age of imperialism' appeared to have passed, the peace settlement worked to extend the territorial boundaries of the British and French empires, and while the so called 'White Dominions' (Canada, New Zealand and Australia) secured self-government, the popularity of notions of imperial economic interdependence among right-wing political groups continued. The growth of the British and French empires was a further source of tension in international economic relations. Indeed, in the 1920s the diminution of Germany's status as a 'great' power (witness its exclusion from the League), coupled with the 'cuts in its national flesh', the loss of over 27 000 km^2 of territory containing around seven million people, served both to break up established economic links within Germany, and to limit German custom and influence in central and eastern Europe.

Reparations and War Debts

It was, of course, for its treatment of Germany that the Treaty of Versailles came to be vilified as the origin of both the Great Depression and the Second World War. The first real salvo against the Treaty from amongst the Allied powers came from John Maynard Keynes, the British economist, with his devastating and highly influential critique, *The Economic Consequences of the Peace* (1919), written after he had resigned from the British delegation in Paris. Keynes argued that the 'honest and intelligible' French policy to weaken Germany, which had gone uncurbed at Versailles, posed a tremendous danger for the 'perpetual prize-fight of European politics'.[7] Central to his criticisms of the peace was the reparation settlement imposed on the new German republic. A 'qualifying note' of the 14 points – the basis of the November 1918 armistice – had demanded 'compensation' from Germany 'for all the damage done to the civilian population of the Allies and their property by the aggression of Germany by land, by sea, and from the air'. At the same time, the Americans insisted there would be 'no punitive damages' and refused to have anything to do with European demands for reparations. The war-dominated election campaigns of Georges Clemenceau and David Lloyd-George soon upped the ante in response to the 'pressure' of public opinion. Turning a deaf ear to American concerns for the economic and political consequences of their demands, both Britain and France promised 'to make Germany pay'. Of all the powers assembled in Versailles, the United States stood alone in refusing to demand these 'tribute payments', but it was powerless to prevent its former Allies from succumbing to popular pressure to secure an indemnity covering the full costs of the war.

The negotiators in Paris balked at settling a final figure for German reparations and after an initial German payment of £1000 million in gold, passed the responsibility onto a newly established Reparations Commission, which reported in 1921. In 1919 Keynes was convinced that the reparation demands, whether in goods or money, profoundly threatened the economic and political stability, not just of Germany, but of all Europe. However, his apparently prophetic claims that the reparation settlement would lead Europe 'into deeper misfortune' should not be taken at face value. The contribution of reparations to the origins of the Great Depression was neither direct nor solely confined to the economic sphere.

Crudely put, the reparations saga which ran until 1932 contributed to the origins of the depression in four principal ways. The first studies of the history of reparations in the 1920s highlighted French determination to render Germany economically and militarily toothless with 'financial clauses ... to be enforced by French bayonets'.[8] But more recent histories of the economic and political impact of the reparations *imbroglio*, notably by Schuker, Marks, Maier, Trachtenberg and Jeannesson, underline the 'honest' and 'intelligible' features of Allied reparation policy in general, and French reparation policy in particular. These accounts explore the contradictions and difficulties which beset the calculation of Germany's reparation burden. After all, although the Weimar Republic was plagued with 'temporary difficulties', the long-term prospects of the German economy still seemed excellent: the former German Reich had been the fastest growing, most advanced industrial economy in Europe in 1913. Indeed, paying reparations, in money and in kind, as officials in the British Treasury pointed out at the time, ran the risk of strengthening and expanding Germany's productive capacity while weakening the manufacturing competitiveness of those countries receiving reparations.

The negotiators at Versailles had been mindful of the problems confronting the new republic, and were not solely intent on placing the prospects of German economic recovery forever in debtors' 'paper shackles' as alleged by Keynes; the interim payment was only £1 billion, while the instalments due to the Reparations Commission 'demanded less than met the eye'.[9] Despite its remit, the Commission was unable to 'scientifically determine' German 'capacity to pay' and so settled on a figure of 132 milliard gold marks (around $33 billion). This sum, in turn, was divided into segments and the London Schedule, as the 1921 commission's report became known, provided for two bond series totalling only 50 milliard gold marks, on which the German government would have to pay interest and amortization (the redemption yield on the bonds). The Reich remained legally responsible for an additional 82 milliards of bonds (known as C-bonds), but this 'funny money' had more of a political than economic significance. The Reparation Commission intended to sell these bonds on the open market only if and when Germany was prosperous enough to service them. In the meantime, the European allies hoped to use them as 'bargaining chips' to persuade the Americans to reduce, and ultimately abolish, war debts. According to Schuker's calculations, under the London Schedule Germany would have had to pay reparations amounting to 5.37 per cent of 1921 national income. Therefore, it was not the volume of German reparation payments, but their interaction with the already complex, sometimes confusing, and certainly damaging network of debt created by the war that marks the first contribution of reparations to the origins of the depression.

The second damaging consequence of reparations and war debts was their impact on European-American relations. In his appreciation of French policy, Trachtenberg demonstrates the essential link between French reparation demands and the American commitment, or rather lack of it, to French economic reconstruction and security. In private, the French government expressed its willingness to reduce its reparation demands significantly if the United States extended reconstruction loans and honoured its promised guarantee to protect France from foreign aggressors as set out in the Covenant of the League of Nations. It is an interpretation that deflects criticism of French policy back onto President Wilson's unwillingness to make concessions to Congress over the Covenant and the latter's subsequent rejection of the Treaty of Versailles. Even more important to the origins of the depression, although also contingent on American policy, was the vexed question of inter-allied debts.

Almost from the outset it was clear that the European Allies hoped to trade any reduction in the volume of German reparations for a reduction in their debts to the United States. In the years that followed, the United States' 'moral' stance of refusing to demand reparations, yet insisting on the collection of, in President Calvin Coolidge's words, the 'hired money' loaned to Europe rang increasingly hollow. The American refusal to recognize any link between Germany's ability to pay reparations and the capacity of Britain, France, Italy and others to make their war debt payments bedevilled European-American diplomatic and economic relations. The burgeoning postwar debt nexus, compounded by the Dawes Plan after 1924 in which almost everyone owed something to someone, undermined efforts to achieve European currency stability. It also meant it was essential that European trade recovered so that debtors could earn sufficient foreign currency and gold to repay their debts. But levels of international trade were slow to revive after the war and, to their chagrin, European governments found the United States more interested in exporting to, than importing from, Europe. Throughout the 1920s, the United States maintained a protectionist wall of 33 per cent (average tariff rate) around its domestic market to politically appease powerful farmers and industrialists. In short, the Americans prevented the Europeans from selling enough to pay back their debts. The interaction between international indebtedness and protectionism was the third means by which reparations and war debts undermined the stability of the world economy.

The final, and arguably most important, contribution of reparations and war debts to the fragility of the interwar economy is the complex story of its relationship to the stability of the international capital market and the impact of foreign loans to Germany in the wake of the 1924 Dawes Plan (p. 37). By the end of 1922, Germany had made only one full quarterly payment, and then exasperated its creditors by manoeuvring 'from one partial moratorium to another until it declined to provide any further payments'.[10] Germany's main excuse was a good one: the inflationary spiral and the accompanying budget deficit which emerged during the war, was now growing beyond the government's capacity to control it. But the German government's assertions that reparations caused the German descent into hyperinflation were misleading.

Inflation and Hyperinflation

The history of the Weimar Republic's 1922–23 inflationary crisis is the best documented of the waves of inflation that engulfed much of Europe from 1919 until 1924. However, France, Italy, Belgium, Czechoslovakia, Hungary, Austria, Poland, Germany and the USSR all experienced serious inflation. In Britain the 1919 inflation rate of 50 per cent was actually one of the lowest in Europe. In central and eastern Europe there were giddy hyperinflationary rates of over 2000 per cent per annum. The consequences of the inflation were more important than its causes to the origins of the Great Depression. In most of these countries the source of the inflation lay in the war-induced expenditure begun in 1914, and which, through civil war, did not end until 1922 in Poland and the new USSR.

In the immediate postwar period, the task of reconstruction and, in addition, serious conflicts over which interest groups should benefit from government spending rocked European society. These political disputes generated a political tolerance to the burgeoning levels of inflation. In November 1919 there was a German 'revolution' and coincident left-wing revolutions in Hungary and Austria. Politicians across the political spectrum feared triggering further social unrest through tax hikes, their anxieties compounded by the desperate need for resources to pay for veterans' pensions, health-care schemes and postwar reconstruction. Governments did not just 'lavish' money on the working classes to cool their revolutionary aspirations. The Weimar Republic, for instance, also gave generous compensation payments to firms that lost assets as a consequences of the territorial changes imposed by the Treaty of Versailles. Across Europe on matters of economic policy, government was no longer perceived as an 'impartial umpire' – it appeared to have become 'a player deeply enmeshed in a game of social and economic bargaining'.[11] The inflationary crisis increasingly laid bare the mechanics of state bargaining between different social groups (like workers and industrialists) as newly democratic governments, in particular, struggled to preserve social peace. Allowing inflation to rise, enabled governments to sidestep awkward political choices and helped to ease the distributional conflict in society.

Weaknesses in the national and international political economy also encouraged inflation to rise. In the face of widespread shortages, the swift removal of price controls and rationing by governments led to inflation. So, too, did bureaucratic ineptitude, which meant that even when taxes were levied they were not always collected. Italy, for example, had high tax rates, even in comparison to Britain and Germany, but the tax burden was poorly distributed and administered. An important, international cause of inflation was the fact that in the period from 1919 to 1920 British and American loans for European reconstruction also declined, triggering additional short-term borrowing and advances from central banks in Italy and France (the Bank of France believed the cost of the loans would be recovered through German reparation payments) and therefore more inflation. Most dramatic was the role of the Hungarian central bank. From August 1921 until December 1923 in Hungary, where the state had little hope of foreign loans to aid

Table 1.1   Industrial Disputes in Germany

	Number	Workers involved (thou)	Days Lost (thou)
1918	532	716	1453
1919	3719	2761	33 083
1920	3807	2009	16 755
1921	4445	2036	25 874
1922	4785	2556	27 734
1923	2046	1917	12 344
1924	1973	2066	36 198
1925	1708	1115	2936
1926	351	131	1222
1927	844	686	6144
1928	739	986	20 339
1929	429	268	4251

Source: B. Mitchell, *European Historical Statistics*, 1750–1975 (2nd edn, London, 1978), C3.

postwar reconstruction, the Hungarian State Issuing Bank succumbed to political and economic pressures to become a leading source of inflation. The bank was not only the chief source of credit to cover the government's growing budget deficit, it also became the leading creditor to the private sector: in December 1923 of the 931 000 million crowns worth of notes in circulation (an increase of over 200 000 per cent on the 1913 level), over 60 per cent of these were commercial bills discounted by the bank. In Germany, too, the Reichsbank played a vital role in discounting the state's floating debt to finance the republic's growing budget deficit. In some instances rivalries between financial institutions also fed the inflationary spiral. During the collapse of 'Liberal Italy', the harsh economic and financial environment of the postwar era exacerbated the long-standing conflict between officials of the Treasury, the Bank of Italy in Rome and financiers of the largest commercial banks in Milan. The bitter arguments between these financiers were dubbed the 'war between the banks' and soured cooperative efforts to control the monetary crisis. The role of banks in the inflation also had long-term implications. The involvement of central banks, notably the Reichsbank, severely damaged their reputations as the guardians of sound currency and led to the imposition of tough restrictions on their ability to discount bills. In Germany this was to have important consequences for the Weimar Republic's ability to fight economic recession in 1928 and world depression after 1929 (p. 125).

As inflation swept Europe, the link between budget deficits and monetary chaos was obvious and it became the single most important lesson drawn by politicians for their economic policy. In particular, it was the famed German hyperinflation which began in the summer of 1922 and culminated in the autumn of 1923 that lingered in the minds of politicians and electorates across Europe. But, in reality, the inflationary episode was a complex and varied ten-year-long affair which, until the collapse into hyperinflation, brought benefits as well as costs to many countries. On a political level, allowing inflation to rise appeared to be the 'least worst' solution to the challenge of maintaining social peace when governments in central and eastern Europe were threatened by revolution. On an economic level, there were also benefits. In Hungary 600 new enterprises were launched between 1921 and 1923. For established manufacturers, the inflation created the opportunity to accumulate assets and pay off loans which had depreciated as a consequence of the inflation, enabling the mechanical and engineering industries to grow by 108 per cent. Industrialists in Germany, too, benefited from the fact that foreign speculation on the mark during the first stages of the inflation created easy credit, and that the subsequent inflation and hyperinflation wiped out German domestic debt and a substantial portion of its foreign debt. It also enabled exporters to capture new markets.

Reparations provided the international dimension to the inflationary crisis. Historians of Weimar's foreign and economic policy contend that Chancellors Wirth (1921–22) and Cuno (1922–23) deliberately postponed balancing the budget and allowed the Weimar economy to succumb to hyperinflation in the hope that the chaos would, in Cuno's words, 'deal with' (read abolish) 'reparations first and clean up the tax problem afterward'.[12] International tension grew as the German Foreign Office misleadingly claimed that it was reparation payments that were generating the inflation. The French took the opposite perspective. Prime Minister Raymond Poincaré's decision to invade the Ruhr in January 1923 sprang, in part, from the French conviction that the Weimar Republic was using the inflationary chaos to undermine the reparations settlement, or as the Germans put it, to put reparations 'on a businesslike' basis. Power politics also came into it. The invasion stemmed from Poincaré's determination to exploit the reparations issue to build on the political and military predominance France had secured after the war to alter permanently European power relationships to favour French, not German or Anglo-Saxon, interests.

The French and Belgian invasion of the Ruhr in January 1923, and Cuno's policy of 'passive resistance', quickened the pace of the now hyperinflationary crisis until the mark collapsed (in January of that year one US dollar bought 7260 marks, by December it bought over 4210 billion marks). The occupation came to an end in September 1923 when Chancellor Gustav Stresemann called a halt to German passive resistance and acted quickly to terminate the inflation. But France suffered too. Poincaré's piecemeal invasion of the Ruhr triggered fierce new inflationary pressures on the French franc. The crisis was only brought to a timely halt by Anglo-American intervention with the Dawes Plan and new proposals to establish financial stability in Europe. The French move into financial crisis was intimately linked with the fate of Germany. After 1919 successive French cabinets and the financial markets buried their heads in the sand over France's growing budget deficit, apparently persuaded by the argument that German reparations would fund French reconstruction. The weakness of the French franc in the aftermath of the 'ruhrnation' of Germany, however, made it plain that the French taxpayer and the international capital market were far more important than reparations to the reconstruction and future health of the French economy. Between 1920 and 1925, levels of indirect taxation had doubled and direct taxation had tripled in France. By 1927 the French government had spent twice as much on national reconstruction as it had received in reparation payments from Germany.

Although it took another two years for France to secure a *de facto* stabilization of the franc, politicians drew some important lessons for future economic policy from the Europe-wide inflationary crisis of 1922–23. Before 1923 the French public, most notably the central bank, the educated public, the press and the overwhelming majority of the parliament, were already hostile to inflation with a zeal approaching 'religious fervour'. After 1923 hostility towards inflation became the *leitmotif* of economic policy across all of Europe. As Feldman makes clear in his richly detailed study of the political, psychological and sociological impact of the German inflation, the political consequences of the inflation profoundly undermined support for the republic, particularly among white-collar workers and *Kleinrentier* who saw their pensions, savings and wages rendered worthless. In France, as in Germany, army officers, magistrates and senior civil servants traditionally lived from their private sources of income and did not rely on their wages. The scale of the postwar inflation changed all this and one consequence was that during the 1920s the question of what we now call 'public sector pay' became a subject of vociferous public debate. The size of the tragedy is best revealed at the level of the individual. In 1923, one sixty-year-old German man who had lived very comfortably before the war on the interest from assets of 60 000 marks, was working for 15 gold pfennigs an hour to try to support his three children: inflation had wiped out his assets. In the same year, the permanently disabled and orphaned daughter of a civil servant watched her 112 000 mark inheritance turn to worthless paper. In despair, she twice attempted suicide (p. 58).

Regardless of some of the economic benefits generated by the inflation, politicians and their constituents across Europe, whether to the left or right of the political spectrum, came to regard the impact of inflation as little short of calamitous. The collective memory of the German people conflated the experience of the inflation with that of the hyperinflation. This produced what Holtfrerich has called 'Inflation psychosis' (a distorted, purely negative view of inflation) that infected all of Europe to varying degrees and had a profound influence on efforts to secure monetary stability in the 1920s and for policy-making as a whole in the depression.

Whatever the short-term benefits of the inflationary crisis may have been, across Europe most people believed that the inflation had almost destroyed the European economy, while the resumption of American loans and the introduction of the gold exchange standard saved it. Yet to historians like Boross and Holtfrerich, the postwar inflation granted an important boost to efforts at reconstruction and, in the case of Germany, provided an opportunity to roll back the gains made by labour during 1918–19 that the Republic's political economy could not sustain. Once currency stabilization was under way, big business secured a realignment of the German state to favour industry rather than workers: working hours were increased, the high level of real wages fell and the distribution of taxation now favoured the interests of industry over the working class. As Walter Rathenau, a leading industrialist and former Economics Minister, put it in 1919, a longer working day 'gave exactly the number of hours needed to pay reparations'.[13]

However, in the longer term the hyperinflation had very damaging political and economic consequences. It generated a deep fear of budget deficits amongst politicians and the public at large, and it made any kind of monetary and fiscal experimentation in the Great Depression politically, technically and psychologically very difficult, if not impossible. As will be shown in Chapters 2 and 3, it also did serious damage to the prospects of European economic and financial recovery. Not only did rampant inflation destroy governments which were unable to manage the political and social conflict generated by the crisis, like that of Italy in 1922, the inflation undermined the sovereignty of European governments on a symbolic level too. The emblems of the nation decorated and distinguished each national currency, and just as the value of every note declined with inflation, so, too, the sovereignty of the state was visibly devalued and eroded. During Weimar's hyperinflation, local government authorities and industrialists printed over 2000 different 'currencies' to pay their workforce.

In the short term, the destruction of the mark also created new difficulties for Germany and the European economy as a whole: in Weimar there was an acute shortage of capital in the factory and in the home; the French franc became increasingly unstable and investment was also in short supply; the vulnerable eastern Europe economy, enduring its own inflationary crisis, suffered from the decline in German demand, and so on. The European economy urgently needed an injection of capital and a successful initiative to stabilize its currencies, and the Americans held the key to both.

The Dawes Plan, 1924

The Dawes plan marked the re-entry of the United States into European affairs. Unlike 1917, this time American intervention was much more in keeping with the traditional economic focus of US foreign policy. Before and during the Ruhr crisis American bankers had been sympathetic to calls for American investment in Europe, and particularly in Germany. Given that there were no international organizations from which to borrow money, and that traditional lenders in countries like Britain, France and the Netherlands tried to husband their financial resources for their own national and imperial needs, American money was central to the stabilization of postwar Europe. This did not mean that British bankers, the dynamic and dominant force in international financial affairs in the nineteenth century, were unimportant. In 1923 and 1924 Montagu Norman, governor of the Bank of England, took a prominent role in encouraging American involvement and defining the parameters of the proposed loan to Germany, although his plan to have the new German currency linked to the pound rather than the dollar (via gold), thereby putting sterling rather than the gold-linked dollar at the heart of the European economy, came to nothing.

The machinery of international economic cooperation in the 1920s was much like that of the nineteenth century. It was dominated more by bankers and businessmen and less by treasury or finance ministry representatives. This was especially true of the United States, where private bankers assumed a powerful role in the creation of the Federal Reserve System, the American 'central bank' in 1913, and the formulation and implementation of American foreign policy after 1919. The national and international power of private businessmen and financiers, like Thomas Lamont, a Director of J. P. Morgan's bank, reflected the spirit of the 'roaring twenties' and the desire of the American business community to secure the European market for American exports. The spirit of competition as much as cooperation motivated American policy in Europe. As the international lawyer and future Secretary of State, John Foster Dulles, bluntly put it in 1922, by depreciating its currencies, 'Europe … is destroying its ability to buy from us, and is increasing its ability to compete with us.'[14] Later, the contribution of financiers to American foreign policy was to be criticized for reflecting the 'selfish' interests of rich bankers and for creating initiatives, like the Dawes Plan, beyond the control of the US State Department and the White House. At the time, however, the 'informality' of the new American commitment to European stability suited successive Republican administrations and American public opinion, all of which were wary of political entanglements in Europe.

In 1924 American financiers were adamant that Germany would not be able to secure international loans unless the burden of reparations on its economy was reduced and European diplomatic relations, notably between Germany and France, were put on a more stable footing. These considerations had an important impact on a conference convened in London that year to resolve the reparations crisis. To put the minds of the bankers at rest, the London conference revised the volume and manner of collection of Germany's reparation payments and, as Schuker has demonstrated, markedly weakened France's ability to enforce the collection of reparations in future. It also redistributed the European balance of power favouring Germany over France, and, once the loan was in place, determined that the Allies would service Germany's loans even if it defaulted on reparations.

The Dawes Plan did not address the issue of Germany's overall liability. Instead, in the words of the committee of experts who reported to the Reparation Committee, the plan offered a schedule of annual payments to restore confidence and thereby facilitate a final settlement. Conditions imposed within the plan demanded that Germany balance its budget, and that the Reichsbank be reformed to act as a bank of issue of notes on a stable basis in relation to gold. In short, the Dawes Plan meant that Germany now had to commit itself to the gold standard. The plan also included a foreign loan of 800 million marks (£40 million) paid directly to the German government. The loan was regarded as essential to the plan's success: partly as foreign currency reserve for the Reichsbank, partly to finance deliveries in kind during the initial period of German recovery, and in general to create an atmosphere of confidence, a necessity if the Dawes Plan was to succeed.

At first the majority of American bankers were pessimistic about the plan's chances of success, although they had secured much of what they had wanted at the London conference to give Germany 'a sporting chance'. Lamont wondered whether Dawes had done enough to give 'the investor in German bonds to suppose that he will have a fair run for his money'.[15] But the sceptics were soon proved wrong. Under the skilful stewardship of Stresemann and the currency commissioner of the Reichsbank who was to become its most controversial director, Dr Hjalmar Schacht, the stabilization of the Reichsmark was highly successful. Both thereby secured their reputations as the men who had brought stability to Germany and Schacht's considerable ego was undoubtedly massaged by such popular tributes as: '*Wer hat die Rentenmark erdacht? Der Demokrat, der Doktor Schacht?*' ['Who invented the Rentenmark? The Democrat, Dr Schacht'].[16] The stable currency and favourable interest rates, prompted foreign investors to purchase huge volumes of German bonds – worth around $2.6 billion – over 60 per cent of which were purchased by Americans, while British and Dutch investors each took around 12 per cent of the German bonds. Thanks to this deluge of foreign credit under the Dawes Plan, Germany was able to meet its reparation obligations in full, although each year there was always a slight default as a 'point of honour'. By 1930 the German economy was hostage to a debt of some 26 billion RM (independent of its reparation liabilities), which accounted for one-third of total investment in the German economy (its national income was around 75 billion a year). At the same time, German loans became an important part of the American economy, as 20 per cent of the American capital market comprised foreign bonds sold in the United States. As we shall see, the pattern of hyperinflation followed by an unhealthy dependence on foreign capital was repeated elsewhere in central and eastern Europe.

American investors were attracted to the high rates of interest and the apparent security of the investment opportunities. Germany's iron and steel industry, the mostly stagnant textile industry, agriculture and municipalities like the City of Cologne, all used their past reputations (rather than their current profit records) and their political muscle to secure a disproportionate share of US dollars; the municipalities alone secured around 12 per cent of all long-term loans issued by the United States. Therefore, despite the flood of Dawes Plan capital, a large proportion of the investment was not productive. The American administration was not ignorant of the dangers of the situation. It issued stern warnings to American investors that their German bonds remained subject to 'the political risks of Europe' and that they would be better off putting their money into 'good safe American securities paying smaller rates of interest'.[17] It also attempted to cool German hunger for American credit, but largely without success.

Six years after the end of the war in Europe, policy-makers had a far better idea of the shortcomings of the European economy than they had in 1918. While the physical losses of property and of life had begun to fade from the agenda of political and economic policy, the challenge of industrial and agricultural change and the financial upheaval engendered by the war were now more prominent and persistent difficulties. Less apparent, but no less troubling, was the fact that the machinery to facilitate international economic cooperation was weak. But foremost in the minds of policy-makers and the general public alike was the devastating impact of currency instability. Inflation had taken a terrible toll on economic prospects and political confidence. However divided workers, industrialists, farmers and professional classes may have been in their political allegiances, by 1924 across Europe the voting public were united in the conviction that the inflation spiral needed to be stopped. Public opinion chimed with views expressed by the majority of politicians, treasury officials, central bankers, economists and industrialists, who all longed for a return to the established and prosperous trading world of the nineteenth century. Indeed, now that the formidable potential of the German economy was ranged behind a gold-linked mark, Germany's economic competitors believed it imperative to stabilize their currencies also. The quest for currency stability became the *leitmotif* of economic policy, with profound consequences for both the parameters of governmental economic policy and Europe's ability to recover from war, revolution and recession.

2

THE PRICE OF STABILITY, 1924–29

The successful stabilization of the German mark made it all the more important for other European powers to stabilize their currencies. In theory there was some temporary advantage to be had for currencies that had continued to depreciate, like sterling and the French franc, against the stable German mark when it came to competing against German companies in export markets. In practice, however, the political and economic uncertainty that continued inflation brought to domestic economies pushed monetary stability to the top of the political agenda. Governments were now highly motivated to squeeze inflation out of the national economy because of the threat it brought to their power and the damage it wrought to finances and trade. Mustering sufficient political will was important, but so, too, was adopting the right financial and economic policies for tackling the crisis.

As European governments vainly struggled to squeeze the genie of inflation – uncorked by war – back into its bottle, speculation almost exclusively centred on the question of when European currencies would be 'returned to gold'. The expression was shorthand among politicians and economists to refer to the widespread desire to resurrect the international gold standard. This was a fixed exchange rate mechanism that had facilitated international exchange transactions with apparent ease and success in the second half of the nineteenth century – the greatest period of expansion the world economy had yet known. During the 1920s, perceptions of how the gold standard had functioned in the past differ considerably from the way that today's historians and economists now believe it operated. This is important because misread lessons of history led governments and central banks to hold incorrect assumptions about how a reconstructed gold standard system would work and what it could achieve.

In the last 20 years economic historians have undertaken considerable research into the impact of monetary policy, much of it focused around the history of the gold standard. European Union plans for monetary union have also helped to revive interest in this system of fixed exchange rates. Most economic historians now agree that the character and operation of the interwar gold standard, more than any other single contributory element, exacerbated many of the problems of the European economy in the 1920s, turned the 1928/29 recession into the deepest depression of the modern world and helped to transmit its effects around the globe. Given all this, it is important to return the gold standard to the political, economic and social context of the 1920s so that we can fully understand its huge appeal.

The Ghost of Gold Standard Past

From the 1870s, the German Reichsmark, the French franc and the US dollar were the key currencies in the gold standard system. There were many other participants, notably Russia, Canada, Belgium and South Africa, but some important countries remained outside the system, such as China, Spain and Austria-Hungary. Significantly, the United States operated according to the conventions of the gold standard from 1879, joining it officially in 1900, but failed to establish an institution which resembled a central bank until 1913 when it set up the Federal Reserve System. In Europe, most, if not all, members of the gold standard boasted some kind of independent central bank which spent considerable energy trying to maintain the value of the national currency. Joining the gold standard made the work of the central bank easier. But although the gold standard was a 'system' for monetary exchange, it was neither as uniform in participation nor as automatic in its operation as came to be believed in the 1920s.

The defining feature of the gold standard was that the currencies of participating nations and empires were stabilized at a fixed exchange rate in terms of gold. This was said to be the 'gold content' of, for example, the pound sterling, the Russian rouble or the US dollar. Gold was the most appropriate monetary base because it had the reputation, undeserved as it turned out, for holding its value steady. From 1879 until 1914, the gold value of the pound was just over 486 per cent of the US dollar, therefore the gold value of the pound was just over $4.86. Surprisingly, in the nineteenth century there was very little debate about how to determine the value of a currency in relation to gold. Nor was there any attempt to correlate the strength of a currency with the stability and strength of the economy in the way there is today. Rather the gold value of a currency largely reflected the volume of gold reserves held in central banks and gold coin in circulation. Membership of the gold standard was supposed to ensure that the paper currency was convertible into gold coin or gold bullion on demand, in unlimited amounts and at a fixed price. Not only was a currency 'on gold' supposed to be fully convertible into gold (all central banks also held foreign currency reserves to supplement their gold cover), currency or other valuables also could be moved freely across national borders. Governments did not impose regulations on the movement of money across their national borders. There were no exchange controls and while a country was a member of the gold standard, it was possible to buy and sell its paper currency, convert it into gold and move it anywhere in the world. The gold standard, in effect, provided a multilateral clearing system (like a huge bureau de change)which meant that money earned or borrowed in one country could be invested or spent somewhere else. This was an important feature of the system as countries rarely imported the same amount as they exported to one another and it greatly facilitated the expansion of international trade and investment. The total value of international trade, estimated at £800 million in 1850, reached a figure of around £2800 million by the end of the 1870s, and rose to £8000 million by 1913.

Exchanging one national currency for another when both came with a solid-gold guarantee removed the element of uncertainty from international currency transactions. In the international economy of the nineteenth century, this had two immediate advantages. Firstly, fixed currency rates helped to stabilize prices and thereby, amongst other things, simplified international trade deals. The gold standard gave buyers confidence in the price agreed for a sale of goods and investors confidence in their investment. Secondly, fixed exchange rates eliminated the risk of competitive devaluation from international trade to make one country's exports, those from Germany, say, cheaper than those of its competitors. But by the 1920s, the reputation of the gold standard's ability to hold prices steady had itself become inflated. In the nineteenth century, prices in Britain (the most 'solid' member of the system) often went up and down, influenced by things like yield of the harvest. But in the climate of uncertainty after the First World War, the fact that prices in the year 1900 were recorded as being the same as those of 1800 was enough to convince many that resurrecting the gold standard was the solution for rampant inflation and all sorts of other economic problems, both at home and abroad.

The fact that the exchange rate was fixed also meant that managing the exchange rate could not be an instrument of national policy. This did not necessarily mean that membership of the gold standard system put the interests of the international economy before the national economy. After all, consumers and producers alike benefited from the stable prices. More importantly, the *automatism* attributed to the system was supposed to keep member countries' rates of inflation in line with each other. The thinking behind this assumption was first laid out by the English philosopher David Hume in 1752. In his forbiddingly titled theory, *The Price-Specie Flow Mechanism*, he argued that if a country experienced a higher rate of inflation than its trading partners, its external balance of payments would slide into deficit as domestically produced goods became more expensive than foreign imports. To meet the resulting deficit, the country would have to both export some of its gold reserve, and raise interest rates to attract money from abroad. This, in turn, would cause domestic money to contract and inflation to slow down.

In fact, economic historians now agree that there is no evidence to suggest that this automatic mechanism operated in the nineteenth-century gold standard system. Instead, many historians' accounts as to why currencies were able to remain on gold, and the particular contribution of the system to the expansion and stability of the world economy, centre on the behaviour of the Bank of England and the strength of the pound sterling, then the world's premier currency. One of the most eloquent and authoritative expositions of the British role as 'lender of the last resort' is to be found in the work of Charles Kindleberger. He argues, in what has become known as the theory of hegemonic stability, that the smooth functioning of an open world economy was dependent upon the world's leading power increasing the level of its lending whenever activity in the world economy turned downward. In the nineteenth century Britain fulfilled its responsibilities as hegemon by lubricating fluctuations in the world economy through its foreign loans – in 1914 Britain owned more than half of the world's international investments, a total of some £4 billion. According to

Kindleberger, the international economy of the interwar era became so unstable because 'Britain could not' act as the lender of the last resort, while the 'United States would not'.[1]

In the nineteenth century British loans overseas were made both more attractive and more secure by the strength of Britain's commitment to the gold standard, and the exchange rate of the pound was virtually unassailable because Britain had a very strong balance of payments. This positive balance was due mainly to the large amount of invisible earnings made on investments overseas (interest paid by lenders on exported capital and charges for financial services like insurance) and income from the colonies paid to Whitehall for running the empire. Providing financial services overseas was a profitable business for the City of London. It also meant that it had the funds and the inclination to invest even more money abroad, usually on a long-term basis – terms which suited the debtor and the stability of the world economy. In the 1920s the gold standard was believed to have contributed greatly to the unrivalled growth in the nineteenth century of both the British and the international economy.

However, as historians and economists have studied both the operation of the gold standard and sterling in greater depth, it has become clear that Britain alone did not 'manage' the world economy during the latter decades of the nineteenth century. Rather, the Bank of England was dependent on assistance from its colleagues in other central and commercial banks, like the all-important help provided by the Banque de France and the Reichsbank during the financial crises of 1907. When it came to managing the international economy, it was more appropriate to speak of a *Pax Europa* than a *Pax Britannica*. In times of crisis, all three governments and central banks had cooperated together (sometimes other European banks were involved too), each drawing on the resources of the other in order to sustain the convertibility of key currencies, like the German mark and sterling, on the gold standard. Their cooperation stabilized the monetary system and the international economy. Teamwork, not hegemonic leadership, was what made the gold standard work, and as in any successful team, the role of the team-captain – in this instance the Bank of England – was important to determine strategy and to coordinate the efforts of its members. In times of crisis, it was the Bank of England which signalled the need for coordinated initiatives and helped to determine what those actions should be. Typically, a country losing gold had to raise its discount and interest rates, while other countries had to lower theirs and make funds available to the country in crisis to top up its bank reserves, strengthening the central bank under attack. In times of quiet, British leadership was equally important, though less pro-active, because the Bank of England's rates were shadowed by central banks across Europe: a reduction or increase in British interest rates was mirrored in Berlin, Paris and Rome.

There were no international institutions, like the Bank of International Settlements (which began operations in 1930) or the International Monetary Fund (set up in 1944), to facilitate this cooperation between different governments and bankers. The channels of communication were informal meetings held in banks, hotels and clubs. Indeed, international cooperation was only pursued when it matched the 'selfish' interests of each nation-state. But governments and banks did share a common set of assumptions about how the economy worked and the function of central banks within it. These assumptions included, above all else, an unquestioning determination to defend the national currency's fixed rate on gold by maintaining a positive balance of payments and a balanced budget (revenue from taxation more than covering the sums spent by government). The main weapon to manage domestic equilibrium and gold standard membership was to raise or lower the bank's rate; in other words, the discount rate (the terms on which the bank rediscounted bills for other financial institutions). These three policies made up what was known as orthodox economic policy. It was an inflexible, deflationary (or in modern parlance dis-inflationary) policy which was sensible enough in a time of plenty – when, for example, inflation threatened to eat away economic growth – but it was to prove disastrous after 1929 in the time of want. It was not just membership of the gold standard that had important consequences for the national economy; equally, if not more important, was the impact of the policy regime designed to keep the national currency convertible with gold. There was no real appreciation by governments or voters that high interest rates discouraged investment and trade or that they encouraged unemployment. In the eyes of bankers and politicians, what was good for the gold standard was good for the interests of the economy at home.

As a number of thought-provoking studies have made clear, the gold standard functioned so smoothly before the war because of the *credibility* of countries' commitment to it, coupled with their ability both to *coordinate* the management of their national currencies by following the same set of economic rules, and to *cooperate* together on an international level to defend the gold parity of a currency under pressure. (Although Flandreau has recently argued that cooperation was limited and the least important element in the smooth functioning of the system.[2]) In fact, in the nineteenth century it was because the British, French and German commitment to the gold standard was so unwavering and their policy responses so consistent that the credibility of their gold parity was rarely tested. It is testimony to the potency of the myth of the gold standard past that its value, and the reasons as to why it appeared to have operated so successfully in the past, remained unquestioned on both sides of the Atlantic until the 1930s.

But by 1919, the world in which the gold standard operated, and the way in which it operated, was radically different to that of 1914. The economic balance of power had swung firmly in favour of the United States and away from Europe; the experience of the war and the political changes effected in its wake, as we have seen, also made the state more responsive to domestic pressure to provide employment opportunities. Changes in the economies of industrial Europe now made unemployment a commonplace, whereas before 1914 it had been a comparative rarity. Economic understanding also grew as economists, politicians and industrialists increasingly appreciated that the high discount and interest rates sometimes required to defend a currency on the gold standard discouraged investment, depressed trade, necessitated cuts in government spending and bred unemployment. As time wore on, gold standard orthodoxy was also challenged by new theories of how supplies of money and credit could be used or managed to reduce unemployment or stabilize levels of production by men like the Englishman John Maynard Keynes, the German Wilhelm Lautenbach and the Swede Gunnar Myrdal.

The Gold Standard Reconstructed, 1920–28

All in all, the title of 'gold standard system' was something of a misnomer, for it was not a system that was organized along clear, invariable lines and administered by a central body; rather it comprised a set of shared assumptions and goals. These common assumptions did not relate merely to the way that the system operated, but also to what the gold standard could achieve. Credited with the unprecedented expansion of the global economy before the First World War, the disintegration of the gold standard in 1919 appeared to have triggered inflation, and even hyperinflation, across Europe. Sadly, this reasoning confused symptom with cause. As we have seen, the reason for the postwar inflation was more complex than this. But the political and economic lessons of the recent past were a powerful influence on European governments. The gold standard offered a 'solid gold' guarantee against inflation, not only because currencies held fixed values, but because participating nations had to follow an orthodox economic policy to keep them there.

Many of the difficulties which were to plague the operation of the gold standard were present in the gold standard of the nineteenth century: the absence of formal channels of cooperation, the challenge of determining the 'right' exchange rate and interest rate, the substitution of gold with foreign exchange in the reserves held by central banks. However, the difference between the title and the reality of the 'gold standard system' grew more pronounced in the reconstructed gold standard system of the interwar period.

When, in 1920, politicians and financiers met together to discuss how to control the inflation that was ripping through their national economies, negotiations soon turned on the question of *when* governments would be able to return the currency to the gold standard, rather than *whether* they should. The desire to return to gold reflected a widespread longing among the traditional arbiters of power, in particular, to restore the stability, prosperity and dominance that the European economy had enjoyed before the First World War. In fact, returning to some form of fixed exchange rate system was so generally accepted on a national level that most of the detailed wrangling, of how currencies could be returned to a stable parity and what kind of fixed exchange system it should be, took place only on an international level.

The first international conference to consider Europe's economic problems took place at Brussels in 1920; a second was held in Genoa in 1922. Each was a high-powered, but loosely organized meeting between government representatives who were accountable to their respective national assemblies and central bankers who were not. At the Brussels conference, political imperatives dominated: the United States refused to attend for fear that proceedings would be eclipsed by wrangling over war debts and reparations (they were right); the governments of Europe complained that without the participation of America, the one country which now controlled over 40 per cent of the world's gold and was its prime source of investment capital, the conference could achieve nothing (they were also right); and the economists and bankers argued over whether it was even the place of governments to concern themselves with economic stability when, for so many years, the prevailing ideology had been to leave it to the market place.

By the time of the Genoa conference, although the United States still refused to participate, Europe's politicians and financiers had grown wise to the dangers of presenting too complex an agenda for international discussion. This time, Britain clearly reclaimed the dominant role it had traditionally enjoyed, although the leverage of the delegation led by the Bank Governor, Montagu Norman, at proceedings did not guarantee that Britain had it all its own way. London was forced to jettison some its schemes for reconstruction – notably its plan to integrate Soviet Russia and the Weimar Republic into the mainstream of European economic life – because France and, from behind the scenes, the United States refused to discuss anything other than issues related directly to reparations and to currency stabilization. Soviet and German delegates abandoned the conference in disgust. On 16 April 1922, while the Genoa conference was still in session, the 'unholy' alliance of Germany and Russia took the bold step of signing the Rapallo Treaty to restore diplomatic and trade relations between their two countries – for the economically needy Soviet state, the economics of the agreement was an essential prerequisite for the political understanding. Further important economic agreements between Germany and the USSR were signed in 1925 and 1926.

On the face of it, at least, negotiations at Genoa were no more productive than those held at Brussels two years earlier. But important progress was made when the Bank of England took the lead in defining the mechanics of international monetary cooperation once countries had returned their currencies to gold: firstly, there was an endorsement of the principle of coordinated central bank operations to secure price-level stability as well as exchange stability. In other words, the big central banks would try to cooperate together to help out any member currency threatened by depreciation. Secondly, given the world shortage of gold, it was agreed that countries could top-up their gold reserves with foreign exchange which was itself backed by gold, like US dollars, to circumvent both the world shortage of gold and to increase global liquidity. Aside from these and other technical agreements setting out the basis for central bank cooperation and international trade relations in the future, the conference delegates in Genoa stressed it was imperative that the United States play a much more active role in the economic reconstruction of Europe.

But the Genoa conference failed to agree any kind of cooperative international strategy to encourage European economic recovery. This had important implications: it condemned most, if not all, European powers to at least two further years of inflation and it made it clear that efforts to achieve currency stabilization would have to be carried out on a national level. In other words, it was the responsibility of each country to build up its own reserves of gold and foreign currency, to bring its national budget into balance, to improve its current account, and to identify a credible exchange rate to return their currency to the gold standard and a bank rate that would keep it there.

The Weimar Republic, of course, did receive international help by way of the Dawes Plan. The severe capital shortage which had gripped the German economy after the stabilization of the mark in November 1923, was resolved by the successful flotation of the Dawes loan in August 1924. Thereafter, the Reichsmark was a fully convertible currency on the gold standard, stabilized at an exchange rate of 4.20 RM to the US dollar – at the insistence of the Americans, it was the same parity as before the war. The burden of adjusting the domestic economy to the fixed exchange rate was born on a national level. In fact, despite anxieties expressed by bankers on both sides of the Atlantic, the return of the Reichsmark to gold was so successful that the Reichsbank was actually able to drop interest rates in the winter of 1924 – itself a further boost to economic recovery.

The return of Germany to the gold standard, coupled with the extensive cooperative links now established between the American capital market and the German economy, threw into sharp relief the question of when Britain would return to gold. Britain's two great commercial rivals, the United States and Germany, now both enjoyed the apparent benefits of being on gold, while the value of sterling continued to fluctuate uncertainly on the international exchanges. The threat to the future of the City of London was particularly grave. Not only did investment from New York challenge British capital exports to Latin America, dollar loans were now financing the rapid revival of German industry and trade, and thereby extending its influence across central and eastern Europe. In an endeavour to prevent this, the Bank of England played the leading role in financing stabilization loans extended to Austria and Hungary during their stabilization crises. But after 1924, with the US dollar and the German mark now fully convertible with gold, British efforts to halt the threatened dollar invasion of Europe were not enough.

With the return of a Conservative government to power in November 1924, expectations that the pound would soon be stabilized began to mount. The City of London, the Bank of England and the Treasury engaged in a concerted campaign to persuade the Chancellor of the Exchequer, Winston Churchill, to return sterling to gold 'to make the pound look the dollar in the face'.[3] These institutions gave Churchill, as the senior official in the Treasury put it, 'irrefutable arguments to support it [the return to gold], whereas if he refused to adopt it he would be faced with criticisms from the City authorities against which he would not have any effective answer'.[4] The financiers marshalled their arguments well. If sterling was not returned to gold, they argued, then not only was London's status as the world's financial capital under grave threat, but so, too, was British commerce (the trade in services like insurance, as distinct from the sale of British manufactures). Further imperial and international considerations were also powerful influences on the British government and its advisors. The Dominions, especially South Africa, were guaranteed a healthy market for gold from their mining operations if Britain, the Empire and the remainder of Europe returned to the gold standard. Membership of the gold standard club also carried the potential not only to reassert British power in Europe, but to improve Anglo-American relations too. From across the Atlantic, successive Republican administrations had advocated that all the world's major economies return to the gold standard, and the persuasive interventions by the charismatic Director of the Federal Reserve Board, Benjamin Strong, encouraged the British to take this bold step. For bold it was as the British government returned sterling to the gold standard at the same exchange rate as before the war: $4.86.

Between 1920 and 1923 the pound had fluctuated between exchange rates of $3.40 and $4.70. Scholars are now in broad agreement that at $4.86 to the pound, sterling was overvalued by around 10 per cent So why did the British government deliberately choose this overvalued exchange rate? The answer lies, in part, in the importance of 'credibility' to the British government in international political and economic policy. The financial and political authorities in Britain shared the conviction that for their commitment to convertibility to be credible to the international exchange market, they had to retain sterling's prewar parity for, so the argument went, any government which tampered with its exchange rate would be treated with suspicion and its currency was more likely to face speculative pressure.

The overvaluation of sterling and the high bank (interest) rates required to sustain it, imposed a severe deflationary burden on the British economy and its people. The government had set its society an almost impossible task as the stabilization of sterling demanded a reduction in wages and overall production costs of around 5 to 10 per cent. British manufacturers and their employees were put in an unenviable position. The two groups were pitched against one another and, as manufacturers struggled to reduce wages, the number of industrial disputes rose. At the same time, both groups lost out because British goods and services were uncompetitive in overseas markets for the remainder of the decade. British policy-makers – in the Cabinet, in the Treasury, in the Bank of England – had made a serious mistake when they failed to consider, in any detail, the implications of this monetary policy for the domestic economy and British society. Churchill and his colleagues recognized that the pound was overvalued at $4.86 and that this would have grave consequences for, in Churchill's words, 'the merchant, the manufacturer, the workman and the consumer ... (whose interests) do not by any means coincide either with each other or with the financial and currency interests'.[5] But this vague appreciation was as close as the government came to any systematic investigation of the political and economic consequences of sterling's overvaluation for the British political economy. But it is also true that both industry and workers' organizations were divided on the issue and failed to mount a campaign of opposition against the move to gold. Economists, too, were largely supportive of the move. There were a few exceptions, notably Keynes, who condemned the act as one which crucified Britain 'on a cross of gold'.

The predicted rise in American prices to help ameliorate this problem was not forthcoming. British advocates of the return to gold argued that because the dollar was undervalued on the gold standard, US prices – according to the mechanics of the system – should rise, but American prices did not rise for most of the interwar period. (The productivity of the average American worker continued to improve, keeping US prices low.) The specific symptoms of gold-induced fever in the British economy were serious, but so, too, was the more general malaise. The deflationary pressures triggered by the return to gold lowered economic confidence and threatened political stability at home. The industrial unrest, present every day since the war, culminated on 3 May 1926 when a miners' strike became a nine-day General Strike. The strike illustrated both middle- and working-class frustration with the levels of pay and the conditions of work for those in employment, and the lack of work for those without. The fact that the strike was neither long-lived nor supported by the Trades Union Congress illustrated that British socialism, like British politics as a whole, were overwhelmingly dominated by moderate politicians determined to preserve the economic policy to keep Britain on gold.

Ultimately, the decision to stabilize sterling at $4.86 was an act of faith – not a blind act of faith, but a myopic one. A selective reading of the 'lessons of history' certainly taught that the gold standard led to prosperity and social stability, and that inflation did not. However, the failure of the British government to consider the adjustment difficulties posed by an overvalued exchange rate for the domestic economy was an important political failure, and the Treasury and the Bank of England were wrong to rule out flatly the possible benefits of devaluation before restabilization, as the experience of France was to show. But there is no guarantee that, even if economists and politicians counselled in favour of devaluation before stabilization, the British public would have tolerated it. In Denmark and Norway, for example, members of the ruling elites attempted in vain to persuade public opinion to devalue. They both returned to the gold standard at their prewar parities (so did Switzerland and the Netherlands) which triggered a depression almost as severe as that to come after 1929.

It was a story repeated, with some variations, across Europe. Britain's return to the system set an important precedent. By the end of 1925, over 35 currencies were stabilized with most returning officially to the gold standard, although some, like the free city of Danzig, joined for the first time. With sterling stabilized, most of the Dominions (Australia, New Zealand, South Africa) and Scandinavian countries (all of whom had large reserves of sterling) soon followed suit. So, too, did Italy, where the inflation which had ravaged its economy since the close of the war was ended with the official stabilization of the lira in December 1927. For Mussolini, the question was not whether to stabilize, but at what rate, now that so many countries were on gold. As in Britain, Mussolini's cabinet knowingly chose an overvalued exchange rate for the lira to underline the credibility of Italy's commitment to gold. Having traded at 153.68 lira to the pound in 1926, it was stabilized at the obviously overvalued rate of 92.46 lira to the pound (19 lira to the dollar) 12 months later. Fascist bravado came into it too. *Il Duce* was determined to make the lira, discredited through years of inflation, into a prestigious currency by returning it to the exchange rate it had enjoyed when he first came to power, in October 1922, of 90 lire to the pound (the fabled *quota novanta*). He proclaimed that his unerring powers of intuition told him 'the fate of the regime is tied to the fate of the lira'.[6] Crucially, Mussolini's decision to stabilize the lira was supported by both the financial and business communities. This was, in part, because of the close relationship between industry and finance in Italy, sponsored by institutions like the *Associazione fra le Società Italiane per Azioni* (Association of Italian Joint Stock Companies). Equally important, though, was the desire of Italy's larger industrialists to lower their costs of production and to see off their smaller competitors – big companies rightly calculated that smaller companies were likely to go bust under the pressure of deflation. The extent of the lira's overvaluation helped to turn the screw.

Morgan's recent study also underlines how far the stabilization of the lira expanded the role of the *Partito Nazionale Fascista* (Italian Fascist Party) in the economic life of the nation. The party's role in implementing wage cuts of between 10 and 20 per cent, agreed in October 1927 and in the new price committees, the *comitati intersindacali*, to ensure price cuts in staples like pasta, rice and olive oil to match, underlines the political implications of economic policy. Although the party was not involved in the decision to return to gold, Mussolini relied upon it to implement the price and wage cuts necessitated by the step and this gave the party an opportunity to wield considerable power at the provincial and local level.

When countries returned their currencies to gold at an overvalued rate, it was not just the exchange rate that was damaging to economic and social stability, but the policies required to keep them there. And the extent of the over- or undervaluation influenced the impact of the policy regime. The point is clearly illustrated in the case of the French franc. Uncoupled from gold, the franc traded at 5.45 to the dollar in January 1919, and by January of the following year, it had slid to 12 francs to the dollar. By 1922 the situation was alarming – it had helped to precipitate the French invasion of the Ruhr – and by the end of 1924 it was almost calamitous. In 1925 the return of sterling to gold at its prewar parity threw into sharp relief the spectacle of continued monetary chaos in France. Nor did the outcome of the London conference and the Dawes Plan help the increasingly embattled French statesmen, for it was now clear that neither France nor Belgium could rely on German reparations to cancel out their spiralling budget deficits – the realization made the struggle to balance the budget even more difficult. Until the middle of 1926, successive left-wing cabinets, and 10 different ministers of finance, grappled with France's antiquated and ramshackle tax system while the franc, despite repeated assistance from the Bank of England and the Federal Reserve System, was subjected to speculative attack after speculative attack on the international exchanges.

There later developed the myth that the Radical and Socialist coalition government were sabotaged by a *mur d'argent* ('wall of money'), a legend erected by financiers and industrialists determined to sabotage any measure introduced by the Left to redistribute the nation's wealth. The legend played an important part in the rise of the Popular Front in 1936. In fact, the efforts of the Cartel des Gauches to balance the budget failed because French monetary policy had been in chaos for many years, and because the Chamber of Deputies could not decide who in French society should bare the burden of increased taxes to pay for reconstruction and stabilization. By the summer of 1926, all sides had grown tired of the disorder generated by the inflation. Middle-class frustration at the declining value of assets, including government bonds bought patriotically during the 'Great' war, was especially apparent in the rising numbers (estimated at some 155 000 in 1926) flocking to join fascist parties and leagues, like the Jeunesses Patriotes, Action Française and the Faisceau. In July 1926 the French government moved to the right with the appointment of Raymond Poincaré, the strong man who had taken France into the Ruhr, as both Prime Minister and Finance Minister. He was granted extensive powers of decree by the Chamber to take unilateral action to bring inflation under control.

Once again, the question of how to end the inflation was posited as one of gold standard membership. But it is here that the story of the French return to gold differed dramatically from that of Britain for, by 1926, the French government and the French people had abandoned any hope of returning the franc to the gold standard at the exchange rate it had enjoyed before the war. French economists made a genuine attempt to calculate the correct, devalued rate for the franc, but as in Britain, Italy and elsewhere, the decision soon turned more on politics than economics. Anxious to avoid making life difficult for French industry, commerce and farming, particularly when it came to exporting their products overseas, Poincaré accepted counsel that warned him against a strong (high) exchange rate in relation to sterling and the dollar. Instead of asking, as they had in London and Rome, how much deflation industry and agriculture could bear, the question was one of how much inflation the French middle classes could tolerate without wiping out their fixed assets entirely. After six months in office, Poincaré pegged the franc to gold in December 1926 (it returned to the gold standard officially in 1928) at an exchange rate of 25.51 francs to the dollar and 124 francs to the pound. In other words, at an exchange rate 80 per cent lower than it had been in 1914. It was a decision that was as good for France, at least until around 1932, as it was bad for the future health of the gold standard system.

Belgium followed a similar path through depreciation and stabilization to that of its ally France. From 1919 to 1925, the Belgian budget deficit grew like Topsy with the failure of German reparations to meet the costs of postwar reconstruction and with its tax system in disarray. The value of the Belgian franc fell consistently, but not alarmingly: in May 1919 it stood at 30 francs to the pound. By May 1925 it had fallen to 96 francs to the pound. Suddenly in the summer of 1926, the inflationary crisis threatened to spin out of control when attempts to negotiate a stabilization loan with the American bank J. P. Morgan failed. The Belgian franc plummeted to a new low. This, coupled with the fact that the public were now heartily weary of the instability, generated a new political will on the part of the three mainstream political parties. They joined together, with support of the King, to form a Government of National Union to impose a new system of taxation and to cut public spending to bring the budget deficit under control. It was now easy to secure an American loan to aid the process of stabilization, and after October 1926 the newly stabilized Belgian franc traded at 14.5 per cent of its prewar parity.

As these examples all illustrate, when European countries 'chose' the rate at which to stabilize their currencies, they did so independently and with no reference to the parities adopted in other countries. The national focus of these decisions compounded the electorate's belief that the nation-state was in control of things that happened to the national economy. Yet the rate at which Europe's wealthiest countries decided to return to gold had important consequences for other members. The stability and viability of the gold standard and the pattern of international trade were dramatically affected by the fact that Britain, Denmark, Norway and Italy were overvalued in the system while France, Belgium and the United States were undervalued. An overvalued currency led to expensive exports, while an undervalued exchange rate produced an export advantage. The development interacted with other forces at work in the European economy, like declining demand for heavy industrial products (p. 10), and heightened international tension as domestic producers increasingly demanded protection from cheap foreign imports.

The experience of some countries in central and eastern Europe illustrates that, despite some of the advantages secured by France and Belgium, stabilizing at even a devalued rate was not necessarily an easy option. Apart from the virtuous exception of Czechoslovakia, which achieved stabilization without international help as early as 1923, elsewhere in the east the process was a long, drawn-out affair. Hungary's route to stabilization mirrored that of Germany. In the wake of a bill for reparations running into some 200 million gold crowns and considerable political conflict, Hungarian stabilization was delayed until 1925 (at 0.0069 per cent of the prewar parity) after the League of Nations extended a loan worth some 250 million crowns. That same year, the crown was also replaced by a new currency, the pengö. As in the west, outside help was indispensable by way of stabilization loans. But here private bankers were at first unwilling to act and the League of Nations had to step in. The League also provided all important stabilization loans to Poland, Greece, Estonia, Bulgaria and Danzig.

Poland, which experienced a more serious and protracted inflationary crisis than Hungary, finally managed to stabilize its currency in October 1927 after failed attempts in 1921, 1923, 1924 and 1926. Here, too, political turmoil played a crucial role in exacerbating the inflationary crisis. From 1919 to 1926 government changed hands 14 times, until General Pilsudski launched his successful military coup in May of that year. With it came a harsh package of fiscal and financial measures to bring an end to the inflationary chaos and, despite the fact that Polish pretensions to democratic politics now stood in tatters, national and international confidence in Pilsudski's firm leadership secured a $72 million loan to facilitate stabilization of the new Polish zloty at a hugely devalued rate.

The Romanian drive to stabilize the leu best illustrates the increasingly nationalist temper of eastern European politics. Romania, like Italy, was a victor of the First World War who came to believe it was a loser in the wake of the peace settlement. After 1919 the battle to contain the inflationary pressures was exacerbated by the Romanian government's wilful determination to stabilize the national currency without foreign help. It took Romania until 1929 to stabilize its currency, demonstrating the difficulty of going it alone. Its lacklustre performance on currency stabilization was underlined by the equally unimaginative slogan: 'We should rely unaided on our own resources.'[7]

The way that countries, from Bulgaria in the south to Estonia in the north, struggled to achieve a stable currency, even at a vastly reduced exchange rate, demonstrates the difficulties most central and eastern European economies faced (particularly when it came to agriculture) and the pressures brought to bear by membership of the gold standard system. Aside from Romania, the new inflow of foreign investment into the region was neither as healthy nor as stabilizing as it first seemed (p. 84). Equally damaging were the deflationary policies that had to be implemented to protect the stability of the newly stabilized currencies, for central and eastern Europe, unlike France for example, was not blessed with large gold reserves or a healthy recovery in the levels of trade. Aside from budget stringency on the part of government, it was also very expensive to borrow money in the region. The National Bank of Austria charged a discount rate of 15 per cent while interest on agricultural loans fluctuated between 25 and 45 per cent and, after currency stabilization in Yugoslavia, industrial and commercial firms, who took out the largest loans, had to pay interest rates of around 16 to 24 per cent. Even the most enterprising and successful of businessmen and women would struggle to make enough in profit to pay off loans at these interest rates.

The manner in which countries returned to the gold standard, coupled with the way the system operated, all stored up trouble for the future. The concluding sections of this chapter explore the implications of the considerable deflationary pressures to which some countries had committed themselves for individuals, interest groups and nations. These are important because even when the fear of inflation began to ease, the technical safeguards introduced to limit the freedom of central banks to expand the supply of money in the economy did not. The policies which accompanied gold standard membership had very important consequences for European economic growth. Even European countries which were free from deflationary pressures – either through devaluation as in the case of France, or non-membership as in the case of Spain – suffered through the interconnectedness of the national, European and global economies. (Spain never joined the gold standard because of the long-established role of silver in its banking system.) There were also technical shortcomings in the way the reconstructed system operated – the 'rules of the game' were violated by leading participants and reserves of gold were in short supply – while the prospects of international cooperation to iron out some of these difficulties were also constrained.

The Experience of Inflation and Deflation

The different national histories of the struggle to control inflation had profound implications for the way that both governments and economies behaved once their currencies had returned to gold. In Europe most countries were engaged in a battle to deflate their economies. If the overvaluation of the currency was large, as in the case of Britain and Italy, then securing membership of the gold standard marked the beginning, not the end, of a struggle to adjust the national economy, by lowering prices and wages, to the international currency rate. The process was politically distressing and socially divisive. The search for credibility, international approval, political prestige and international capital prompted Britain, Italy and Germany to overvalue their currencies and condemn their economies to deflation. There were only two ways out: to make considerable gains in productivity so that costs and prices would fall, or to devalue the currency and return to gold at a lower exchange rate. But the whole question of devaluing currencies and then restabilizing them on the gold standard was ruled out at the Genoa conference. Thereafter, the gold standard offered no remedy for an overvalued exchange rate other than price or wage deflation or persistent unemployment. At the time deflation seemed a price worth paying for stability. For societies torn asunder by high levels of inflation, gold standard membership offered a gold-backed guarantee against repeating the experience. Although deflation was to exert its own pressures on the state, member nations clung to gold, even after 1929 when economic circumstances deteriorated so dramatically as to make gold standard membership, and the policies necessary to maintain it, wholly inappropriate.

Social historians have been at great pains to point to the great diversity of experience within class groups according to age, gender, location (urban or rural), and ethnic or religious group. But it is still possible, albeit crudely, to show how the experience of inflation and deflation affected different groups of people in the interwar period. If you were an industrial worker, inflation brought a rising cost of living, but often better employment opportunities and rising wages. You would quickly notice that your wages were falling in real terms; if you were Polish or Hungarian, by as much as 65 per cent in 1919. Deflation, on the other hand, brought lower pay, and the greatly increased threat of unemployment. Once jobless, any payments you might receive from the state were also at risk from cuts as the Chancellor of the Exchequer or Finance Minister struggled to balance the national budget. Young people entering the job market for the first time grew disillusioned and pessimistic about the future – a trend which made the radical, militaristic youth movements on the left and right of European politics all the more appealing.

If you were a member of the middle class, then your experience of inflation would be almost all bad. Of course, the first thing to note is that you abhor the very concept of class and see yourself more as a member of an important status group. In Germany you are a member of the *Mittelstand*, a group made up of rentiers, artisans, shopkeepers, civil servants and white-collar workers. The heady rates of inflation would cut, or even wipe out, your fixed income from savings, government bonds, salary or pension, and you would be conscious, most of all, of your loss of privilege and social status. Your only gain would come if you had outstanding debts or a mortgage on your home: these would be significantly reduced in real terms. Deeply, perhaps even violently, hostile to the threat of renewed currency instability, you would be most anxious to see your nation's currency returned to gold. Only in time do you discover that gold membership does not improve your sense of security. True, the value of your assets and income is steady, but the pressure on government to save money in order to balance the national budget means that your wages, even your job, are now at risk. As the owner of a small business, your experience of inflation and deflation would be rather similar to other members of the middle class, although if your business had survived the threat of bankruptcy through deflationary pressure, you would also face increased competition from larger business rivals. Big business was far better equipped to cope with a competitive economic environment that included high interest rates designed to preserve gold parity, but which also made credit expensive.

If you were the head of a large manufacturing concern, in Germany, for example, inflation had brought the opportunity to rid your business of debts, expand your export markets overseas, and invest in new equipment. Growth was possible as long as the demand for higher wages from your workers did not lead to massive strikes, accompanied by distressing political and social upheaval which threatened your factories' output and economic confidence. However, once loss began to outweigh gain, then a stable currency rate in which both domestic and foreign investors had confidence became imperative. Deflation, on the other hand, meant reducing costs and protecting profit margins by making your employees work longer hours for less pay; a strong currency, like sterling, the Reichsmark or the lira, meant you also enjoyed lower prices for your imports of raw materials. More importantly, every European business, large or small, also faced renewed competition from foreign exporters, notably from the United States and France, whose exchange rates on gold were lower. Already fierce American competition, facilitated by new products and new methods of production, received an additional boost after 1924 because the dollar was undervalued in relation to many European currencies. Increasingly, in the face of such strong foreign competition, businessmen across Europe began to demand that government protect the home market for domestic suppliers, by way of tariffs, quotas or price cartels; a trend which violated the spirit and the principles of the gold standard.

If you were a farmer in Europe, the experience of deflation would be especially trying. Inflation enabled you to pay off your debts and to secure a good price for your produce relative to industrial goods. The downside was that if you had any savings, they were lost in the chaos of hyperinflation. Deflation was only more painful. It meant the value of your produce now fell relative to manufactures (deteriorating terms of trade), making it much more expensive for you to buy goods for your farm and home. Unlike manufacturers, you do not benefit from cheaper import prices as you do not need imported goods to help you to tend your herd or grow your crops. Already fighting sluggish demand for European agricultural produce, once the national currency is stabilized, the subsequent pressures of gold standard membership, especially if the currency is overvalued, would prompt you to demand more protection against already strong competition from overseas farmers. If you lived in central and eastern Europe, you would also demand some cuts in the amount of taxation you were expected to pay: your group, amongst the poorest in society, bore the lion's share of the tax burden. At the same time, any mortgage secured on farm land would become increasingly expensive as interest rates rose, carrying with it the spectre of foreclosure and destitution for you and your family. The growing pressure on farmers in the 1920s also had important consequences if you were a financier or a banker, traditionally one of the strongest supporters of the currency stability and freedom of exchange offered by the gold standard. As the deflationary pressures across Europe took their toll, however, you would find your profits falling and some of your customers, notably farmers, experiencing great difficulty paying off their debts to you. A large enough number of defaults on loans by farmers and businessmen, and the viability of your bank and your livelihood, too, could be under threat.

After 1923 the fear of inflation among all groups in society meant that the utility of the gold standard, regardless of how it functioned, was not questioned. Instead, by 1930 the political pressures – generated first by inflation and, subsequently, by gold standard membership – obliterated political support for internationalism. In countries as diverse as Britain, Germany and Italy, the painful outcome of international cooperation, off and on gold in the 1920s, made many voters demand that politicians work even harder to protect the national interest first. The nationalist trend was reinforced by the fact that two countries, the United States and France, appeared to do particularly well out of the gold standard. Indeed, the problems for overvalued currencies were compounded both by the fact that the gold standard also contained undervalued currencies and by the way in which those undervalued currencies operated within the system. The nationalism which paralysed efforts to revive the global economy on an international level in the Great Depression had its roots in the lessons learned from international cooperation in the 1920s.

Shortcomings of the Gold Standard 'Order'

The experience of inflation had made almost everyone hostile to the notion of floating currencies. To European minds of the 1920s, exchange rate instability and runaway inflation were regarded as interchangeable – this was, and is, simply not the case. The political determination to avoid all threat of inflation was underlined by the resolve of government to liberate further the management of the economy from domestic interference. Once on gold, the central banks were free from political involvement in determining the rate of discount and interest rates. They were shielded further from political pressures by legislation designed to limit the banks' freedom. The intention was to prevent central banks from contributing to inflation in the way, for example, that the Reichsbank and the Central Hungarian Bank had in 1922 and 1923. The banks now faced strict limits on their freedom to mount open market operations. These operations reinforced any change, up or down, in the discount rate. They were facilitated by stocks of public debt which the central bank sold when it wanted the supply of money to tighten, thereby supporting an accompanying increase in the discount rate, and bought them back when it wanted to expand the amount of money available in the national economy. The new restrictions on the central bank's freedom to increase money supply had dramatic consequences for a number of countries, especially Germany, in 1929.

Indeed, long before the decade's end, two vitally important central banks failed to behave as they could, and should, have if the gold standard was to work properly: the Banque de France and the Federal Reserve Bank system of the United States. As in Hungary and Germany, the Banque de France was implicated in the 'crime' of postwar inflation and legal steps were taken to prevent a recurrence. The French government imposed strict legal limitations on the volume and character of open market operations undertaken by the Banque de France. The Federal Reserve System, too, faced limits on the volume and character of its market activities, although the United States had not experienced anything like the inflation which had gripped France. After 1927 the strength of both the American and French economies (demonstrated by their balance of payments surpluses) encouraged a huge inflow of gold into their countries.

With gold pouring into the coffers of the Banque de France and the Federal Reserve, France and the United States should have responded, according to 'the rules of the gold standard game', by lowering interest rates and mounting open market operations in order to encourage the supply of money to rise and, ultimately, to allow some of this gold to flow out again. But both countries violated this rule. Instead of allowing their money supply to grow commensurate with the inflow of gold, they stashed most of the gold away in their reserves – contemporaries dubbed the process gold sterilization. Of course, if France and the United States had begun to buy and import more foreign goods, gold would also have left their countries. But this did not happen. It was, and is, very difficult for governments or other institutions to arrange the buying habits of the nation.

In 1927 and 1928 the Federal Reserve Bank did relax its discount rate and engage in small-scale open market operations (the French complained bitterly about America's 'irresponsible' actions). But it needed to have done so on a much greater scale to be able to extend credit to those countries which were experiencing the gold outflow. As it was, the French and American failure to play by the rules made it much more difficult for countries overvalued on gold and for those who were already short of gold. In effect, the Americans and the French were using the gold standard as a buffer to protect their national economies.

The fact that, by the end of the 1920s, France and the United States were draining the world of its gold reserves (between them hoarding more than half of the world's total gold supply) had a number of serious consequences, both for the long-term viability of the gold standard and for the health of participating domestic economies. Firstly, any country that experienced an outflow of gold, because investors chose to sell their pounds or zlotys in favour of French francs or US dollars, found their reserves of gold and foreign exchange diminishing fast – an intolerable situation if they wanted to stay on the gold standard. The drain on the national reserves forced the central bank, albeit reluctantly, to raise interest rates, regardless of the repercussions. Of course, countries were anxious to avoid this situation, and the larger the reserves of the central bank, the longer it was possible to postpone a raise in the discount rate. But, and this brings us onto a further flaw in the operation of the gold standard, from the outset, most countries (with the obvious exceptions of France, the United States and South Africa) were very short of gold, both when it came to accumulating reserves in preparation for returning to the gold standard, but also after they had rejoined it. Central banks across Europe struggled to find gold. Instead, as we have seen, countries used foreign exchange to build up their reserves. However, large reserves of foreign exchange in place of gold, a commonplace of monetary policy at the end of the twentieth century, had consequences for which central banks and governments were, in the latter 1920s, largely unprepared.

To explain: gold was never the only valuable held by central banks as reserves to support their currency. They held silver and other foreign currencies too, but in the nineteenth century gold reserves made up the bulk of valuables in the vaults of central banks; by 1927 this was true only of the United States and France. Most countries diluted the gold content of their currencies with foreign currency, preferably one which was gold-backed like the US dollar or the French franc. Sterling also was a very popular choice of reserve currency in Europe as well as in the Empire. In the hands of continental bankers, sterling could be readily exchanged for another currency, say French francs, or gold in order to trade, to supplement central bank reserves, or simply to make a profit on the transaction. Therefore, when Britain wanted to discourage investors from exchanging pounds for gold or some other national currency, it had to maintain competitive interest rates – usually the higher the discount and interest rate, the more attractive the currency to foreign bankers and investors. This had important implications for domestic investment and employment, as well as for stirring up ill-feeling between countries which needed to cooperate together to make the system work. At the end of 1926, for example, Schacht, the head of the German central bank, wished to slow down the massive flow of foreign capital into Germany. Rather than lower domestic discount and interest rates, he elected to convert the Reichsbank's reserves of sterling into gold. In response, the Bank of England should have increased its interest rates in order to protect its gold reserves, thereby tightening money supply and, as Schacht calculated, slowing down the rate of foreign investment in Germany. Instead, Norman, who was at the height of his powers at the Bank of England, chose to lose gold. He calculated, based on noises coming from the Treasury and the man in the street, that the political cost of raising interest rates at home was too great. This episode, and there were others like it, illustrated that regardless of whether countries experienced an inflow of foreign investment or an outflow of gold, central banks tried to minimize the impact of these flows on the domestic economy. Even at this early stage in the life of the reconstructed gold standard, it was clear the system did not work automatically, and that domestic considerations took precedence over the international obligations of gold standard membership.

It was possible to paper over the cracks in the system provided that countries experiencing difficulties had continued access to credit from the United States and Britain. These two countries had provided the stabilization loans that had helped Europe back on the gold standard and helped to keep countries in deficit on gold by continuing to supply the all important credits to bolster dwindling national reserves. Much of central, eastern and southeastern Europe, for example, ran a persistent current-account deficit (they imported more than they exported), putting confidence in their currencies at risk. The inflow of dollars and sterling helped them to sustain their membership of the gold standard without repeatedly having to raise interest rates, an action that would only have increased the deflationary pressures on their economies. Provided that confidence in the system and in continued economic growth remained, and provided that American and British loans continued to flow into countries running a deficit, in theory at least, the reconstructed gold standard could have continued indefinitely.[8] But none of this happened automatically. From the outset, the reconstructed system was dependent upon continued, close cooperation between the central banks of the main economic powers, for if private investors did not step into fund a country's deficit, then it was up to the central bankers to do so. (Leading central banks also supported loans arranged by the League of Nations to central and eastern Europe.)

One central bank could not alone save the system. If a country experienced a run on its currency, then international cooperation between the world's most important bankers was essential: Governor Norman of the Bank of England; Benjamin Strong, governor of the Federal Reserve Board in New York; Émile Moreau, governor of the Bank of France and Hjalmar Schacht of the Reichsbank. But there is plenty of evidence to suggest that while these staunch advocates of the gold standard were happy enough to extend loans to countries in order that they might stabilize their economies to join the gold standard, they were less willing to continue to extend credit so that a country carrying a budget-deficit could remain on gold. This unwillingness only became apparent in 1928, when pressures on the gold standard, for reasons which will be outlined below, began to mount.

Even during the supposed heyday of effective cooperation between central bankers during the 1920s, there was plenty of evidence of tension over policies and between personalities. In contemporary documents and diaries, Norman and Moreau, to give two prominent examples, often expressed their frustration with the malfunctioning gold standard, and problems in international relations in general, in strongly personalized terms. When they met for the first time in July 1926, Moreau recorded the following, unflattering impression of Norman:

> He seems to have walked out of a Van Dyck canvas: the long face, the pointed beard, the big hat lend him the look of a companion of the Stuarts ... He doesn't like the French. He said to me literally: 'I want

very much to help the Bank of France. But I detest your Government and your Treasury. For them I shall do nothing.'[9]

Views such as these have prompted historians to spend a great deal of energy exploring how far personal friendships (like that between Norman and Schacht), personal animosities (between Norman and Moreau) and the death of the charismatic Strong in 1928 disrupted international cooperation. Personalities mattered because of the absence of formalized structures to facilitate cooperation. Yet for all the personal and sometimes xenophobic complaints that pepper the private records of the bankers and financiers, the records equally reveal the strong commonality of aims and objectives among the central bankers, particularly when it came to the contribution of the gold standard to economic well-being.

Genuine bad feeling among the bankers was generated by differences in national policy, not personality. For all their claims of independence, central bankers were highly susceptible to domestic political pressure, and when domestic priorities diverged, international cooperation suffered. True, most central bankers were free from direct government interference when it came to setting the bank rate, but they tended to share the world view of their governments when it came to economic and foreign policy. Norman's attitude towards issues like inflation, the sources of British economic prosperity and the French echoed the views of successive British cabinets and Whitehall mandarins towards, for example, French reparation policy and the extension of French power over Germany and southeastern Europe. In fact, until the 1930s, there was very little political dispute about the power wielded by central bankers, who were unaccountable to the public because their priorities chimed so precisely with those of the government. At the same time, bankers were increasingly sensitive to the deflationary impact of the interest rate on the domestic economy. In Britain, for example, the bank rate was changed 18 times between May 1925 and September 1931 (an average of three times a year). Indeed, the primacy of domestic interests over international cooperation was an accepted rule of the 'gold standard game'. Cooperation was only expected in so far as there was no sacrifice of national interest. If this was defined broadly enough, then national and international welfare begin to merge, but if national interest was narrowly defined there remained little scope for cooperation. In the interwar period there was no international institution to act as an arbiter, however imperfect, to resolve conflicts that arose between national and international interests. International consultation was on an *ad hoc*, informal basis, and such cooperation as there was, was bedevilled by the differing interpretations of what was understood by the term 'cooperation' on the part of individuals and institutions.

In short, the problem with the gold standard was not simply that it failed to function as it should have or that exchange rates were too high, and the subsequent policy regime too demanding. Many of these problems could have been overcome if the political will for international cooperation had been strong enough. After all, the declared outcomes of the gold standard – to limit exchange rate fluctuations, to facilitate the international movement of capital and goods – were goals all of Europe shared. There were ways to improve international monetary relations, but these measures demanded greater imagination on the part of politicians and bankers to think beyond the resurrected gold standard as *the* policy tool to achieve all their economic goals. They could have chosen other than to return to gold or to change the way the system operated. But once on gold, it became all the more difficult to abandon a policy that, for many, had demanded considerable sacrifice or had brought apparent prosperity. Having committed themselves to gold and ostensibly to internationalism in the 1920s, European leaders (and those of the United States) wanted to make the gold standard work, but failed to regard international cooperation as a common good. Disputes over questions unrelated to the gold standard – naval rivalry between Britain and the United States, Anglo-American hostility towards French rearmament plans – were also allowed to muddy the waters of economic cooperation. It was more than the failure of one country to lead, it was the failure of all the system's participants to cooperate, not just to defend fixed parities on gold, but to appreciate fully their common interest in a healthy international economy.

3

A EUROPEAN REVIVAL? 1925–28

In 1925 it became clear how far the monetary balance of power had shifted away from Europe and towards the United States. For 300 years, the American economy had been dependent on European capital, but now the trend was reversed as huge sums of American investment flooded into Europe. From 1925 to 1929 over $5.1 billion of foreign loans were floated in the United States, most of them destined for Europe. Germany was the largest international borrower, receiving over 50 per cent of all the money invested into Europe, although Austria, Italy, Romania, Poland, Hungary, Greece, Belgium, Norway, Yugoslavia and Bulgaria were also significant beneficiaries. While struggling to compete with the might of Uncle Sam, British and French loans were also important to Europe, with each contributing some $1.3 billion over the same period.

Foreign loans played an important role in reinforcing the connections between the American and European economies determined by the gold standard and by patterns of international trade. By the middle of the 1920s, it at last seemed as if the European economy had recovered from the damage and dislocation of the First World War. The revived economy led to a new interdependence. The complex network of loans and debts helped to reinforce the dependence of European economies on each other and on the health and conduct of that of the United States, although these facts were quickly forgotten with the onset of depression in 1929. Money and trade were not the only links between Europe and the United States. America's reputation for innovation in the organization of its production and work force, borne out in America's unparalleled levels of industrial growth, also had an important impact on the character of Europe's economic development.

The influx of foreign investment helped to paper over many of the cracks both in the European economy and in the faulty operation of the gold standard. Thanks to this infusion of foreign investment, the European economy recovered at a reassuring, although hardly spectacular, rate in the second half of the 1920s. Taking 1925 as the base line (1925:100), the index for production in European industry rose to 123.1 by 1929 and, over the same period of time, the index for European agriculture reached 122.2. European growth was facilitated by monetary stability at home and abroad, the return, in some measure, of business and consumer confidence, and the impact of postwar industrial and agricultural reconstruction. Levels of trade had recovered also, although a cautionary note was sounded by the fact that it took until 1929 for trade within and beyond Europe to reach the level enjoyed in 1913. Indeed, this was only when the scale of European trade was measured by value. The overall volume of European trade was still lower in 1929 than it had been in 1913; in Britain's case the volume of its export trade in 1929 was a full 20 per cent down on what it had been in 1913.

The patchy character of European growth after 1925 was also worrying. There was considerable variation within and among European states: Britain, Denmark, Norway, Greece and Austria, for example, all recorded rather modest levels of growth; in Belgium, France and Sweden, on the other hand, growth was fairly rapid. The continued difficulties faced by European farmers were not encouraging. Agricultural output and prices in Europe, particularly to the east of Berlin, did not compare favourably to levels of industrial growth. This had important consequences for the level of trade protectionism – it rose throughout the period – and the ability of European debtor countries to pay off their ever mounting debts.

The United States in Europe, 1925–28

It was the combination of prosperity and low interest rates at home and the sweet smell of opportunity abroad that encouraged Americans to invest overseas in search of a larger profit. In the 1920s, many more American citizens purchased foreign bonds than ever before. American banks and finance houses, though inexperienced in the vagaries of foreign investment, happily encouraged the expansion and received generous commissions for underwriting such loans. Now that the gold standard was back, borrowers and lenders alike were able to forget the economic chaos which had engulfed Europe in the wake of the First World War. Many became convinced that Europe, like America, had entered a period of unparalleled prosperity and growth. Central Europe, in particular, benefited from low interest rates and the expansionary monetary policy pursued by the Federal Reserve Banks – these policies helped to attract money into Europe where interest rates were higher. Large, American-sponsored loans were their reward for the, usually draconian, austerity measures necessitated by the return to the gold standard.

As we shall see, the underlying performance of the European economy in general, and the German economy in particular, merited neither the confidence nor the money invested in it by foreign lenders. The attitude of American financiers towards Europe can best be understood through the domestic context: their optimism grew out of the tremendous expansion taking place in the American economy. The epithets applied to the decade – the 'roaring twenties', the 'New Era', the 'Age of Ballyhoo' – confirmed American society's unprecedented and unquestioning optimism in the future. Helped along by low interest rates at home and a devalued exchange overseas, certain sections of the American economy, notably the new motor vehicle industry and the construction industry (aided by innovations like quick drying concrete) enjoyed spectacular levels of growth. Between 1899 and 1929 the total output of American manufactures grew by 264 per cent and by 1928 the United States, with only 6 per cent of the world's population, produced over 57 per cent of the total world output of machinery. The competitiveness of the American economy was underlined to its commercial rivals in Europe by the fact that the expansion of the American economy was facilitated largely by great improvements in manufacturing productivity. American workers, on average, produced twice as much for every hour worked as their European counterparts and national levels of unemployment appeared to remain very low.[1] For many Europeans, America was *the* economic model to emulate.

But even in America, all was not as rosy as it seemed. As in Europe, the United States experienced significant levels of regional unemployment. Even those in work feared the relentless march of the machine would soon push them out of a job. It was an anxiety more usually associated with the European reaction to the new American methods of 'productivity' and 'rationalization'. (These were catch-all terms used at the time to denote methods of scientific, efficient production through standardization, time and motion studies, market analysis and mass assembly.) Again, as in Europe, regional unemployment was brought about through the decline of staple industries, like shipbuilding, railways, coal mining and footwear, while even the parts of America that had experienced tremendous growth in the New Era did not share the benefits of the new prosperity equally: workers' wages rose by 11 per cent, corporate profits rose by 63 per cent and share dividends by 65 per cent, with the top one per cent of the population earning 15 per cent of all income. A particular sense of grievance was harboured by American farmers, a fact that would have surprised their counterparts in Europe who believed they were much worse off than their American cousins. In the United States, the farming community had done very well out of the sharp rise in commodity prices during the First World War, but it was hit hard by the collapse in primary prices of the 1920–21 slump, the creeping protectionism that shielded overseas markets from American agricultural exports, and the massive increase in the cost of land at home triggered by speculation in the real estate market. The United States then, although much more prosperous and confident than Europe, also shared common problems, notably in the difficulties faced by some of the 'old', established industries like mining and the growing perception amongst farmers that they were worse off than everyone else.

The Recovery in Industry

After 1925 in Europe the picture of national recovery and growth remained a varied one, although many more regions of the world participated in this period of economic growth than in the short-lived boom after the First World War. When it came to the health of industrialized Europe's 'old' industries, problems present at war's end – declining demand, static levels of productivity and fierce competition from within Europe and, more significantly, outside it – continued to dominate (p. 9). A sense of excitement, innovation and progress was limited largely to the so-called 'new' or 'sunrise' industries. Sometimes these terms can be misleading. What was considered an old, established industry in one region of Europe was a dynamic, new industry somewhere else. A good example is the textile industry that was in sharp decline in Britain and Italy, but was thriving in Hungary and the Benelux countries. The term 'new' industries is best understood in relation to the adoption of new methods, new technologies and changing markets, and the truly new industries were those which combined new methods with new technologies. The best examples are the motor vehicle industry, the petrochemical industry and manufacturers of new products set to change life at home and at work dramatically – refrigerators, radios, cars, new types of office machinery and aeroplanes. In France, for example, the real winners in the 1920s were the men and women who made artificial fibres and who refined petrol shipped in from oil-fields in the Middle East, an industry wrested from German control at the Paris Peace Conference that helped to trigger the explosive growth of the French automobile industry. Citroën, Renault and Peugeot were at the forefront of European automobile production until the 1930s, when British companies who manufactured cars and vans gained the upper hand in Europe.

But many of the 'new industries' made a difference only at a regional level, with new factories concentrated near large, urban markets around Manchester, Liverpool, London, Paris and Berlin. Levels of production, on the whole, remained too small in Britain and Germany to soak up workers laid off from the declining, old industries, a trend reinforced by the new industries' preference for semiskilled or unskilled labour that was generally young and often female. As the challenge of recovery became one of converting industrial resources to new methods and technologies, there were other problems. Much of European industry was not adapted to produce those goods where demand was growing fastest and the question of change was made more complex for industrialists because demand was spread over a far wider range of commodities than it had been in the nineteenth century. It was also much more sensitive to the vagaries of what was to become known as 'consumer confidence'.

In 1925, the picture was especially bleak in Britain as far as the 'old' industries were concerned. Although world output in iron and steel began to rise that year, technical backwardness and high prices helped to push nearly half of British pig-iron capacity and three-fifths of its steel-making capacity into idleness. The combination of the industry's physical stagnation (old-fashioned plants and machinery) and the British government's determination to maintain the gold pound also meant that the financial position of British industry deteriorated. Once the pride of the British-led 'industrial revolution', heavy industry was now trapped in a vicious cycle of decline. Inertia characterized the response of industrialists and government to the problems of replacing machinery, modernizing methods of production and whether industries should be relocated; the fact that gold standard membership pushed up the cost of investment did not help. Yet, it was not until the late 1920s that doubts about the long-term future of heavy industry in Europe were being voiced on both a national and an international level.

In France and in Belgium the picture was more complex. With much of their heavy industry destroyed or damaged in the war, reconstruction was the first order of business, a challenge greatly facilitated by the inflation that had eased the burden of national debt and encouraged investment. By 1925 the French government had processed around three million claims for assistance and had helped to rebuild roads, railways, factories and mines. As in Belgium, the government took the opportunity of reconstruction to modernize and mechanize many of its working mines – 300 coalmines now included new electrically powered equipment. But almost 8000 of the French factories rebuilt with government aid were simply restored to their original state. By default more than design, the French government rejected the opportunity to effect a throughgoing modernization of European-style factories that were comparatively small, labour-intensive and family based. Across western Europe textile centres, still largely an artisan industry in countries like Germany and France, continued to be hard-hit, unable to compete with foreign competitors who employed new methods and offered new products and cheaper prices.

In Belgium the restabilization of the currency in 1926 (at an exchange rate somewhat higher than that of the French franc) triggered a slowdown in the rate of economic recovery, but the signs still appeared good. By 1927 Belgian pig-iron production was half as large again as it had been in 1913. In France and Belgium industrial production continued to grow strongly from 1928 until well into 1930. In the case of France, high levels of industrial output were maintained until July 1930 – at a level 44 per cent higher than it had been in 1913 thanks to the devalued exchange rate of the franc. It was significant, indeed, that while countries like Germany, Norway and Britain were struggling to recover the levels of international trade they had enjoyed before the war, by 1929 French trade overseas was two-thirds higher than it had been in 1913. Economic growth in Europe after 1925 proceeded more rapidly in countries that had joined the gold standard at a devalued rate than those which vigorously pursued policies of deflation to stabilize their currencies at the levels of 1913: the economies of France, Belgium, Hungary and Italy (until 1927) grew much more quickly than those of Britain, Norway, Sweden and the Netherlands (p. 54).

Some of the signals that European industry was recovering its prewar competitiveness were more apparent than real. The emergence of industrial cartels in the 1920s was a good example of how change had both good and bad effects on the European economy. In an effort to cope with the changing composition of global demand, the pressure for productivity and foreign (especially American) competition, European manufacturers, particularly in the west, sought to eliminate inefficiencies by forming large-scale production and trading units and by setting up price cartels (p. 183). This became known as the 'rationalization mania' and it sponsored some of the leading industrial mergers of the era: the creation of Vereinigte Stahlwerke (United Steel Works) and I. G. Farben in Germany, the Imperial Chemical Company (ICI) in Britain, the French metallurgical and armaments concern Schnieder based at Le Creusot and the Czech iron and steel conglomerate Prodejna sdrueznych ceskoslovenskych zelezáren (Selling Agency of the United Czechoslovak Iron Works). The difficulties in evaluating whether these kind of mergers were beneficial are enormous. The high degree of economic organization, for example, helped to ease the transition from one set of technologies to another (evident in the chemical and steel industries). It also offered greater opportunities to control the workforce and advantages through the economies of scale. The downside was that 'rationalization' also skewed patterns of investment and shielded some uncompetitive companies from the pressure to modernize until it was too late.

The patchy nature of Europe's recovery in the 1920s was underlined by the comparatively high levels of working-class unemployment, although France was a notable exception. In Britain, unemployment averaged one million throughout the period. In Germany, too, unemployment never fell below a million after 1925. The figures for Scandinavia were even more dramatic. Expressed as a percentage of the working population registered to receive unemployment insurance, joblessness in the period from 1925 to 1929 in Norway, for example, averaged 19. 5 per cent and in Denmark, over the same period, it was 18.5 per cent. As we have seen, principal among the causes of unemployment in western Europe was the decline of heavy industry and the impact of gold standard membership. For the continent as a whole, the problem was made all the more visible by the loss of emigration opportunities which had distinguished Europe's high growth, low unemployment economy of the nineteenth century.

Table 3.1   Unemployment in Europe, 1921–28 (as a percentage of the workforce)

	1921	1922	1923	1924	1925	1926	1927	1928
Belgium	11.5	4.2	1.3	1.6	2.4	2.0	2.5	1.7
Denmark	19.7	19.3	12.7	10.7	14.7	20.7	22.5	18.5
Germany[2]	2.8	1.5	9.6	13.5	6.7	18.0	8.8	8.4
Netherlands	9.0	11.0	11.2	8.8	8.1	7.3	7.5	5.6
Poland	-	-	-	-	-	-	7.4	5.0
UK	14.8	15.2	11.3	10.9	11.2	12.7	10.6	11.2

Source: International Labour Organization, *Yearbook of Labour Statistics* (Geneva, 1935).

In western Europe the persistence of comparatively high levels of unemployment coincided with the growth of organized labour. This has prompted some scholars to explore how far unionization and successful collective bargaining made the labour market inflexible and unresponsive to economic change. Certainly, at the time, commentators on the right of European politics made great play of this by pointing to the fall of the average working week from 54 hours to 48 hours, with more workers than ever before enjoying paid holidays. But the vast majority of workers in Europe were not union members and they were, for the most part, far more productive after the First World War than before it. The highest increases in productivity were recorded in Switzerland, Czechoslovakia, the Netherlands, Norway and France, where the amount each working person produced each year grew, on average, by 2.4 per cent (in the case of France) to 3.2 per cent (in the case of Switzerland). Of the major industrial economies in Europe, it was German and British productivity which remained low. Although, even in Germany, which had one of the most unionized and politicized workforces in Europe, recent research into the German labour markets of the 1920s has challenged earlier assertions that German wages were too high and unresponsive to change (or as economists would put it, too 'sticky'). The issue remains controversial, but Balderston's recent work argues that while wages for workers in the Weimar Republic continued to rise after the restabilization of the mark in November 1923, increased pay-levels were matched by increases in the amount produced by each worker. (Wage rises were also triggered by labour shortages as certain types of skilled labour were in short supply in most European economies.) In Britain, however, early studies point to a different conclusion. There is evidence that British wage rises were not matched by commensurate gains in productivity and workers were less sensitive to the problems confronting employers who were anxious to become more competitive.

Economists have also explored whether unemployment benefits, introduced in many countries for the first time during this period, served to encourage unemployment. Throughout the 1920s, successive administrations of the United States, where the unemployed had to rely on charities for help, certainly considered western European levels of benefit far too generous. So far, there is very little evidence to support claims that state benefits encouraged joblessness because the sums paid in state unemployment insurance were not enough to prompt workers to opt for unemployment benefit over regular work. But unemployment insurance was a burden on economic recovery in other ways. Most importantly, programmes of government assistance were a persistent drain on the state budget. This did not just raise painful political issues of increasing taxes and deciding who to collect them from: if the country in question was a member of the gold standard, a persistent state deficit threatened the government's entire monetary strategy. It was no coincidence that the looming budgetary crisis in Germany in 1927 came at the same time as the Reichstag passed a drastically underfunded unemployment insurance scheme. Within four years, the deficit on this one account would claim over 14 per cent of all taxes collected by the Reich and the Länder put together. In Germany the burden of social spending had profound implications for currency stability and the continued flow of credit into the country.

Analysts at the League of Nations were more impressed by the very high levels of industrial growth achieved in central and eastern Europe during this period than by the recovery of the west. Between 1925 and 1929, manufacturing grew by over 26 per cent in Czechoslovakia, 48 per cent in Hungary, 36 per cent in Poland, and 48 per cent in Romania, while Bulgaria's rate of growth was the highest in the Danubian region.

Of course, one of the principal reasons why these figures were so impressive was the low base from which industrial production expanded. It was hard for the west not to notice that the most substantial industrial growth in the east was in industries traditionally considered the strongest in western Europe: coal, iron and steel, cement, oil production, raw material extraction and food production. Modernization, where it happened, produced some startling gains in productivity; in British coal mines output per shift rose by only 14 per cent between the wars compared to 54 per cent in Poland, although mines in the Ruhr and in the Netherlands became more productive by 81 per cent and 118 per cent respectively.

But for the most part, with the exception of Czechoslovakia, the region struggled to match developments in new methods of production and factory layout, in business organization, in rationalization and in exploiting new sources of energy. Firms in central and eastern Europe also found it hard to specialize in producing select lines of quality products because most goods manufactured east of Germany were sold at home and the domestic market was fairly underdeveloped. Instead, firms opted to produce a variety of mediocre products. In Hungary, for example, the iron and steel factories have been described as 'general stores' because they produced so many items in such small quantities. Here, as in the west, the influx in foreign investment was important, but, continuing the prewar trend, the state also continued to take a prominent role in developing the economy. It encouraged industry by subsidies, import controls, tax relief schemes, high tariffs and export bounties. The higher levels of state intervention in the economies of the east did not always help, for government policies often lacked coherence and consistency. In Romania, for example, any business employing more than 25 workers, or with a power capacity of more than five horsepower, was entitled to tax exemptions, railway subsidies and free access to around 5 hectares of land for 90 years. The scheme did not address the real needs of Romanian industry and, because it was indirectly protectionist, also generated new problems.

Neither state intervention, nor foreign investment had a wholly beneficial impact on the development of central and eastern European economies. As in the Weimar Republic, foreign investment was often squandered on projects designed to impress – munitions production and fancy construction projects (p. 89). But most damaging to its prospects of continued growth were the persistent troubles of the primary industries.

Problems for Farmers

The troubled health of agriculture, especially in eastern and southern Europe, was the most serious drag on European economic growth. Here the year 1925 did not mark a turning point in the difficulties which had plagued the agrarian sector since the end of the First World War: competition from producers in the Americas remained fierce, levels of productivity failed to improve and in some regions, notably the Balkans, yields of the most important crops were down by as much as 13 per cent. What was needed, scholars have argued since, were policies designed to reform the pattern of landholding and to improve methods of agricultural production to make eastern and southern European agriculture as intensive as farming in northern Europe and in Canada and the United States. But, if anything, the determination of eastern European statesmen to 'modernize' their countries led them to give priority to industry over agriculture.

The situation in Poland was bleak and typical of the problem. Many landholdings were simply too small, with only 17 per cent of the peasant population owning farms adequate to earn a livelihood. In 1931 the census in Yugoslavia listed two-thirds of all farms as measuring less than 5 hectares – the minimum necessary to sustain a peasant family. In the east, Czechoslovakia alone recorded consistent improvements in its yield from 1913 to 1929. Here the state successfully intervened to reform the pattern of landholding and offered technical and financial assistance to farmers who modernized their farms and concentrated on more profitable produce, like sugar-beet. Elsewhere, however, many peasant farmers, despite the hardships they faced, were often opposed to new techniques and mechanization, and methods of farming remained remarkably static. Such problems were not confined to the east. Patterns of agricultural production in southern and, to a lesser extent, western Europe (as in France) were also behind in relation to competitors in North America, but agricultural backwardness was a much more serious issue for eastern Europe because of the economy's reliance on agriculture.

In much of central, eastern and southern Europe, the condition of agriculture came to dominate the political agenda. European farmers faced common problems that had important implications not just for their own well-being – farmers in Italy, for example, found their civil liberties constrained by government policies designed to stop the rural unemployed from migrating to the cities – but also for the health of their respective national economies and the international economy as a whole. In the 1920s the region's problems were much the same as they had been before the war: the dominance of peasant self-sufficiency in smallholdings; overpopulation; primitive production techniques; low capital accumulation accompanied by high levels of indebtedness; and high interest rates. It all added up to very low levels of efficiency and helped to make life as a farmer a hard and precarious existence.

Life as a tenant farmer was little better. Levels of productivity on these farms were somewhat higher, particularly on the large estate farms in Catalan Spain. But tenant farmers here, like their counterparts in southern Italy, had grown to resent these traditional patterns of landholding that milked them of their labour without enabling them to enjoy the benefits of owning their own land. The large estate farms in Spain were run on a factory-style system, and employers, with the excuse of a competitive marketplace for their produce, were able to keep wages close to starvation levels because of the large pool of unemployed labour. Throughout the 1920s in Spain, agrarian unrest was widespread and sometimes erupted into localized conflicts or 'civil wars', contributing in the long run, of course, to the civil war that engulfed all of Spain in 1936.

There were bright spots in primary production. Farmers who switched to fruit, vegetable and/or animal production, and away from cereals, found themselves considerably better off. So, too, did those who opted to cooperate with each other. Danish agricultural cooperatives provided a model emulated by countries like Estonia and Latvia. Farmers in the Baltic republics became, like their Danish counterparts, particularly successful at exporting butter and bacon. Even more impressive was the strong demand for industrial raw materials, like Romanian oil and Yugoslavian metal ores, with exports rising very rapidly until around 1928. Tobacco and forestry production also grew increasingly important to the region – by 1926 one-third of Bulgaria's export earnings came from tobacco.

But the variety of new goods produced for export in eastern Europe could be counted on the fingers of one hand, and most of these were raw materials or agricultural products. Around three-quarters of all exports from eastern Europe were commodity exports; as so often, Czechoslovakia was a notable exception with only one-third of its exports taken up with the primary products. This was not a healthy situation given the rise of new global competitors to the west and east, the deterioration of commodity prices and the changing patterns of food consumption. The problems of oversupply in world cereal production, already evident in the immediate aftermath of the war, especially when it came to wheat, continued unabated throughout the 1920s. The world was awash with wheat. Between 1924 and 1929, world wheat output rose by almost 17 per cent above the 1909–14 average, yet consumption rose by only 11 per cent. For eastern Europe (excluding Russia) the news was even worse, for its proportion of the world's wheat export market declined in relative and absolute terms: from 1909 to 1913 cereal exports from the region had averaged 8 million tons a year, but from 1925 to 1929 they stood at only 0.61 million tons.

Even without this bad news, much of central, eastern and southern Europe was already in trouble, with the threat of more on the way, because of its overdependence on the international commodity market and the inflow of international credit. Commodity markets were notoriously volatile, largely because demand for agricultural goods remained quite constant. Any sudden changes in supply, such as the very good harvest of 1927, had a very dramatic (downward) effect on prices. This vulnerability was reinforced by the fact that most countries, in eastern Europe in particular, were heavily dependent on the production and export of one or two key commodities. All it took was the price of tobacco to fall on the international market, as it did in 1926, and the whole economic, financial and political stability of an entire country, in this case Bulgaria, was called into question.

Life grew increasingly difficult for eastern European farmers, in particular, but it is important to remember that *all* of Europe was adversely affected by increased international competition in the international commodities markets and changing patterns of demand. Between 1925 and 1929, raw material prices fell by 18.8 per cent and food prices by 14.1 per cent (1923–29), while the price of manufactured goods fell by only 10.7 per cent. The fact that the terms of trade had shifted against farmers by around some 5 per cent, made it increasingly difficult for eastern Europe to pay for imports, such as industrial machinery, which were essential if it was to modernize, to diversify, and thereby to strengthen its economy. The collapse of primary prices, also made it difficult to pay off debts, both at home and abroad.

The political turmoil which racked eastern Europe in the 1920s, destroying virtually all traces of democracy by the end of the decade (again, Czechoslovakia was the exception), is eloquent testimony to the impact of the agrarian crisis on politics. The new nations of eastern

Europe had overcome some of the disruption to their traditional markets by the break-up of the Austro-Hungarian Empire by developing trading links with the United States, Germany, Britain, France and Italy. In contrast, intra-regional trade had declined to one-third of total trade in the region. But these links could become a source of weakness if the economy of the west should turn downwards, particularly given that the poor country cousins to the south and east had little diplomatic or economic leverage to persuade the wealthy countries to keep their markets open in the face of domestic pressure for trade protectionism.

Rising Protectionism

During the 1920s, despite the lofty rhetoric of returning to the prewar, albeit largely mythical, freedom of unregulated trade, European governments succumbed to political pressure and gradually reintroduced protectionist measures. Primary producers demanded protection in the face of falling prices and the fear that cheap imports from the Americas and the Far East would be dumped on already vulnerable markets. Across Europe political pressure led to the imposition of tariffs, import quotas and other, more indirect, forms of assistance by way of subsidies and sanitary restrictions (prohibitions made on 'health' grounds). Moreover, when traditional party politics and methods failed to meet farmers' demands for protection and recovery, farmers were drawn to political parties which proclaimed a special national role for those who tilled the soil. In the 1920s, increasing frustration with the new interest group politics encouraged many in farming communities to support fascist parties, who claimed that conflicts of interests (between industry and agriculture) could be overcome and that all groups in society could and should work together to build a strong national economy. As Hitler asserted, he wanted to lead 'not a class party, but a party of honest producers'.[3]

There was a growing realization on the part of government, regardless of its political complexion, that agriculture was not like other industries. For one thing, it was more difficult for farmers than industrialists to respond to changing patterns of demand because it took several years to switch from one product to the next; for another, it was clear that, on an individual basis, Europe's farmers were helpless in the face of market disequilibrium, and more particularly, the growing disparity between industrial and agricultural prices. Protecting national markets seemed to be the only answer of governments from east to west. With the conclusion of the Locarno Treaty in 1925, Germany regained its right to protect its domestic market, and did so – immediately introducing tariffs at approximately the same levels as they had stood in 1914. France was far from perturbed, for it had already reintroduced a moderate degree of protection in 1919, reinforced it in 1926, and then, in the context of a commercial agreement with Germany in 1927, revised and extended its quotas and tariffs. Norway, too, introduced measures to protect its farmers and lumberjacks that year. But it was the Italian tariff, made law in 1922 to inhibit Italy's 'overdependence' on foreign grain imports as part of the fascist Mussolini's nationalist 'Battle for Wheat', that pointed to the potent fusion of agricultural crisis and nationalism that was to grip first eastern, and then central Europe in the decade to come. By 1927 in western Europe alone, France, Germany, Italy, Belgium, Switzerland, Austria, Sweden and Finland had introduced agricultural tariffs ranged from 15 per cent to 50 per cent.

In central and eastern Europe, the year 1924 marked the turning point. New customs tariffs were introduced in Austria, although, in deference to the notion of free trade that had governed economic relations within the former empire, the levels of protection remained comparatively low. By spring 1925, tariffs were implemented in Hungary and Yugoslavia. Here protectionist barriers were set at much higher levels than before the First World War. Hungary's prewar tariff had been 20 per cent, after 1925 it stood at 30 per cent; Yugoslavian protective tariffs were raised from their former level of around 10 per cent to stand at between 20 per cent and 26 per cent on agricultural goods, rising to between 70 per cent and 170 per cent on industrial products. The most dramatic tariff hikes came in Bulgaria and Romania where effective tariff rates were increased to between 50 per cent and 300 per cent, with a prohibitive tariff barrier raised in every field that domestic industry was active. Even Czechoslovakia succumbed to the trend after the election victory of the Agrarian party in 1925.

At a time when agricultural exporters were increasingly desperate to sell at almost any price, tariff hikes were not enough to protect the domestic market from cheap foreign imports. The 1920s witnessed the emergence of new and increasingly inventive forms of indirect protectionism. One of the best examples of this was the 'milling ratio' for wheat and rye flour: millers were legally obliged to use a prescribed minimum of home-produced wheat in their grist. First introduced in

Norway in 1927, it was instituted in France and Germany in 1930 and became widespread across Europe during the 1930s. Like the increasingly popular import quotas, legislation that determined the consumption of domestic over foreign goods according to fixed ratios (like the inclusion of domestically produced alcohol in imported petrol) provided a highly effective, and price insensitive, type of protection. It did not matter how much competitors overseas dropped their prices, there was no way around these restrictions. But even something simple, such as the provision that imports should carry a mark of origin – the legend 'Made in Scotland', for example – led to all sorts of unforeseen complications in international relations. First came the sensitive questions: which were the 'recognized' countries of Europe? Which cities or regions could have their own marks of origin? Copenhagen? Sheffield? Solingen? Bavaria?

In the 1920s, however, creeping rather than spiralling protectionism remained the norm, moderated as it was by both political pressure from domestic export industries and the ethos of free trade implicit in the reconstructed gold exchange standard. Politics and history, as well as economics, played a role in the national and regional debates of tariff advocates, who sought to underline the historic contribution of landowners and peasants to national life. In 1927 the League of Nations convened a World Economic Conference in Geneva to slow down, and preferably halt, the rising tide of protectionism. The 194 delegates and 226 experts from 50 countries gathered together to pay lip-service to the principles of internationalism and the need to liberate national economies from protectionist practices, but there was no political agreement as to how this might be achieved. All of the European delegates at the conference agreed that it was essential to stop the 'balkanization' of their continent through tariffs and quotas, particularly given the formidable economic advantage enjoyed by the 'internal free market' of the United States. But here unanimity ended for they could not agree on how to do it. The political will necessary to effect genuine cooperation was found wanting.

The scale of the problem was best illustrated by the chequered history of the principal of *unconditional* most-favoured-nation (MFN) status, the principal tool for securing tariff reductions in international trade treaties. In the final resolutions of the Genoa Conference of 1922, it was decided that the widespread adoption of the unconditional form of the clause in commercial treaties would go some way toward rehabilitating international trade. When the Netherlands and Britain, for example, extended unconditional MFN to one another, it meant that the Netherlands and Britain could both claim for themselves the low tariff rates one or the other of them had granted to a third party. The United States finally adopted this form of the clause in 1923, but did not employ it until 1934. A large number of European countries, notably Germany and France, regarded unconditional MFN as something that had to be bargained for and did not accept the clause as a general principle of policy. Successive French and German governments justified their position, in part, by pointing to countries that maintained high, non-negotiable tariffs while at the same time benefiting from all reciprocal tariff reductions negotiated between other countries – the United States was widely regarded as the leading villain. Throughout the 1920s, even in Britain, internationalists enjoyed few easy victories over those who advocated regional tariff arrangements.

By 1927 the rising tide of protectionism held serious implications for the future health and prosperity of the world economy. Unless something was done the sluggish revival of international trade after 1924 was set to end, jobs would be lost and friendly relations between states put in jeopardy. Crucially, protectionism also meant countries would find it increasingly difficult to pay off their debts and to secure continued access to foreign capital flows.

The Role of Foreign Investment

The final impetus that put an end to economic growth came not from trade wars, but through the collapse of international investment and policy decisions taken by governments in the context of their continued membership of the international gold standard. The year 1927 saw the beginning of a sharp decline in the levels of foreign investment in eastern Europe, and by 1928 the volume of foreign capital entering Germany dropped sharply too. As we have seen, foreign investment was vital both to the stabilization of the German economy during and after 1924 and to the, sometimes Herculean, effort required to reinstate the gold standard system in Europe. According to Feinstein and Watson, some $7.8 billion was lent to Europe's debtors in the period from 1924 to 1930, averaging around $1.0 billion a year. Much of the money, some 60 per cent of world loans, came from the United States. It is testimony of their continued economic strength that Britain and France advanced around 15 per cent of the total world loans, although Britain, the larger creditor of the two, preferred to lend to its empire and Latin America over Europe. The Netherlands, Switzerland, Czechoslovakia and Sweden exported more modest amounts of capital.

The amounts invested in central and eastern Europe, in particular, were enormous, with Germany receiving over $4 billion – some 50 per cent of the total inflow into Europe. Austria and Italy together received around $1.5 billion, while Romania, Poland, Hungary and Greece also between them secured around $1.5 billion. Without going into too much detail regarding the different types of investment, it is significant to note the tremendous growth of short-term in relation to long-term investment in Europe. Short-term loans made up 55 per cent of the investment entering Germany and 37 per cent of the monies entering the remainder of central and eastern Europe. This was important because, once financiers began to doubt the wisdom of their loans and whether the debtor nations of Europe would continue to be able to service the debts, it was much easier to curtail their commitments to Europe than if the investments had been made on a long-term basis.

During the 1920s Europe had grown increasingly dependent on foreign loans to sustain economic growth and monetary stability. There were nationalists who claimed that their country had no use for foreign capital. But the low level of domestic savings and the like meant that domestic banks (inflation and hyperinflation seriously undermined public confidence in banks) had precious little capital, far less than they had before the war, to invest in the economy. Take the example of Hungary. In 1914, domestic capital accumulation averaged around 10 per cent; after the war, the average was closer to 5 per cent of net national product. (Even before the war, economic growth had only taken place thanks to substantial injections of foreign capital.) Estimates suggest the shortage of capital in the Balkan countries was even worse. It meant that foreign creditors could obtain rates of interest of between 20 per cent and 25 per cent on any investment made in the Balkans and so foreign capital seeped in to fill the gap left by the collapse of domestic loans. In Poland the ratio of domestic to foreign capital was 4:6, with foreign participation in Yugoslavia and Hungary even higher. But as in the Weimar Republic, the inflow of capital did not necessarily strengthen national economic performance.

Examples of poor investment abound in agricultural Europe as the poverty and traditional attitudes of the peasantry meant it was easier to obtain investment than to put it to good use. In the case of Hungarian agriculture, one-third of the foreign credits raised were invested in farming, but it had very little effect on levels of productivity. In Romania one-third of foreign investment was spent on the civil service and on projects dedicated to generating prestige. Matters were no better elsewhere in the east. It has been calculated that of the $604.6 million invested in Hungary, Bulgaria, Yugoslavia and Poland on a short- and long-term basis, over half was used to finance an import surplus of goods and services, one-tenth was used to purchase gold (duties performed as part of gold standard membership), while the remaining two-fifths were used up servicing outstanding loans. In the case of Estonia, the figures made even worse reading: over 70 per cent of the foreign capital went straight back out again to service its loans. Not only did this foreign credit largely fail to make these economies more productive, servicing the loans meant that earnings from agricultural exports were also diverted from productive use. Hard-earned foreign currency was spent on loan payments when it could have been used to buy new machinery for industry and agriculture that would have made a genuine contribution to the task of modernization.

The need to service burgeoning levels of international indebtedness also triggered more protectionist policies that were not in Europe's best interests in the long run. The failure of foreign investments made after 1924 to self-liquidate (in other words, profits made from investments were insufficient to pay off the loan) meant that foreign debt absorbed a steadily increasing proportion of eastern Europe's precious export earnings. By 1928 external payments on such debts swallowed up around 40 per cent of the capital flowing into Hungary and 28 per cent of the money entering Poland. In order to meet these payments, countries attempted to boost exports, but this proved difficult. When the strategy failed, European governments increasingly resorted to tariffs and quotas to limit imports, and thereby protect foreign exchange needed to defend gold convertibility and to service their debts. International trade, as ever, was vital to the well-being of the debtor countries of Europe because it helped to pay off loans that, in turn, encouraged fresh foreign investment into Europe.

In short the inflow of foreign capital into Europe had helped to disguise, but not effectively treat, the maladies of European industry and agriculture, and problems in the operation of the gold standard. The cracks in the facade began to show in 1927, when the levels of foreign capital entering Europe dropped sharply. They were not to recover again until after the Second World War. In 1927 and 1928 some

$1.7 billion was invested in Europe. By 1929 the figure had fallen to $1 billion and it stood at less than half that by 1930. Why? In large measure, of course, it was because the reality of Europe's patchy record of industrial growth in general, and the persistent problems of the agricultural sector in particular, made it increasingly unlikely that debtors would be able to pay back what they had borrowed. As foreign investors themselves had come to realize, the fact that European debtors were prepared to pay high rates of interest did not reflect their real ability to pay off their debts, and the whole cycle of indebtedness was now serving only to weaken the prospects for economic growth. Indeed, the rising level of protectionism was symptomatic both of the problems facing the European economy and a reason why it would be so difficult to tackle these problems.

As the levels of investment fell away, the debtor nations in Europe did not just look to their own backyards for the source of their renewed troubles. An accusatory finger was also pointed at the largest source of their capital, the United States. At the same time as America had become the largest foreign lender, it had also become a significant import market taking in more than 12 per cent of the world's total imports, the majority of which were primary products. The interaction between American investment flowing out and foreign imports flowing in was essential. European debtors needed access to American markets to earn US dollars to make payment on war debts and commercial debts (and, indirectly, reparations) to their American creditors. But by the end of the 1920s, the falling prices of agricultural goods had triggered new protectionist barriers around the United States. (We have seen how the agricultural depression fostered the same trend within Europe.) The development made it clear to European producers that the American 'Open Door' increasingly swung open only to let American exports out, and exhibited a growing tendency to swing shut when it came to letting foreign imports, particularly agricultural ones, into the United States. The situation was vividly summed up by B. M. Anderson, an American banker: 'The debts of the outside world to us are ropes about the necks of our debtors, by means of which we pull them towards us. Our trade restrictions are pitchforks pressed against their bodies, by means of which we hold them off.'[4]

4

INTO THE WHIRLWIND, 1927–31

From 1927 to 1929 the European economy *appeared* to perform to a respectable standard. There was still cause for concern regarding aspects of agriculture and heavy industry output, and most countries remained a long way off the spectacular rates of growth achieved by the United States. But the general atmosphere was one of optimism about the future, reinforced by political stability in much of Europe and new-found international harmony in the wake of the Locarno treaties. As events during the next three years were to demonstrate, confidence in all these aspects – political, diplomatic and economic – was gravely misplaced. The first signs there was a storm brewing came as early as 1927 in Germany. As one of the best studied and most important economies in Europe, the 'late' Weimar economy provides the opportunity to explore the complex nature of economic recovery in central Europe in the 1920s. The history of the Weimar's low performance economy and its interaction with other countries also underlined how far, and in what ways, the fate of national, regional and international economies was linked.

Critics of Europe's performance in the second half of the 1920s were particularly worried about reparations, and spiralling levels of international indebtedness more generally. They argued 'the only thing it [American lending] really taught us, is that it is extremely easy to pay old obligations with new debts.'[1] In 1929, the issue took on a strong contemporary significance because the Wall Street Crash coincided with international negotiations for the Young Plan, a new scheme designed to keep the reparations settlement afloat. Histories of the Great Depression traditionally date the onset of the crisis to the collapse of the American stock market, although historians have long recognized that the Wall Street crash did not lead inevitably to the global slump. Its most notable effect on Europe was a further downward slide of prices for agricultural goods and primary products. But by 1930, many of the problems already evident in European agriculture in the preceding decade now took hold with a vengeance. It took a while, however, for policy-makers, and society as a whole, to recognize the magnitude of the crisis that confronted them. The early policy response to the economic downturn only worsened matters. The lessons of history were a vital force in shaping the way European governments understood the onset of the depression and informed their policy response to it. One of the most striking features of the period as a whole, was the way the 'golden twenties' continued to be identified as the decade of inflation, when, for the most part, it had been a decade of deflation.

The 'Special Case' of Germany

The collapse of the Weimar economy at the end of the 1920s, lays bare many of the problems in the way that capital operated in both the domestic and international economy, and the relationship between these two levels. The role of foreign credit in the German economy has come in for particular scrutiny by historians for a number of reasons. First, the republic received the largest amount of the foreign monies entering Europe in the 1920s; second, the severity of the economic depression in Germany was, next to the USA, the most acute of any industrialized economy in the world. Third, as one of the continent's largest economies, the health of the German nation was vital to the well-being of the whole. Fourth, and most compelling of all, was the close correlation between the collapse of the economy and popular support for the German National Socialist Party (NSDAP) which, by January 1933, was to see the end of the republic and the first signs of German economic recovery. (As Chapters 5 and 7 illustrate, the relationship between the two events is complex.)

It might have been reasonable to expect that the huge inflow of foreign investment into Germany from 1924 – some $7 billion over the next six years – would mark the dawn of a new period of growth and investment. Certainly, the scale of foreign investment meant that German industrial firms appeared to be financially much stronger than their competitors to the east and west. But, once again, much of the vaunted capital, most of it American, was sunk into staid, unproductive companies that failed to make the most of it. Rather than use it to modernize plants and products and to improve productivity, foreign capital was often used simply to effect industrial mergers – the steel industry is a classic example. Harold James is certainly dismissive of the German rationalization movement, arguing that 'modernity took place on the cinema screen and in the novel, but on the whole not in the German workplace.'[2] This view has been challenged recently by Mary Nolan, who argues that the effects of rationalization in German industry were not so much insignificant as contradictory. In either case, overcapacity in German industry remained a considerable problem until the mid-1930s. Even the German automobile industry, which was one of the most rationalized and productive industries, had to work hard to compete. The German car industry was divided between an efficient sector and a host of small producers who had to work hard to build inexpensive cars for a mass market. As a result, Germany came an embarrassing eighth when it came to the world index of car ownership per head of population, behind America, Britain, France, Denmark, Sweden, Switzerland and Belgium. Many historians have also been critical of the large amounts of foreign investment spent on building and public transportation projects to modernize civic life and maintain social peace; sports stadiums and swimming pools, exhibition halls, underground systems in Hamburg and Berlin, airfields and tram networks. These projects brought political, social and cultural benefits, although they have proven more difficult to measure.[3] Indeed, the trend was not confined to Germany. Municipal authorities in Britain spent comparable amounts on public works.

The governments of creditor countries, notably successive Republican administrations in the United States, were not oblivious to the risks being taken by American investors who chose to put their money into Germany. So why did the American government fail to reduce the volume of dollars entering the Weimar Republic? The explanation lies first and foremost in the fact that these were private loans. The American government relied upon private bankers to follow its recommendation to extend loans for 'reproductive [sic] purposes only' and to refrain from lending to German municipalities. Yet determining whether a loan was likely to be productive was 'not a subject for mathematical determination [but] largely a matter of opinion'.[4] The Republicans had neither the political will nor the legal power to intervene directly in what were private transactions between investor and debtor. While American confidence in European, and America's continued prosperity, remained strong, loans to Germany continued; when that confidence evaporated, then so too did domestic and foreign investment.

The record of unemployment in Germany in the period from 1924 to 1928 underlined the republic's patchy recovery since the stabilization of the mark. Although levels of unemployment fell to 7 per cent in 1925, they rose to 18 per cent the following year. By 1927 they dipped again to around 8 per cent and 9 per cent but then, in the final months of 1928, began an ascent which became unprecedented and did not stop until the spring of 1933. For historians of the Weimar Republic, the evidence of persistent and serious weaknesses in the German domestic economy prior to October 1929 has impor'ant implications for the heated debate as to whether the Weimar Republic was doomed long before the onset of the Great Depression. As we have seen, of all the European powers, Weimar experienced the greatest range of industrial, agricultural, monetary and political problems in the 1920s: constitutional challenges, high levels of state spending and a crisis of legitimacy. The republic was trapped in a low-growth economy that made it highly vulnerable to a new downturn after 1929.

It is now clear that Germany's slide into depression began as early as 1928, for it was then that output began to decline and investment in the economy began to dry up. Historians now largely agree that many of the short- as well as long-term causes of the decline were domestic. One of the first things to fail was business confidence, in the wake of renewed wrangling over the state budget and the threat of further tax increases to hit employer and employee alike. The growing disquiet of German business was reinforced by a deliberate initiative on the part of the Reichsbank to check the boom in the stock market. (It triggered a crisis in the price of stocks and shares that did not recover until the end of the depression.) In 1928, as part of the effort to cool down the market for foreign credit in Germany, the Weimar government led by Hermann Müller withdrew tax concessions enjoyed by foreign investors and this, combined with the now miserable economic climate, led to a serious decline in foreign investment.

The close link between the economic health and political viability of the republic was underlined by the consequences of these economic developments for political life. The decline in foreign investment meant that at every level of government – state, regional, municipal – there was a desperate shortage of money. Budget deficits began to grow at an alarming rate. By 1929 many regional and municipal governments, such as those of Berlin and Cologne, were facing bankruptcy. Indeed, falling levels of economic activity and employment only made the budget deficits grow larger. The relationship is clearest at the national level. Every year from 1925 to 1932, the Reich ran a budget deficit. In itself, this was not unusual and the deficits generally were not large. But the damage done to the German capital market by the hyperinflation, alongside the legal restrictions placed on regional and national budgets and on the operations of the Reichsbank, made it very difficult to finance even small amounts of government debt. History played a central role in the growing conviction that the Weimar economy was in serious trouble. The confidence of German investors had been badly battered by the republic's history of revolution, reparations, hyperinflation and sluggish economic growth. Moreover, the foreign investment, which had helped Weimar to acheive recovery after 1924, was now increasingly seen as a source of weakness rather than strength. There was a growing conviction, at home and abroad, that the Weimar Republic was carrying far more debt than it could ever pay off. As a consequence, the volume of *German* investment in the German economy fell off rapidly after 1927.

In 1927 and 1928 two developments helped to cover up the fact that the Weimar Republic was running out of cash and out of time. The first was a sharp rise in interest rates. As the logic of gold standard membership demanded, rising budget deficits helped to trigger a further increase in Germany's already high interest rates. Although the interest rate hike tightened the monetary vice around the German economy, it also revived the flow of foreign credit into Germany and, superficially at least, this foreign capital continued to lubricate the otherwise jolting performance of the German economy into the middle of 1928. The reinstatement of tax concessions to foreign investors also helped. Beneath the surface, however, the renewal of foreign loans only exacerbated the problems the nation was to face thereafter, for most of the loans surging into German banks, and from there on to German industry, were made on a *short-term* basis only. The trend had numerous political and economic implications. As the Treasurer of the City of Cologne explained to its Mayor, Konrad Adenauer: 'We will thus have to make do with further short-term credits for all the fixed expenditures. But, as you can see by looking at the example of Düsseldorf that could lead ... [to] quasi-legal control [of the city] by bankers.'[5] These short-term loans also made the German economy even more vulnerable to the mood-swings of foreign investors and dependent upon the health and stability of the American economy.

The Role of Reparations

The second development to forestall the onset of the German depression came in 1929 with a fresh initiative to create a new, permanent and final plan to secure the payment of reparations. It was a mark of growing international concern about the stability of the German capital market, as well as renewed international tension over the Allied occupation of the Rhineland. In 1929 the brains behind the Dawes Plan, Owen Young, the Chairman of General Electric, tabled the new scheme, soon dubbed the Young Plan. The scheme attempted to reconcile Allied demands for reparations, German reluctance to pay them, and the United States' unchanging determination to collect the 'hired money' extended to its allies in the First World War. In it German reparations were reduced once again and new credit arrangements were established. The tone of the negotiations was difficult – typical was the acerbic comment of the French journalist Pierre Hamp: 'America declares a plan the way Germany declared war'.[6] The misplaced American optimism that the Young Plan would revive US loans soon evaporated in the face of the global economic collapse after 1929. Significantly, the former European allies and the German delegates, in a special arrangement made outside the terms of the report, agreed that German reparations would be scaled down if and when the former allied powers secured any reduction or cancellation of war debts from the United States. The development was an indication of the deterioration of relations between debtors and creditors that was to come after 1929. It also raised the spectre of a 'united front' of European debtors to provoke the ire of the American people and the Republican administration. In the long run, the sole positive contribution of the Young Plan was to establish the Bank of International Settlements (BIS) in Geneva to provide a much-needed agency for international cooperation amongst the central banks – its other function, to receive and to disburse reparations, remained unfulfilled.

In the autumn of 1929, while talks regarding the Young Plan were still under way, events took a worrying turn with a new fall in the amount of foreign investment entering Germany and the collapse of the

American stock market on Wall Street. By 1931 these two events were seen to have heralded the beginning of the world's economic crisis. Before going on to consider whether this was so, it is important to note the apparent link between the reparations and the incipient economic depression. The fact that the negotiations for the Young Plan were still under way when the American stock market fell so spectacularly, coupled with the monetary history of the 1920s, left Germany well-placed to exploit the widespread perception that reparations had done irreparable harm to the German economy. Despite the complex and largely domestically generated causes of the slump that was to grip Germany after 1930, in the eyes of the German public it was internationalism in general, and reparations in particular, that were to blame for the crisis. After December 1929, public hostility to the Young Plan, and its association with the rapidly deteriorating health of both the German and global economy, translated into significant support for political extremists, notably Adolf Hitler. The populist message that reparations were to blame for all Germany's woes was an easy and seductive one. In the wake of the banking crisis in the summer of 1931, the argument gained increasing acceptance outside Germany too, and, as we shall see, came to dominate much of the international diplomatic efforts to tackle the economic crisis.

The respite provided by the revival of international lending to Germany in the first half of 1928 proved to be temporary. In 1929 the once mighty stream of foreign investment into Weimar became a trickle, and then, in 1930, pretty much dried up altogether. For Europe as a whole, with the notable exceptions of Sweden and France, the problem was no less serious. In 1927 and 1928 the volume of foreign capital invested in Europe stood at around $1.7 billion a year. In 1929 it dropped to $1.0 billion and fell to less than half that figure by 1930. Why such a dramatic turn of events? What had changed was not so much the reality of the economic situation in Europe, as it was perceptions of that reality. The patchy record of Europe's economic performance since the war had finally caught up with it. In the summer of 1929, all sorts of indicators revealed the economy was in decline. It was clear the crisis in agriculture was getting worse, not better, and that the problems in industrial performance had not been resolved by inward investment. The growing perception that Europe was entering a period of recession caused the confidence of foreign investors to turn to anxiety in the face of the enormous accumulation of European debt and the apparently dwindling ability of countries, especially

Germany, to continue to meet these obligations. The loss of confidence was reflected in the fact that most loans to Germany in 1929 were made only on a short-term basis. This development merely made things worse: the more the short-term debt increased, the greater the perceived threat to German stability, and the scarcer foreign credit became. As events during 1930 and 1931, in particular, made clear, this short-term borrowing laid the Weimar Republic open to financial pressure at moments when it was most vulnerable. Any political disputes about taxation increases, government spending cuts and paying public servants also had an impact on Germany's financial health. The Weimar Republic was caught in a vicious circle: increasingly bitter political arguments over the budget helped to put off foreign investors; the ensuing decline in the availability of short-term credits triggered a new round of political wrangling over the government budget.

By the middle of 1929, the Reichsbank had little alternative but to borrow on a short-term basis because long-term American capital was no longer available to sustain German budget deficits. However, recent accounts of the crisis, notably by Balderston and Schuker, have thrown the spotlight back on the shortcomings of the German response to the crisis. Firstly, they argue that the Republic failed to make the most of the economic boom in 1927 to reduce its budget deficit. Instead, the reverse was true as government spending continued to rise well into 1929. The reflections of S. Parker Gilbert in 1927 proved remarkably prescient. As the American Agent-General for Reparation Payments put it: overspending and overborrowing on the part of the German authorities would, if unchecked, 'lead to severe economic reaction and depression and ... encourage the impression that Germany was not acting with due regard to her reparation obligations'.[7] Secondly, it was not just Americans who now were loathe to invest long-term in the German economy. So, too, were the Germans. The monetary history of the Weimar Republic and the rapid deterioration of conditions in 1929 meant the German people themselves quickly became reluctant to put their savings into banks and to buy government sponsored bonds. The political context did not help. As 1929 became 1930, it was apparent that the politicians had no easy answers to the growing crisis. Political disputes over the levels of taxation and spending were growing ever more acrimonious. This political failure made the crisis of 1929 to 1930 all the more severe.

Europe and the Wall Street Crash

Developments on the other side of the Atlantic also played a crucial role. In the summer of 1929 the hitherto booming economy of the United States began to exhibit signs of indigestion. It, too, was hard hit by falling agricultural prices and, with levels of consumption in decline, industrial production fell by 2.5 per cent. Some sort of recession in America now seemed increasingly likely. In 1929, however, signs that the economies of America and Europe were slowing down were not the most important determinants of American policy. Uppermost in the minds of American bankers and politicians was the spectacular boom taking place in the stock market on Wall Street. Between 1925 and 1929, the value of stocks and shares traded on Wall Street had risen by some 250 per cent. Indeed, by 1929 the stock market boom had become such an irresistible attraction to many investors that it helped to draw credit away from Europe because the American economy seemed to offer better opportunities to make a profit. It was in its efforts to cool the speculative fever in the stock market that the United States took steps that had profound implications, not just for the American economy, but for the future health of national economies around the globe, and therefore the international economy as a whole. In early 1929 the Federal Reserve Board undertook a campaign of 'moral suasion' in an attempt to cool the speculative fever of the stock market. This was followed in August by more dramatic measures. The American discount rate was raised from 5 per cent to 6 per cent in a concerted effort to reduce the amount of money circulating in the American economy. But the impact of these steps was not contained within the USA.

In the 1920s the United States had become the most important source of investment for the global economy. Yet its willingness to support the 'system' of investment it had helped to create was not tested until 1928. In a time of crisis, the question remained: would the United States give precedence to other countries' dependence on American dollars over the apparent needs of the American economy? Events after 1928 were to make clear that the health of the US economy took priority. American policy was dictated by considerations of national self-interest. At the time, few were surprised given the priorities of the Federal Reserve Board and the primacy of national over international considerations in the reconstructed gold standard. International considerations played almost no role in the deliberations about the bank rate rise at the Federal Reserve Board nor, according to the rules of the gold standard game and the principles underpinning central banking cooperation, should it have done. Indeed, even if there had been consultation with other powers, there is no guarantee things would have turned out differently. On a visit to New York in February 1929 Montagu Norman, reflected the mind-set of bankers everywhere when he urged the Federal Reserve to take 'sharp, incisive action' by raising bank rates to break the speculative demand for credit around the stock market boom in the United States.

The logic underpinning American policy was at work in Europe too. Germany, Hungary, Austria, Poland and other debtor countries, whose economies began to be squeezed as a consequence of the loss of investment and the contraction of American money, had to look no further than France for evidence of a similarly tight and self-interested monetary policy. After the successful stabilization of the franc in June 1928, France failed to play by the 'rules of the gold standard game' and its monetary policy did nothing to ameliorate the downward pressure on its neighbours' economies (p. 62). In theory, the French government had the power to do so because of the large amount of gold flowing into the vaults of the Banque de France. In the period from 1928 to 1932, French gold reserves rose from 29 billion francs to 82 billion francs, yet over the same period, the amount of notes in circulation rose by only 22 billion francs. Recent studies of French monetary policy have demonstrated how the intellectual and psychological constraints imposed by the history of inflation on French statesmen, coupled with the legal restrictions on the Banque de France, meant that the rapid accumulation of gold did not lead to a loosening of French monetary policy. Inside France, the rising tide of gold only confirmed the wisdom of its commitment to the gold standard. Membership of the gold standard had become an article of faith in French political life, regardless of the negative effects on its neighbours of stockpiling gold. At the same time, it is far from clear that an easing of French monetary policy would have solved all the problems the European economy faced after 1929. It would have contributed little, for example, to solving the crisis of investor confidence in central Europe or the declining volume of European trade. A large-scale foreign investment programme, sponsored by France and managed by the League of Nations, might have helped, but given the history of huge losses sustained by French investors in Imperial Russia such a step was very unlikely.

None the less, economic historians agree the effects of the tightening of American monetary policy were dramatic both within the United States and without. Firstly, it encouraged investment to remain in America where it might previously have gone to Europe or elsewhere. Secondly, in an effort to attract back the foreign investment on which much of Europe had become dependent, the central banks of Italy, Germany and Britain sought to match bank rates now offered in the United States. On 26 September 1929, the Bank of England was forced to raise its discount rates from 5.5 to 6.5 per cent. In Europe, with the important exception of France, the step had little effect in luring back dollars. What the interest rate hikes did do, however, was to increase the already considerable deflationary pressure on the economy. The monetary vice around Europe was turned ever tighter.

The response of European governments to the decline of foreign investment in 1929 underlines the importance of government policy to the origins of the Great Depression. Without foreign investment to oil the operation of the gold standard, the deflationary pressures of membership increased and the shortcomings of the European economy were laid bare. Although the loss of foreign investment did not necessarily mean a great depression would follow, European determination to stay on the gold standard made it increasingly likely. Yet governments across Europe were resolved to remain on gold. Indeed, the decision to shadow the interest rate increases of the Federal Reserve Board was also determined by the logic of gold standard membership, and it was this which was to pitch Europe into depression.

In 1929 and 1930 politicians across the political spectrum in Europe continued to argue that membership of the gold standard guaranteed stability and prosperity not poverty – a message that was reflected in, as well as shaped by, public opinion. Membership of the gold standard club meant that European governments could not take steps to alleviate the impact of the Europe-wide recession and the American contraction on their economies. Introducing policies to spend money to encourage employment and consumption, like investing in public works, were rejected largely for fear of putting additional pressure on the national budget, and thereby jeopardizing the credibility of the exchange rate. Nor could European banks lower rates of interest to encourage domestic investment and to alleviate the burden of debt on businessmen and farmers. Central banks rejected lowering discount rates because this, too, would encourage gold to flow out of national reserves into the bank vaults of France or America where interest rates were higher, and, once again, put membership of the gold standard at risk.

The spectre of Europe's recent inflationary history continued to determine policy choices as Europe slid deeper into depression. Haunted by fears that a more liberal credit policy would bring inflationary chaos and social upheaval, politicians and bankers held fast to gold. It was European membership of the gold standard that enabled American and French policy in 1929 and beyond to have such a decisive impact on Europe. For this reason, it is no longer useful to write of the Great Depression beginning in the United States and being transmitted to Europe, or of the European recession acting as the catalyst of the American depression. The relationship between the two was symbiotic. The determination to maintain fixed exchange rates, evident in the policy choices on both sides of the Atlantic, determined that all the economies would sink together. The mechanics of gold standard became the means by which the depression was transmitted from one country to the next.

Table 4.1   Fall in Wholesale Prices (in per cent)
Average from Jan. to June, 1929 = 100

	France	Germany	USA	UK
June 1931	76	83	76	72

Source: League of Nations, *The Course and Phases of the World Economic Depression* (Geneva, 1931), p. 222.

Of course, in the short-term, the policy actions of the Federal Reserve Board had the desired effect of breaking speculation in credit and shares in dramatic style with the collapse of Wall Street on 24 October 1929. Historians have long been in agreement that the crash itself had little direct impact on the American economy or beyond because the amount of wealth lost as a result of the stock market fall was comparatively small. Yet the Wall Street Crash continues to be synonymous with the Great Depression and a potent symbol in political culture. The answer as to why this is so lies in the way that the images of the stock market crash – flashed around the world on cinema newsreels – conveyed, and came to symbolize, the collapse of confidence in the future. For Americans, to whom the 1920s had brought prosperity, the events of 'Black Thursday' marked the end of the heady optimism that had distinguished the decade. The collapse in stocks and shares was also transmitted to European markets: the Belgian stock market fell by a full 30 per cent, although the British fall of around 16 per cent was more typical. Cultural critics, like the Frenchmen Bernard Faÿ and Robert de Saint-Jean, now claimed victory over America, the nation they earlier denounced as materialist and machine dominated. In Germany, too, those on the right who demanded a return to *völkisch* ('pure German') traditions also appeared to triumph over the advocates of Weimar's 'modernizing' intellectual and artistic movement, the *Neue Sachlichkeit* ('New Objectivity'). But for the many Europeans to whom the 1920s had delivered neither prosperity nor security, it was difficult to take much *Schadenfreude* out of the magnitude of the American crash. European confidence in progress had died already in the First World War and an economic situation that many Europeans in the 1920s believed could not get much worse promptly did.

Agriculture and the Crash

The most immediate casualties of the crash on Wall Street, apart from the distraught shareholders, were farmers and primary producers. As we have seen, prices for primary products were already falling before 1929. Thereafter they went into a tailspin, driving farmers ever deeper into debt and despair. The American stock market crash triggered the first price collapse that hinted at the troubles to come for European farmers and primary producers. Most commodities were shipped to the various ports of the world on consignment. This meant the goods, like wheat, sugar, tobacco, were ordered, but not paid for in advance. In the wake of the Wall Street Crash, confidence collapsed that goods, for example on their way from European farms to the commodity markets of the United States, would find a buyer. Commodity brokers became desperate to sell their wares and dramatically dropped their prices. The impact on primary prices was immediate and world wide. The price-falls on the American markets were quickly mirrored around the globe because the United States alone accounted for more than one third of the world's demand for primary products. Worse was to come over the next three years. Primary producers were hit hardest of all by the collapse of confidence and the decline of industrial activity that was due largely to the ever-tightening deflationary pressure of the gold standard.

Between 1929 and 1931, demand for primary products collapsed and the prices, particularly of agricultural exports, fell through the floor. By 1931 the price of wheat sold on the Liverpool Exchange had fallen by 50 per cent and the prices for meat dropped by 40 per cent. Farmers were now earning less than half what they had before 1929 and found they were considerably worse off than their compatriots who worked in industry. By the early 1930s, a Polish farmer who paid 100 kg of rye to buy a new plough in 1929 found that the same plough now cost 270 kg of rye. At the level of European nation-states, the collapse of primary prices meant that industrial economies were able to slash dramatically the terms of trade for the agrarian economies of central, southern and eastern Europe. Polish and Bulgarian imports, by no means atypical of the region, fell in value by over 75 per cent after 1929. Not only was it difficult for farmers to find any kind of market for their goods, agricultural exports sold for so little that it was well-nigh impossible for agricultural countries to pay off overseas debts or, where needed, to buy in essential industrial products. This was also bad news for European manufacturers who now lost important markets. Between 1828 and 1930, Yugoslavia's drive to make agriculture more productive, for example, benefited from the importation of over 30 000 tons of machinery, implements and tools. In the six years from 1932 to 1937, the figure fell to a mere 8000 tons. True, the agricultural depression in the east was made all the more severe because agriculture there had not adjusted fully to the changes triggered by the war. But the 'scissors crisis' wrought by the depression (agricultural prices falling sharply in relation to industrial ones), coming as it did after a difficult decade for agrarian countries, was the most challenging problem of all. As we have seen, agricultural growth had been unimpressive before 1929, but the unparalleled fall in prices, together with the bankruptcy of thousands of peasant farmers, hindered further development in the 1930s.

The response of policy-makers to the crisis only made matters worse. Raising prices by relaxing the nation's monetary policy was out of the question, thanks to Europe's continued commitment to the gold standard. The impulse to protect the domestic economy, already a feature of European economic policy in the 1920s, grew much stronger after 1930. The burgeoning regionalism of the 1920s was transformed into the competing trade blocs in the 1930s. In the years between 1923 and 1926, the average tariff level was around 11 per cent; after 1931 the average was closer to 18 per cent. The deteriorating economic climate encouraged levels of protection to spiral upwards more quickly, and to higher levels, than they had in the 1920s. Of course, in theory a tariff is an expansionary policy because it encourages consumers to buy domestically produced goods and dampens down demand for foreign produced goods. But the practice after 1930 was much more messy. If the tariff did its job and prices for domestically produced butter and the like begin to rise, then consumers started to complain. The rise in food prices, in turn, triggered demands for higher wages from the workers and increased costs for their employers. The same workers and employers, engaged in the production of manufactured goods, now found that foreign powers were angry that their agricultural products faced steep tariffs and retaliated by imposing tariffs on manufactured exports. Manufacturing, already at risk from becoming uncompetitive through high wage demands and poor productivity, now found export markets closed off too. (This dynamic can be traced clearly in the 1932 and 1933 German-Dutch trade disputes over Germany's butter tariff.) In political terms, protectionism not only ran the risk of setting nation against nation, it also set farmer against consumer and export manufacturers, and marked a considerable threat to social peace.

The liberal trade regime, already under pressure in the 1920s, was now swept away by a new, anarchic international trade regime. As we shall see in Chapter 5, this undirected process was given a further boost by the banking crisis which ravaged much of Europe in the summer of 1931. After 1929 tariff barriers were raised to new, higher levels. The new political systems established after the war in many European countries continued to make it easy for lobby groups to exert powerful pressures on governments to protect the domestic market (p. 23). And with legislation already in place in many countries, it was a comparatively quick and easy matter of increasing the level of protection. Relations between European countries quickly deteriorated in this bitterly competitive environment. Farmers in northern and western Europe were agitated by the reasonable fear that hard-up farmers in the east would dump their commodities onto western European markets given the dramatic fall in commodity prices after 1929. This was good news for the consumer, but bad news for the local producer, so to protect their own farmers, France, Belgium, the Netherlands, and others, introduced new quota systems. In 1930 the

American decision to expand the Smoot-Hawley tariff to cover almost all goods entering the USA at an average rate of 40 per cent drew stringent international criticism. At the time, European countries argued that America's actions forced them to retaliate, but it is now clear that domestic political pressures were the greatest influence in the growth of economic nationalism. Inside Weimar Germany, where the debate about economic policy was among the most politicized, bitter and divided of depression-bound Europe, all the major political parties courted the vote of German farmers by offering protection. Even the Socialist Party (SPD) attempted to attract the peasant vote. Over the next two years, the few remaining countries unprotected by tariffs and quotas became favoured dumping grounds – Britain was one of the most popular. By October 1931 food imports into Britain were running at 35 per cent above normal levels.

The huge increase in protectionism across Europe was evidence both of the problems faced by primary producers and of their political muscle. Countries that imported food and raw materials, and exported manufactures were in a better position to help domestic producers and to bargain with other countries than those who depended solely on the export of primary products. To the east, only Czechoslovakia fell into the category of an industrial power. Here the state increased tariffs on imported wheat and flour by 300 per cent and took steps to regulate their importation. At the same time, the new *Centrokooperativ* (central cooperative) dictated a higher price for home-grown produce. Similar initiatives were launched across Europe. While such schemes did help to raise domestic prices, seen from a European-wide perspective, they sometimes exacerbated the problem of oversupply. Farmers who had not grown wheat now switched to producing it. The end result was even more wheat that the state then had to 'dump' abroad through exporting at subsidized prices. Not that this made Czechoslovakia, or the many other countries that indulged in such practices, any friends abroad.

In central and eastern Europe, too, despite the continued orthodoxy of their monetary policy, governments became heavily involved in trying to help agriculture. The scale of state intervention here was anything but orthodox. The introduction of state monopolies was one of the most significant steps taken. These semiofficial bodies had exclusive rights to buy and sell certain agricultural products on foreign markets. The monopolies offered a guaranteed, minimum price and, over time, did help to raise agricultural prices. Hungary introduced an extensive system of monopolies that, by 1939, controlled around 85 per cent of all Hungary's foreign trade. But there was also a sinister aspect. Central and eastern Europe's desperation to sell its agricultural products, coupled with greater levels of state intervention in the economy, made it easier for Germany to sign mutually beneficial trade agreements in the region. After 1933, these trade agreements also gave Nazi Germany a political toehold in eastern European countries where it had expansionist designs. Take, for example, the history of German-Polish trade negotiations in the fist half of the 1930s. By 1932 the higher levels of protection around German farmers meant that the German government, for the first time since 1925, was able to offer some concessions to Polish farmers wanting to export to Germany, without alienating primary producers at home. The Polish-German trade agreement signed in March 1932 lowered the tariff on Polish butter entering Germany from 170 marks per ton to 100 marks per ton. (Although a significant reduction, the protective barrier around German butter producers was still high.) Hitler subsequently built on this agreement in 1933 with new German-Polish trade negotiations designed to calm European fears caused by Germany's withdrawal from the League of Nations and the Geneva Disarmament conference. The trade negotiations also fed into talks, held in 1934, for a non-aggression pact with Poland. By the late 1930s, as we shall see, the political dimension to Germany's trade policy was more overt now that the Third Reich had moved from seeking trade agreements to demanding 'living space' for ethnic Germans (p. 174).

Farmers, from Poland to Peru, faced the same challenges. Not only were industrial products now priced beyond their reach, the collapse of commodity prices and trade also made it very difficult to pay off their debts. Farmers had faced these problems in the 1920s, but with European food prices falling by an average of 28 per cent in the first 12 months after October 1929, the problems of indebtedness grew much more severe. At the level of individual farmers, these debts covered, for example, bank loans taken out to buy more land, new equipment and chemical fertilizers. Farms in Europe were not repossessed by the banks on anything like the same scale as in America. Instead, the growing burden of debts was hidden beneath a decline in efforts to invest and modernize farming practices and, in central and eastern Europe in particular, beneath mounting poverty and despair. By the mid-1930s governments had introduced measures to ease agricultural indebtedness by introducing debt moratoria (holidays) of anything up to five years in length and even paying off the debts on behalf of their impoverished farmers. Governments learnt the hard way that allowing the problem to fester threatened social cohesion and political stability. Typical were the sentiments of an Australian farmer who wrote to Keynes of the long hours and reduced wages of farmers across the commonwealth: despite 'our best efforts, we cannot keep up to the demands of the financiers and owing to the fall in values the whole lot of us are in varying stages of bankruptcy'. After a heated meeting between farmers and the local banker, 'we left immediately, with hot blood in our heads, to go home and organize a rifle club.'[8]

Relations were to grow equally acrimonious on an international level. If much of central and eastern Europe was struggling to service its foreign debts before 1929, thereafter it was almost impossible. It was a vicious spiral of falling prices, surplus stock and rising debts which spelled potential bankruptcy for families and countries alike. The collapse of prices and trade meant that most countries were paying out more than they made and the strain on their balance of payments grew acute. Indeed, prices were falling because there was no new lending, and there was no new lending because prices kept on falling. If the international economy had been working properly, the decline in the ability of poorer countries in Europe to export their products, both agricultural and industrial, should have been matched by increased borrowing by the wealthier nations – the United States, Britain, France, the Netherlands, Switzerland – to stimulate demand and to raise prices. A revival of international lending would have enabled increased state spending and industrial development. Instead, loans to Europe's poorer nations dried up at the same time as the volume of their exports fell dramatically. The debtor nations of Europe began to lose reserves from their central banks as confidence and their balance of payments deteriorated yet further (p. 45). Deeply and emotionally committed to gold, these developments at first prompted all European governments to redouble their deflationary policies by raising interest rates and cutting spending yet further. It was a 'triple-whammy' for the European economy from which France alone, and then only temporarily, was spared.

The Policy Response: Fighting the 'Last War'

By 1931 most Europeans began to feel as if they were being engulfed by a 'tidal wave' of history which could not be reversed. Commentators wrote of 'whirlwinds', 'landslides' and 'global shocks' in a language that suggested that society believed it was caught up in a natural disaster. In reality, the crisis was largely man-made. The sense of helplessness that infected 'ordinary' people and members of the elites alike stemmed, in part, from the fact that after 1930 conditions in the economy and society continued to deteriorate when it had been widely predicted they would improve. Feelings of frustration were also generated by the political response to the crisis as governments across Europe continued to offer more of the same: gold standard orthodoxy and deflation.

One of the great difficulties in determining the right policy response to tackle the onset of the depression was recognizing the crisis for what it was. In 1930 it was hard to foresee how deep and protracted the economic collapse was to become. Economic forecasters observed the changes that were taking place around them, but this did not make them alter their expectations about the future. The Harvard Economic Service, for example, argued in 1930 that the worst of the crisis was over. They accepted that a decline in business had taken place, but did not expect it to continue. Typical, too, was the view of a leading Belgian economist, L.-H. Dupriez, who that year claimed: 'Nothing in the current state of affairs leads us to believe we are threatened with permanent unemployment.'[9] In 1930 forecasters understood the crisis in terms of the 1920–21 depression that had come in the wake of the postwar spending boom. They did not recognize that the deflation taking place in 1930 and 1931 was substantially different to that of the early 1920s. How so? Firstly, the downturn in demand was more fundamental and widespread at the beginning of the 1930s than the 1920s. When the boom ended in 1920, spending soon shifted from buying, or investing in, commodities unavailable or damaged in the war to new products and methods of production. After 1930 demand for all goods, 'new and old', failed to recover and remained severely depressed for the next three years. Secondly, and much more fundamental to recovery after 1921, was the expansionary monetary policy pursued in Europe and America. In the early 1920s European monetary policy was very relaxed with governments and banks across Europe permitting, indeed, in some cases, downright encouraging inflation in order to facilitate economic growth and minimize social conflict. And finally, America's new found status as the world's leading creditor had also given it an appetite to invest in Europe.

Economists and historians today are in agreement that the collapse in demand in 1930–31 was far more serious because these three elements were absent, yet the apparent parallels with 1920–21 fooled economists, bankers, politicians, alike. By 1930 the public demanded solutions, but they, like the politicians and their advisors, understood the causes of the depression through the perspective of past problems. Public and political concern continued to revolve around fears of inflation and monetary chaos that had come so quickly in the wake of the 1919–20 boom. It was, as the British economist Ralph Hawtrey later put it, like shouting, 'Fire, fire in Noah's flood.'[10] As a consequence of this mindset, the deflationary shock emanating from the United States continued unchecked into the European economy. American monetary policy eased only slightly in 1930 and the change was not enough to trigger a significant reduction in European discount and interest rates. As Eichengreen, Temin, and others, have made clear, the restrictive monetary policy in the United States greatly exacerbated the depression because it induced restrictive monetary policies amongst members of the gold standard around the world (p. 43).

So long as countries were determined to maintain the fixed parity of their currencies on the gold standard, they could not protect themselves from the deflationary impulse coming from America. The only way European countries themselves could beat deflation and depression was to take expansionary measures, like a significant reduction in discount and interest rates or a large increase in public spending. But, of course, taking such steps on a scale large enough to produce an upswing in demand violated gold standard orthodoxy. Any country adopting reflationary measures, or any country that failed to control the mounting pressures on the national purse, ran the risk of triggering a convertibility crisis that would force their currency out of the gold standard. For European casualties of the 1920s inflation, taking any action that risked gold standard membership was an unthinkable step (in the case of some countries it was barred by international treaty) (p. 58).

The fact that by 1931 the prices for industrial goods, as well as agricultural products, had fallen dramatically was particularly worrying. It was a further indication that the gold standard was not regulating the world economy as it was expected to. As detailed above, in theory the collapse of agricultural prices should have brought some benefit to industrial countries. The calculations made by the British government offer a good example of the continued widespread belief in the self-righting properties the gold standard offered the world economy. The Treasury recognized the hardship brought by the fall in primary prices to their imperial partners, but calculated that these falls would translate into benefits for British industrialists who imported most of their raw materials. Falling primary prices meant falling costs, which translated into falling prices for manufactures – in theory a stimulus to demand. But demand for industrial products did not revive in 1930 or 1931. Instead, manufacturers cut back on their purchases of raw materials like cotton, iron and steel and coal. Industry and agriculture were now two drowning swimmers locked in a deadly embrace. Demand in both areas of the economy fell further to become the severest contraction the world has ever known. In the three years after 1929, industrial output fell by one-third, with Poland, Germany, Austria, Czechoslovakia and Yugoslavia the worst hit countries in Europe.

The continued deterioration of the financial sector made matters worse. In 1930 and 1931, central banks across Europe once again raised their domestic interest rates and restricted the provision of domestic credit to protect the gold parity of their currencies. By this time, gold and foreign exchange had begun to flow into America at an alarming rate. In Europe, France was the only country to enjoy a similarly strong financial position. But neither country opted to ease its monetary policy to encourage gold to flow out again, thereby violating some of the basic principles of the gold standard and increasing the pressure on European countries losing gold (p. 62). Life was little easier for Europe's commercial banks. As we have seen, there had already been a flurry of banking failures in the 1920s. In the summer of 1931, the flurry was to become a storm as European banks strained to cope with the deflationary pressures imposed by gold standard orthodoxy.

Indeed, European banks were not the only ones under pressure through the deteriorating economic climate. In the winter of 1930, and again in the summer of 1931, numerous small, 'pioneer days' banks in America failed – in a two-week period in November 1930, over 120 banks in Tennessee, Arkansas, Kentucky and North Carolina alone collapsed. There has been a heated debate amongst historians of the American depression regarding how far these bank failures made it difficult for American farmers and industrialists to lay their hands on capital that would have helped numerous companies to survive. The controversy need not concern us here, except to note the continued deterioration of the American economy had only bad consequences for Europe and the rest of the world. American loans to Europe continued to fall, although the losses were not borne by Europe alone. Debtor countries around the world, especially in South and Central America, acutely felt the withdrawal of American financial support. The United States lost out too. European demand for American exports, industrial and agricultural, fell dramatically. In 1929 American exports to the rest of the world made up 7 per cent of its GNP. Over the next two years, they fell by 1.5 per cent of 1929 GNP, and by 1936 they stood at only 3.8 per cent of GNP. Aside from the damaging effects this had on the already parlous condition of the United States economy, in the long run the development also had very serious consequences for American diplomatic relations with Europe. After 1931, the apparent uncoupling of America's economic fate from Europe, and the magnitude of the American economic collapse, made it increasingly difficult for both President Herbert Hoover and his successor, President Franklin D. Roosevelt, to sell involvement in European problems to the American people.

The Vicious Circle of Financial Crisis

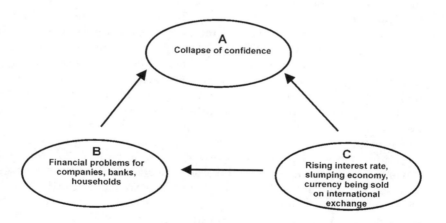

The vicious circle can start at either A, B or C.

After P. Krugman, *The Return of Depression Economics* (London, 1999), p. 94.

5

IN THE DEPTHS OF DEPRESSION, 1931–32

In the late spring and summer of 1931, the European economy began to crack under the strain of deflation and depression. Economic, financial and political pressures combined to produce a financial crisis that swept across Europe like a flash flood. It was only then, as Brüning put it in July 1931: 'the realisation slowly dawned that the world is facing a situation without parallel in history.'[1] Until the summer of that year, government policy, in large measure, deepened the impact of the economic downturn. The crisis underlines the way economic history has consequences for every strata of society ranging from the individual, through the local, regional and national, to the international level. The history of Europe in the depths of depression is an extremely eventful one on all fronts, political, social, economic and financial. Unsurprisingly, these treacherous waters have attracted considerable attention from scholars, and histories of the period are replete with 'turning points', policy avenues taken or rejected. However there is also a consensus amongst historians that the wave of banking crises in 1931 was the key 'turning point' of the Great Depression. In its wake the health and prospects for the European economy and society deteriorated yet further.

For those in political office at the time, the pace of events was often overwhelming; their experience was in sharp contrast to the millions of Europeans who found themselves unemployed or underemployed, and with plenty of time on their hands to contemplate both their own future and that of their country. Mass employment had a profound effect on society, and one result was that by 1932, most European governments, as much by default as design, had become much more involved in managing the domestic economy. New economic and financial agencies were set up, and many governments begun to plan and to introduce large-scale public work schemes, although Britain was a notable exception.

The banking crises which swept first central and eastern Europe and then Britain in 1931 form the fulcrum of the Great Depression. In central and eastern Europe, commercial banks had strong links to industry and the breakdown of one had serious implications for the other. Particular attention will be paid to events in Germany – the region's best-studied collapse – to explore how the failure of commercial banks altered the prospects for industrial and agricultural recovery. The banking crisis also put unbearable strain on the Reichsbank and on the German people, who were faced, as in 1922–23, with widespread financial chaos. The banking failures had important consequences within and beyond German frontiers. German recovery policy deserves the disproportionate attention it is given because it had implications for economic recovery across central and eastern Europe, in Scandinavia and for international diplomatic relations (p. 181). The German banking crisis also helped to create the context in which the National Socialist German Workers' Party (NSDAP) was able to generate mass support within the German electorate – one of the most far reaching outcomes of the Great Depression for Europe's future.

Events in 1931 altered the landscape for financial and economic policy for the rest of the decade. A very different banking crisis shook Britain in 1931. Here it was the Bank of England and sterling that came under pressure. The financial crisis culminated in Britain's abandonment of the gold standard in September 1931, an event which, by 1933, had led some 15 other countries to join Britain off gold. The flotation of sterling is one of the key turning points in the monetary history of the twentieth century. It marked the beginning of the end of the gold standard order and pointed the way to genuine recovery. The improvement in Britain's economic and financial prospects was soon noticeable, although it was not as dramatic as it might have been. For countries that abandoned gold, the deflationary pressure at last began to ease. But there were limits to recovery. Moreover, the nationalism which imbued so much of European policy, notably when it came to trade, had less beneficial consequences. The events and the choices made from 1930 to 1933, in the realm of politics as much as economics, helped to shape national and international history for the remainder of the decade.

Society in Depression: History's Playthings

There was a widespread conviction among almost all political parties in Europe that there was little alternative but to maintain gold standard orthodoxy. When it came to formulating policies to combat the depression, European governments and most of their advisors were busy fighting the last war – against inflation. It gave economic policy the appearance of inaction, and individuals were left feeling powerless, cast adrift in stormy seas. Falling levels of productivity and profits and increasing bankruptcy engulfed Europe in the coming years. On a human level, the most visible measure the world economy had failed was the tremendous and unprecedented surge in the levels of unemployment. The official figures are impressive, but it is very likely that the real figures were even higher. Rural unemployment, too, led to acute poverty, but was often disguised by underemployment. Unlike the 1920s, unemployment was now indiscriminate – it hit blue-collar, white-collar and professional groups alike. Nor was the experience short-lived. Many of the unemployed remained without work for three or four years, with younger age groups hit disproportionately hard. Even men and women fortunate enough to remain in work found their hours cut and levels of pay threatened.

Table 5.1   Unemployment in Six European Countries, 1929–34 (as a percentage of the workforce)

	1929	1930	1931	1932	1933	1934
Austria	12.3	15.0	20.3	26.1	29.0	26.1
Denmark	15.5	13.7	17.9	31.7	28.8	22.1
Germany	13.1	22.2	33.7	43.7	...	...
Norway	15.4	16.6	22.3	30.8	33.4	30.7
Sweden	10.7	12.2	17.2	22.8	23.7	18.9
UK	10.4	16.1	21.3	22.1	19.9	16.7

Source: I. Svennilson, *Growth and Stagnation in the European Economy* (Geneva, 1954), p. 31.

Social tension increased considerably, notably the rising intolerance within nation-states towards perceived 'economic rivals' and 'outsiders'. Many Europeans began to blame their neighbours for the economic collapse, be it other countries or competing economic groups in society – industrialists, bankers, farmers, workers – or simply people who they perceived to be different from themselves, like the gypsies and Jews. The depression also served to heighten the division of experience between men and women. One of the most neglected areas of scholarship of the Great Depression is its impact on gender relations. While a great deal of new work has been done on women's role in the creation of 'maternalist' orientated welfare states in Europe during and after the First World War, the interwar period tends to be treated as a whole. There may be good reasons for this, but one consequence is that we lack a clear picture of the impact of the depression on the lives of women and children in particular. (Kramer's study of women in Frankfurt is a rare example of a detailed examination of women's employment in the depression.) In some countries new legislation was enacted to force women from the workplace. Steps taken in the Weimar Republic to discriminate against so-called 'double-earners', married women whose husbands were expected to bring in a 'family wage', is a good example. At the same time, there are also cases where employers preferred to sack the males and keep their female workers because they were cheaper. The sacrifices made by women to keep the family going during times of extreme hardship have been the subject of greater study. In homes where the main, usually male, breadwinner was unemployed, women – mothers, daughters, grandmothers, aunts – waged a full-time battle against poverty. Their skills at penny-pinching could make considerable difference to the family's prospects for survival. Informal and irregular sources of income from cleaning, taking in laundry and child minding became vital to the family economy.

Undoubtedly, the depression took a heavy toll on children and the men too: infant mortality began to rise; unemployed men suffered physically and psychologically. Young men were especially hard-hit by the social and psychological effects of unemployment. The effects on a community could be devastating where, as in Hamburg, almost half of all young men between the ages of 20 and 25 found themselves among the long-term unemployed. Malnourishment was also widespread and its effects on national health long-lasting. In the mid-1930s a routine medical inspection identified 21 per cent of schoolchildren in Pontypridd as malnourished. It is all too easy to treat the jobless as mere statistics, or the nameless objects of political debate or social welfare. Indeed, some politicians and economists fell into this trap at the time. However, the need for brevity prevents further discussion of the wealth of materials historians have uncovered which convey the subjective experience of what it was like to be unemployed in the Great Depression.

There was not much help to be had from state-led efforts to help the jobless. Although many states in Europe had welfare systems – some more rudimentary than others – the very scale of the problem, coupled with budget orthodoxy, soon exhausted the welfare budget. As so often, the Weimar Republic provides the most clear-cut example. In August 1930 some 453 000 workers were dependent on welfare support (around 15–17 per cent of the total registered as unemployed); one year later there were 1 131 000 (26.8 per cent) and by August 1932 the figure had risen to 2 030 000 (38.9 per cent). Private charities and small relief schemes tried to step in to fill the breach left by the state's failing programmes, however, their efforts were often but a drop in the bucket of need.

In 1930 and 1931, as we have seen, the majority of established democratic political parties in Europe offered no alternative to trade protectionism, which had a mixed effect on employment, and belt-tightening determined by gold-standard orthodoxy. The financial conservatism of politicians and financiers was heightened by the deterioration of the political climate triggered by the economic collapse. It is important not to oversimplify the relationship between economic misery and political radicalism. Many countries around the world experienced intense economic hardship, but did not succumb to political extremism; the example of the United States, which endured the most acutely depressed economy in the western world, is the most notable. However, in much of central and eastern Europe, the coming of the depression seemed to validate all the criticisms made of the democratic system by those on the right and the extreme left of the political system. (Right-wing parties proved more successful at seizing power.) Most insidious was the idea that an effective policy response to the depression could only be found through a change of political regime to produce an authoritarian reform of the constitution, or even a dictatorship. Pilsudski's manoeuvrings in Poland are as illustrative of the phenomenon as the collapse of democratic politics in the Weimar Republic.

There was plenty of finger-pointing at the international level too. The American President, Herbert Hoover, wrongly presented the depression to the American public as a disaster that emanated from Europe and engulfed the United States. Many European governments, on the other hand, claimed the destabilizing impulse had come from America to Europe. The European critics were closer to the truth. The contraction of the American economy had such dramatic effects because it was so large and because governments across Europe chose to tighten the hold of orthodox economic policies to maintain their membership of the gold standard. The deflationary impulse emanating from the United States was transmitted to Europe through the 'mechanics' of the gold standard. The problem could have been tackled most effectively by international cooperation: a coordinated devaluation of currencies on gold, coupled with the introduction of reflationary measures. But one of the defining features of the depression after 1929 was the rapid disintegration of international cooperation, such as it was, on all issues but reparation payments. The depression was a global crisis. No one was left untouched by its impact, yet nationalism dominated the political and popular response to the crash. Looking back on the 1930s, it is all too easy to categorize the experience of people and their political representatives, regardless of country, as broadly the same. It did not seem that way at the time. The severity, duration and timing of the crisis varied considerably and these disparities, coupled with the primacy of domestic political and economic concerns, greatly complicated the context of international relations; the problem is typified by the trade protectionism that swept Europe (p. 137). History also played a role. It was not easy for governments and their advisors to conceive of international cooperation outside the framework of the gold standard. The gold standard gave a focus to all efforts at cooperation in the 1920s and the experience of the past continued to shape expectations of the future. If cooperation failed within the gold standard, then nationalism appeared to be the sole alternative.

Opting to fight the economic depression while remaining on gold meant that governments, determined to balance their national budgets, found themselves growing increasingly short of 'cash'. Government spending was rising while tax yields were falling – thanks, in large measure, to the declining numbers of employees, investors and businessmen who were in a position to pay taxes. Political debate became increasingly acrimonious as to how best to deal with the budgetary crises, and this also put political pressure on incumbent governments. So, too, did the atmosphere of social tension epitomized by widespread 'Red Scares'. The fears of the propertied classes were not helped by the Soviet Union's crowing that the depression marked the beginning of the predicted and inevitable collapse of capitalism. But while Communist economists revelled in what they called the 'bankruptcy of the bourgeois political economy', the Soviet Union also exploited the capitalist crisis for its own ends.[2] In the spring of 1931 the USSR secured a new loan of 300 million Reichsmark from a Weimar government desperate for export orders (it now owed Germany the massive sum of RM 1100 million). The Soviet Union then went on a shopping spree, buying up German machinery that was going cheap thanks to the depression, to meet the remaining requirements for industrial imports of the Five Year plans.

In European politics, some of the bitterest political disputes were fought not between party-political opponents, but within the political party of the ruling government or coalition. The trend was especially marked in governments dominated by socialist or labour political parties where there was a dramatic divergence between electoral promises to generate employment and greater social equality, and the orthodoxy underpinning economic policy. It was a problematic position given that the government would spend vast amounts on social programmes to provide relief for the unemployed, but would spend comparatively little on schemes to generate employment. (A good example of this tension is found in Britain in the summer of 1931.) Indeed, as the economic and financial climate deteriorated in 1930 and 1931, those who advocated expansionary policies or implementing measures to improve living standards sometimes became isolated and defensive.

The question as to how far incumbent governments enjoyed the freedom to make economic policy as they would have wished demands a complex answer. The ability to make 'effective' economic policy was, and is, determined not just by the economic conditions, but by the domestic political, social and cultural context of each country. So much of the domestic environment that shaped economic policy depended on the impact and perception of the recent past: the magnitude and memory of the inflation; the power and perception of interest groups; the exchange rate at which countries returned to the gold standard; the legal restrictions imposed on central banks; the degree to which the domestic financial system was dependent on the importation of foreign capital; the types of goods a country produced and traded, and so on. The international context was important too. No country had sufficient diplomatic leverage to make the United States or France play by the rules of the gold standard (by allowing gold to flow out) or to lend more money. Moreover, once nationalism dominated one country's policy response to the crisis, it provoked, and offered justification for, the implementation of nationalist policies elsewhere.

The issue of 'freedom' was especially problematic for Europe's debtors. Countries that were dependent on imports of foreign capital to maintain their economies had to be seen to play by the rules of the gold-standard game if they wanted to maintain the credibility of their currency on gold and to lay their hands on foreign capital in the future. Indeed, the need to appear financially 'responsible' did not diminish when countries abandoned gold. After 1929, in order to make up for the decline of American capital entering Europe, the debtor countries had to compress spending and to limit demand for foreign imports in order to safeguard their precious gold and foreign currency reserves. Of course, despite the attempts to axe spending, government budgets continued to slide into the red. As the economy slowed down and people were laid off, levels of unemployment (and therefore social expenditure) rose as dramatically as the yields from taxation fell.

Germany and 'Hunger Chancellor' Brüning

The debate about how much 'freedom to manoeuvre' democratic governments had when it came to formulating an effective response to the depression has become particularly heated among historians of the Weimar Republic. The cabinet of Heinrich Brüning, a minority government, took office on 30 March 1930 and its travails illustrated in dramatic style the dilemma faced by all European debtors in 1930. Brüning's government, of course, is famed for its austerity measures and the exploitation of emergency Presidential powers under Article 48 to push them through the Reichstag. After the budgets of October and December 1930, Brüning became known as the 'Hunger Chancellor' because he raised unemployment contributions, cut civil servants' pay and reduced the amount of taxation transferred by the central government to the state (*Land*) and local level. Historians now argue that these spending cuts, when measured in real terms, were not as severe as they appeared, with expenditure falling by only 9.8 per cent between 1931 and 1932. Indeed, as a percentage of GNP, government spending was actually higher in 1931 than in 1930 or in any year in the 1920s. None the less, the budget cuts had a strongly detrimental effect on the German economy because it was in such a weakened condition already. They served only to depress further prices and employment opportunities in Germany with the attendant social and political costs – notably the electoral success of the NSDAP and KPD.

Nevertheless, Brüning increased the deflationary pressure on the Weimar Republic when the opposite was needed. There is still a lively debate amongst economic historians regarding Borchardt's once controversial contention that the Republic had lost whatever 'room to manoeuvre' it had to make economic policy with the onset of the depression – in other words, Brüning had few policy options available to him by the time he had taken office. Most historians agree that Chancellor Brüning did not tighten the deflationary screw around the German economy because he lacked the imagination to do anything else. Important contributions to the debate have been made recently by James and Balderston who demonstrate that, even before the depression struck, the Reich was able to carry only a very small debt. As we have seen, the German capital market had failed to recover from inflation, with German investors struggling to build up their savings in banks after 1923, making it difficult for business and government to borrow money. The government was also desperately scratching about for money to pay for the most basic of services because restrictions imposed on the Reichsbank prevented it from printing money (monetizing its debt) to help out the government. It was the threat of state bankruptcy, and not the fear of inflation *per se*, that limited Brüning's room for manoeuvre.

Economists continue to explore whether there were any genuine alternatives to the disastrous course taken by Germany. They are rightly asking important questions about how governments should handle major economic crises that may be of value to policy-makers in the future. But for historians trying to understand why Germany's depression was one of the most acute in Europe and why Weimar failed, the significance of what actually happened is measured against what the evidence shows might have happened or almost happened. The question is not what Chancellor Brüning *should* have done, but what he *could* have done to improve the economy. At the time, a number of German economists did advance proposals for public works schemes to stimulate economic recovery (p. 141). A possible devaluation of the Reichsmark was also discussed. (The move was prohibited by international treaty.) But these plans were not supported by any of the mainstream political parties, including the Social Democratic Party (SPD). Undoubtedly, the Hunger Chancellor's own precarious political position also played a role in shaping his conventional and inflexible approach to the crisis. Given that, even today, German popular culture continues to be particularly fearful of inflation, it is extremely unlikely that abandoning the gold standard in 1930 or 1931 would have won Brüning political support.

There was more to Brüning's economic policy than flagellation in search of salvation. Brüning and his advisors argued that Germany could only ease the pressure of deflation, spend more, and encourage desperately needed foreign investment back into the country, by showing the world that Germany was determined to impose deflation and spend less. As we have seen, Germany was exceptionally dependent on external financing – and hence vulnerable to political pressure from the international financial community. Brüning had to appear to go along with what foreign and domestic bankers wanted if his government were to secure additional foreign credits (negotiations for new loans under the Young Plan were under way) and stay on the gold standard. But by imposing new budget cuts, the German electorate believed Brüning was simply ignoring the desperate pleas of Germany's growing millions of unemployed. His policy choices further exacerbated the already deep divisions in Germany society. Surprising as it may seem, Brüning calculated that, in the long run, his strategy would liberate Germany. The Hunger Chancellor, like many on the right of the German political spectrum, recognized that if Germany managed to balance its budget without the help of additional foreign loans, then it was on its way to regaining its financial and economic independence. A very helpful next step would be to abolish German reparations and scale down its other commercial debts overseas. After 1931 regaining national autonomy became the watchword of Germany's external economic and foreign policy.

The Banking Crisis in the Heart of Europe

Ironically, the enthusiasm of bankers for the gold standard and for orthodox economic policy proved their undoing, as many commercial banks in the interwar period proved highly vulnerable to the deflationary pressure on the economy. As we have seen, the crisis in agriculture had long weakened the position of many European banks. It also increased the value of European debts by, according to some contemporary estimates, as much as 50 per cent. In 1931 the deteriorating prospects for industry combined with renewed anxiety about the solvency of many banks joined together to whip up a storm in European banking. A further irony of the banking crisis was that it made bankers one of the most unpopular groups of people in Europe, and seemed to pitch the interests of industry and agriculture against banking in much the same way as the increasingly nationalist response to the crisis appeared to set the interests of one nation against another. But it is important to step back from the climate of recrimination that characterized the interest-group politics of the time. An understanding of the processes under way in the banking crisis underlines how far the interests of farmers, businessmen, workers and bankers were all bound up together.

Banking structures across Europe varied considerably, both at the level of commercial and central banks. Local features played an important role in determining the effectiveness of the banking structures in supporting industry and agriculture, and in withstanding the crisis of 1931. Banks in central and eastern Europe were especially vulnerable to collapse for two main reasons. Firstly, these countries had become highly dependent on foreign capital. This had almost dried up completely by 1931 so public and private sectors were both chasing the dwindling supply of domestic capital. Banks were caught in the middle. They could only lend more money to government by reducing the volume of loans extended to private corporations and businesses. Secondly, commercial banks in central and eastern Europe had particularly close links with industry. The well-being of one directly affected the health of the other. The interdependency of their relationship, typical of the great 'universal' banks of the region, is crucial to understanding the mechanics of the banking crisis which enveloped central Europe in the summer of 1931: with interest rates still rising thanks to gold standard orthodoxy, it became prohibitively expensive for many industries to borrow money. As a result, companies were forced to reduce stocks of their goods by dropping their prices. As prices fell, so, too, did the value of securities given by the companies to commercial banks to secure their loans; as the value in the securities fell, so the banks demanded additional securities to cover loans; if these were not forthcoming, then the next step was for the banks to call in the loans. Businesses began to fold. When the chain reaction reached this point, and banks were unsuccessful in redeeming their loans, then depositors lost confidence and a run on the reserves of the commercial bank in question quickly followed. The process could have been stopped by vigorous intervention by the central bank to help the commercial banks and by an easing of the deflationary pressure applied by governments and central banks: both measures ruled out by gold standard orthodoxy. In 1931 the results of this process were disastrous for banking, industry and agriculture alike.

The banking collapse began in earnest in Austria in May 1931. In retrospect, neither the location nor the timing of the crisis was surprising. Although mergers to salvage ailing banks had become commonplace in 1920s Europe, Austria had experienced more than most. The disintegration of the Austro-Hungarian empire, rampant inflation, agricultural depression and, after 1929, industrial collapse had all taken their toll. So, too, had the intimate relationship between industry and banking. Austrian industry was exceptionally dependent on bank loans, while the banks, in turn, owned very high levels of stocks in their client companies. The relationship was too close to be healthy. To sustain their own creditworthiness, the banks had to keep industry afloat, and worked hard to cover-up industrial losses and to create an illusion of prosperity. Neither party gained in the long run. When industry failed, so did the banks; when the banks failed, so did industry. Banking mergers offered a temporary respite, but the result of each merger and consolidation was that the surviving banks had an even greater number of potentially insolvent companies dependent upon them. It was no accident that the Creditanstalt, Austria's largest bank, which crashed spectacularly in May 1931, itself had merged with the nation's second largest bank, the Bodencreditanstalt, in 1929.

With the onset of depression and the evaporation of foreign credit, it became increasingly difficult for Austrian banks to maintain the façade of solvency. The reality was revealed on 8 May when auditors informed the Austrian Finance Minister that the bank had incurred recent losses amounting to some 140 million schillings. In the weeks that followed, no bank in Austria, including the House of Rothschild, could offer sufficient support to bail out the Creditanstalt. Between 11 and 23 May the bank lost over 300 million schillings in domestic withdrawals, and a further 120 million schillings were taken out by foreign investors – the bank extended its opening hours until 8.30p.m. to cope with the volume of withdrawals. Only after weeks of financial chaos did the Austrian government become heavily involved by extending loans to its failing commercial bank. By the end of the crisis, the Austrian government ended up owning the Creditanstalt, and in consequence, owning 64 different companies and 65 per cent of the nominal capital of Austrian businesses. Foreign creditors, too, did their best to ease the financial crisis. Their most important contribution was their agreement to a set of standstill agreements that froze their loans inside Austria.

The run on the banks also triggered a loss of confidence in the Austrian schilling. In the five months following the announcement of the Creditanstalt's difficulties, the Austrian National Bank lost around 700 million schillings in foreign exchange. On 9 October 1931, the government finally acted. Rather than abandon gold, the central bank introduced exchange controls to direct the amount and destination of gold and foreign currency leaving Austria. These became an elaborate network of bilateral payment agreements. Organized on a country-by-country basis, earnings were collected and payments deducted, usually through clearing accounts set up in pairs of central banks. It was a highly complicated system and made the machinery of international trade very cumbersome indeed. Austria retained the appearance of remaining on the gold standard, but the state now had the power to limit its impact on the Austrian economy. From 1931 exchange controls became a vital tool in the management of most central- and east-European economies. In Austria the state-led exercise in financial reconstruction also had important long-term consequences. State intervention reinforced the already highly concentrated structure of banking and industry, and put most of it directly at the service of what became the Austro-fascist state. In 1938 it made the Austrian economy all the easier to absorb into the German Reich after the *Anschluß* and to put efforts to plan the economy of the Third Reich to the service of the National Socialists.

Banking panics like the one that gripped Europe in the summer of 1931 do not recognize national frontiers. The movement of money links the fate of the national with the international economy like no other medium. The banking crisis of 1931 underlined the limits of the nation-state and the importance of international cooperation when it came to defending the nation's currency and financial system. The new political frontier between Austria and Hungary did not prevent the collapse of confidence in the Austrian schilling from moving to the Hungarian pengö or the German mark. However, the Austrian crisis also demonstrated clearly that international monetary cooperation was absent. Europe's 'lesser' powers, as the countries of central and eastern Europe were sometimes disparagingly labelled, became increasingly resentful of 'great' power failure to staunch the crisis. Neither the interventions of the Bank of International Settlements in Geneva, nor a cooperative bank credit organized by the leading European and American central banks was sufficient to halt the banking collapse.

The collapse of the Creditanstalt also had implications for Hungary because the bank was the major source of capital for the Hungarian banking system. The pattern of events here was much the same as in Austria. International assistance failed and Hungary's government was forced to come to the aid of its largest bank, the General Credit Bank, by lending it some 40 million pengös. By the middle of July, as in Austria, the Hungarian banking crisis had resulted in greater state intervention in the economy and exchange controls designed to limit the outflow of gold and foreign currency from Hungary. These steps restricted the impact of the gold standard on Hungary's economy. Bulgaria, Yugoslavia and Czechoslovakia all experienced comparable problems and reached for similar nationalist solutions. By the latter half of 1931, they had all introduced exchange controls. So, too, had Romania in May 1932. Only Poland was able to remain free of exchange controls, and then only until 1936.

Italy, too, experienced a commercial banking crisis in 1931, but neither the Italian people nor foreign governments were aware of it. Italy's three largest banks, the Credito Italiano, the Banca Commerciale and the Banco di Roma (with close links to the Vatican), all experienced difficulties – the latter was bailed out with a secret government-sponsored loan of one million lira. The fascist government and the Bank of Italy both worked hard to keep these worrying financial developments secret. Negotiations usually involved no more than two or three people, and often the Bank's board of directors were kept completely in the dark. The strategy was a success and helped to forestall the widespread panic which helped to undermine banking structures elsewhere. In December 1931 the government established the Istituto Mobilare Italiano (IMI) to support commercial banks and this, coupled with a decline in the overall number of commercial banks – from 457 in 1931 to 266 in 1933 – stabilized Italian finance.

The stability of the Spanish banking system during this period was the exception that proved the rule. Spain had never been a member of the gold standard, in part thanks to the peculiar role of silver in the evolution of its economy. While this had, in the past, left the Spanish economy damagingly isolated, during the 1930s this exclusion also insulated Spain from the worst of the destabilizing impulses and deflationary pressure generated by the gold standard. True, Spanish agriculture faced long-established difficulties, but Spain was spared the worst of the Great Depression. In 1933 the League of Nations estimated that Spanish industrial production had fallen by only 15.6 per cent below its peak in 1929. Harrison, however, has shown this insulation was not complete. Spain was hit hard by the collapse of international trade (the slowdown in the French economy after 1931 was especially damaging) and by the reduction of emigrant remittances to dependants back home. By December 1933, 12.8 per cent of Spain's insured population were out of work, with the southern agricultural regions of Andalusia and Extremadura worst affected. Here unemployment affected more than one quarter of all workers.

The German Banking Crisis

By June 1931 events in Austria set alarm bells ringing inside Germany. With so much already going wrong inside Weimar, historians have found it difficult to determine how far Austrian developments triggered the German banking crisis.[3] That summer confidence in the stability of Germany's banking system, and in the German economy as a whole, was undermined yet further by a number of developments. On a political level, there was continued disquiet about NSDAP and KPD electoral successes, and continued calls from the Socialist (SPD), KPD and Centre (Zentrum) parties in the Reichstag that Brüning stop ruling by emergency decree and return to more democratic practices. Nor did Brüning's efforts to outmanoeuvre his critics at home ease the concerns of worried investors abroad. Indeed, large parts of his political strategy embraced steps that were bound to unsettle them. First came the call in May 1931 for an Austro-German Customs Union that contravened the terms of Versailles and infuriated the French. It was followed by Brüning's ill-advised publication of a *Tributaufruf* (reparations manifesto) in the first week of June 1931. The *Tributaufruf* raised new questions about Germany's ability to pay off its overseas debts – political and commercial – just when the republic was trying to negotiate a new international loan under the Young Plan. Creditor confidence was drastically undermined by the manifesto's assertion that the German government was using the 'last power of reserves ... to tell the world: the limits of privations we have imposed upon our people have been reached.'[4]

Yet for all the furore surrounding international reparation negotiations held at the British Prime Minister's Chequers residence that June, the real causes of the banking crisis lay within the German economy. Of course, the collapse of the Austrian banking system was a worrying backdrop to developments in Germany. So, too, was news that some German banks might be in trouble because loans extended to Austria were now frozen under the Austrian standstill agreements. But it was the deteriorating condition of German banks and their relationship with public and private debtors, on the one hand, and the Reichsbank, on the other, which made the German banking crisis so severe. The drama began on 1 July when news broke of the expensive gamble taken by the giant German textile concern, Nordwolle. Early in 1931 it had bought over a year's supply of wool in anticipation of higher prices, with money borrowed from the Darmstädter und Nationalbank (DANAT Bank). But prices had continued to fall, and they took Nordwolle and the DANAT Bank with them. The dam now burst and the dynamic which had undermined Austria's banking system and its currency now swept through Germany (p. 120). The withdrawal of credit from the biggest commercial banks in Germany quickly became a flood. In June alone, the DANAT Bank lost over 40 per cent of its deposits (RM 847.8 million), the Dresdner lost 10.7 per cent (RM 218.1 million) and the Deutsche Bank 8.2 per cent (RM 321.5 million). In an effort to hang on to their reserves, the banks put up their interest rates and cut back on loans to business. Many of the poor investment decisions made in the 1920s were now coming home to roost (p. 38). Companies across Germany were now under pressure to repay their loans quickly – even firms that normally would be seen as healthy had their credit withdrawn and faced the prospect of bankruptcy.

The role of the Reichsbank now became crucial. Statutory responsibilities and good sense determined that the Reichsbank should act to help out Germany's commercial banks. But as soon as the Reichsbank began to use its gold and foreign currency reserves to discount bills from the commercial banks, people began to question the Reichsbank's commitment to defending the Reichsmark – speculative pressure on the mark soon followed. The fact that the Reichsbank was also having great difficulty funding the German government's relatively small debt (remember Brüning's efforts to reduce the German budget deficit) only served to undermine confidence in the mark further. By 22 June the Reichsbank found it could not serve the needs of private and public finance at the same time as it was struggling to safeguard Germany's position on the gold standard. The reserves of the Reichsbank were not large enough.

With its gold reserves dwindling rapidly, the Reichsbank soon reached the legal limit of 40 per cent gold cover imposed in 1923. New loans from Britain and the United States in June 1931 were too small to help, and by 1 July the Reichsbank could not replenish the shrinking reserves of German commercial banks because no more foreign loans were forthcoming. The Reichsbank was working very hard to defend the parity of the mark, but now had to stand idly by and watch as the crisis in the domestic banking system continued. The alternative for the Reichsbank was to put all its efforts into stabilizing the domestic financial system at the expense of Germany's membership of the gold standard. But to allow the value of German mark to fall was an unthinkable step at home and abroad.

The spectacle of financial pandemonium greatly unnerved the German people as German banks, as they had in 1923, once again began to close their doors on their customers. As the Director of Commercial School in Berlin wrote in the thick of the crisis, pressure on the mark 'presented to the German people the dread spectre of a new inflation. The people were willing to undergo the most gruelling privations, provided the stability of the mark could be maintained.'[5] In the midst of the deepest deflationary crisis in modern history, the German people continued to worry about inflation! Much of the political debate surrounding the financial crisis, whether in international negotiations or in the more acrimonious forum of German domestic politics, continued to focus on the past. Once more, debate turned on the destructive impact of reparations on the German economy and the role of foreigners in orchestrating the chaos – the French, in particular, were condemned for withdrawing funds from Weimar and refusing to lend more. Governor Norman, on the other hand, won public praise for his efforts to help Germany. Yet the careful calculations of James and others demonstrate that German investors and companies were the first in the queue to withdraw their money from German banks (interestingly, American creditors were among the last). Recent history had made German investors timorous and, although they were inappropriate, the lessons of Weimar's inflationary history were applied swiftly. In June 1931 German companies moved quickly to transfer their deposits to Belgium, Switzerland and the Netherlands; private German investors moved quickly to withdraw their cash from banks. These were all skills picked up in the hyperinflation.

The Hoover Moratorium

Germany's need for foreign money and gold to stabilize its financial system, and the inability of either Britain, the United States or France to supply it, meant that, once again, reparations became the focus of attention. Throughout the banking crisis, political debate inside Germany, coupled with the diplomatic efforts of the British government outside, stressed that Germany could no longer afford to pay its reparation bill. Seen from within the cauldron of German politics, Brüning's strategy makes perfect sense: reparation payments were the one aspect of his chancellorship where he stood a chance of broad political and public support. Indeed, when, on 21 June the Americans announced the Hoover Moratorium, a 12-month postponement of all payments of reparations and war debts, the Chancellor's strategy appeared to have paid off. But the Hoover Moratorium did nothing to still the German banking crisis. Debt payments were undoubtedly a burden on the German budget, but they were not fuelling the run on Germany's banks. The moratorium's failure only underlined that the dynamic behind the banking crisis was taking place within the German economy. Nor did the Moratorium do much to help countries who owed war debts to the United States. In fact, during the depression war debts were as much a political as an economic problem. Although America's position on 'hired money' remained the same, a series of international negotiations in the 1920s had considerably reduced French, Belgian, Italian and, to a lesser extent, British debts as well. By 1930 the United States had, for example, waived 35 per cent of Italy's debt, 65 per cent of French and Belgian debts, and 35.1 per cent of British debts. The allied debts did not constitute a great burden on the balance of payments of these debtors, but the debts were a cost to the exchequer that had to be included in national budgets, although some governments, notably Britain, stopped including them in 1932. War debts were as much a political as an economic problem for the United States too. The Republican administration had grown increasingly weary of the war debts saga, but Hoover knew that neither Congress nor American public opinion would accept their cancellation. As *The Economist* noted in May 1932: 'The United States is in the throes of wrestling with the largest budget deficit the world has ever seen in the time of peace. Therefore, it is not to be expected that she should be willing to write off a substantial amount of income from abroad.'[6]

Consequences of the Banking Crisis

Chaos reigned in the German financial system until the 13 July, when all German financial institutions closed down. Within two days many banks reopened on a limited basis, with business confined to paying out salaries, wages and pensions. By 5 August German banking appeared to have returned to normal, however, things were not quite as they seemed. As in Austria and elsewhere in central Europe, government intervention had proved crucial to saving the financial system. The German government had set up a new Akzept- und Garantiebank (acceptance and guarantee) bank to help out the commercial banks and to replace foreign credits that had been withdrawn from Germany. The Republic also had frozen a great mass of foreign credit – around 6.3 billion Reichsmark – inside Germany under the standstill agreements of July 1931. Established as a temporary measure to ease the banking panic, over the coming years the standstill agreements became an increasingly complex system of managing the German economy, particularly with regard to Germany's international trade. The standstill agreements also gave the German government bargaining leverage with foreign debtors whose assets were frozen inside Germany. The agreements were linked to new exchange restrictions to limit the amount of German gold and foreign exchange leaving the country. James's work has also made clear that the Reichsbank discreetly allowed its reserves to drop from 40 per cent in relation to the notes in circulation to 10 per cent, enabling Germany to begin reflating its economy on the quiet. In short, though the German mark notionally remained on the gold standard, the Reichsbank no longer played by the rules of the game. German officials quickly grew to appreciate this new freedom to make economic policy as they wished, not as the international community wanted them to. All of these measures made it easier for the National Socialists to manage the economy after 1933. Indeed, the impact of the banking crisis on central and eastern Europe as a whole made it clear that monetary chaos did not have quite the revolutionary consequences prophesied by the Communists. Rather than mark the dawn of global Communism, the banking crisis led to a closer relationship between the state, banking and industry that produced higher levels of industrial concentration that has come to be called 'state capitalism'.

The banking crisis also had important consequences at the level of the individual. In the wake of the crisis, German savers found they could now only withdraw small amounts from their deposit accounts. There were also new restrictions on foreign travel, designed to prevent middle-class Germans taking suitcases stuffed with Reichsmarks out of the country – dropping in at a Swiss bank while *en route* to a rest cure at a sanatorium was a popular choice. After January 1933 these restrictions on the movement of individuals and money were put to a more sinister purpose. As one German-Jew later reflected: 'Ever afterward this exchange control continued; it greatly facilitated the plundering of Jews by Nazis'.[7] Indeed, bankers in Germany were now almost social outcasts and the common association of the Jewish community with banking and finance was infamously played upon by the Nazis. After 1931 the Weimar Republic's political structures and its ethnic minorities bore the brunt of society's increasingly violent frustration with the gyrations of capitalism.

It is difficult to underestimate the social, political and economic impact of the banking crisis on Germany and the rest of Europe. It certainly made the depression a great deal worse. The prospects for a recovery in industry and agriculture now deteriorated rapidly: levels of investment, already poor before the summer of 1931, fell further and confidence was shattered. The early summer of 1931 marked the point at which optimistic predictions that the crisis was nearly over were replaced by pessimistic ones that the world had not reached the bottom of the depressive pit. Deflationary expectations became self-fulfilling. Business and consumers now anticipated that prices would keep on falling so they held off making big purchases or investments, in the expectation that they could buy them more cheaply some time in the future. Europeans everywhere expected the economy to sink further, and that is exactly what happened.

The lessons of the banking crisis in central Europe also shaped the way many economists and politicians thought about economic recovery. Although the crisis had been caused by the inability of European banks to cope with such a sustained period of deflation, it did not cure Europe of its fetish for orthodox policy. Indeed, the role of the government deficit in the German banking crisis had made many in Europe and the United States only more suspicious of budget deficits. This lesson was reinforced by the sterling crisis detailed below. The deflationary vice of gold standard orthodoxy remained in place. Most governments continued to exclude significant increases in government expenditure as a policy antidote to combat the crisis in employment.

The Emergence of the Sterling Bloc

In most histories of the Great Depression, accounts of the German banking crisis stop abruptly in the middle of July 1931. This is because, although the German banking crisis did not end until August, international attention had long since switched from Germany to Britain where a new banking crisis was under way. The sterling crisis, which ran from July to September 1931, became one of the turning points in the monetary history of the twentieth century and marked the beginning of the end of the gold standard system. In Britain it was not the commercial and savings banks that were under pressure, but the central bank, the Bank of England. From 13 July onwards, the gold pound was sold heavily on the international exchanges and the Bank of England had to work hard to defend sterling's parity with gold and currency reserves. Once again, 'foreigners' were blamed for selling the pound in favour of gold, with the British press singling out the 'greedy, irresponsible French bankers' for particular criticism. The Americans, too, were condemned for their unwillingness to extend new loans to the Bank of England. Now that the richest members of the 'gold club' were under pressure (they were also the leading democratic powers), they began to fall out with one another. It was a worrying omen for the prospects of future international cooperation. Ironically, if any single overseas power was responsible for the pressure on sterling, it was Germany, for the timing of the crisis was precipitated by revelations of the volume of British loans frozen inside Germany – some £62 million – under the standstill agreements. These came on top of similar arrangements made with Austria (covering some $27 million) and Hungary, and widespread debt default in Latin America.

The true causes of the run on sterling, however, lay at home. At the heart of the crisis lay the persistent frailty of the British economy. It was widely perceived that the return to gold had not brought the benefits promised by Churchill in 1925. By 1931 Britain had a chronic balance of payments crisis: invisible earnings from the financial services, shipping and overseas business profits had all collapsed; so, too, had British exports. (Although the prices for imported commodities on which Britain was heavily dependent had fallen dramatically since 1929, it was not enough to offset these problems.) The final blow to the gold pound came in August 1931 when the minority Labour government was unable to resolve the growing crisis over the budget. For much of the 1920s the British economy had been one of the most depressed in western Europe – since October 1929 it appeared to have fared better than many other countries, in part because it did not have so far to fall. Ramsay MacDonald's Labour government, like the equally ill-fated Grand Coalition led by the SPD in Germany, had come to power shortly before the onset of the Great Depression with a pledge to tackle Britain's persistent unemployment problem. The issue had dominated campaigning for the 1929 election, but the minority Labour government found itself quickly overtaken by events. Labour's ministers, like their luckless socialist counterparts across Europe, had no new weapons to combat the slump. Jimmy Thomas, Britain's Minister for 'Unemployment', had plenty of ideas to expand existing national relief schemes, but the usual budgetary constraints stood in the way. Europe's socialist parties continued to demonstrate they were much better at devising palliative schemes to provide financial and social assistance for the unemployed than they were at creating policies to improve the performance of the economy.

Quite how much the Labour government was constrained by the growing budget deficit was revealed by the findings of the May Committee on 31 July. Published on the final day of the parliamentary session, the report pointed to the serious problems in British industry and finance. It was estimated that by April 1932 the British government would be £120 million in the red. The Committee urged the British government to increase taxes and introduce economies, largely by cutting unemployment benefit. It was the latter demand which split the Labour movement: on the one side was the TUC and cabinet members like Arthur Henderson, who believed any reduction of benefits was a betrayal of party principles in general and the working class in particular; on the other, a group, including MacDonald and the Chancellor of the Exchequer, Philip Snowden, who asserted that reducing expenditure was the only way to preserve the stability of the British economy. Although disputes and potential splits were a way of

Table 5.2 Industrial Output During the Depression, 1927–33
(percentage grouping by relationship to the gold standard)

1937=100

	1927	1928	1929	1930	1931	1932	1933
Gold Bloc							
France	109	126	123	123	105	91	99
Belgium	106	115	115	97	88	73	76
Exchange control							
Austria	84	92	94	80	66	58	59
Czecho	92	99	104	93	84	66	63
Germany	78	78	79	69	56	48	54
Italy	80	88	90	85	77	77	82
Depreciated							
Denmark	63	68	74	79	74	67	77
Sweden	58	63	66	68	64	59	60
U.K.	75.3	73.3	76.9	73.6	68.9	68.6	73.1
Non-member							
Spain	94	96	100	99	93	88	84

Source: I. Svennilson, *Growth and Stagnation in the European Economy* (Geneva, 1954), p. 230-50.

life in the Labour Party, this time the Party was unable to resolve the divisions within it. On 24 August 1931, it was replaced by a National Government. MacDonald stayed on as Prime Minister and was joined by representatives from the Liberal, Labour and Conservative Parties, although the last soon came to dominate. These political changes, plus emergency measures to cut the pay of public employees and the amount of interest paid on the national debt, were not enough to banish the cloud of foreboding which enveloped the country. It would take more than a change in government to resolve the economy's plight. The most dramatic development came on 15 September 1931, when 12 000 sailors based at Invergordon refused to work after learning of further pay-cuts. Alarmist voices likened events in Scotland to the Kronstadt naval rebellion that presaged the Russian Revolution in 1917. As elsewhere in Europe, the pressure to resolve the budget crisis was being played out in society.

In September 1931 Snowden's hastily cobbled together public-sector pay cuts were the government's last gasp attempt to save British membership of the gold standard. By 17 September international cooperation among the world's most powerful central banks in Britain, Paris and New York had failed to stave off the collapse of the pound, and on 20 September Britain was 'forced off' the gold standard. The end of the gold pound, however, was not so much a defeat as a surrender. It is clear that by the summer of 1931, many in parliament, the Treasury, and even some officials within the Bank of England, had lost faith in the benefits to Britain of gold standard membership (at least until the system was reformed). In effect, the British government and the Bank of England had given up trying to preserve sterling's fixed parity of $4.86. Where recent history had taught countries like France, Germany and Hungary the horror of inflation and the sanctity of gold parity, Britain's less than illustrious economic history since returning to gold had taught the opposite: the gold standard was a recipe for economic and social misery. It meant that, unlike in much of continental Europe, the political costs of allowing sterling to float on the international exchange were not very high.

What of the economic risks? For Britain there were only benefits, as we shall see. The costs were borne by those powers which remained committed to the gold standard, notably France, Belgium, the Netherlands and the United States. Interest and discount rates were lowered as the British government embarked on a policy of 'cheap money' to encourage demand and investment.[8] The British government continued to claim it had been 'forced off' the gold standard, but in time it became apparent Britain had no intention of returning to the system. Over the next six months, partly by accident and partly by design, the British government developed a national and regional strategy for economic recovery. Interest rates were reduced and the pound was allowed to depreciate by around 30 per cent relative to countries which had retained their fixed parity with gold, most notably France and the United States (the bank rate fell from 6 per cent in September 1931 to 2 per cent in June 1932 and stayed there until the outbreak of war). The Bank of England also lost some of its independence in determining monetary policy, although it was put in charge of the new Exchange Equalization Account (EEA) set up to smooth out fluctuations in sterling's exchange rate. Currency depreciation underlined a trend that had been under way since 1929:

economic and monetary policy was now much more a matter for governments than banks.

For countries still on gold, notably the United States, the EEA became the focus of frustration with Britain's new regionalism. As Senator Borah, Chairman of the Senate Committee on Foreign Relations, fulminated in a radio broadcast, the EEA was 'being used to depreciate the pound and appreciate the dollar, thereby giving Britain an advantage in world markets against the United States'.[9] It is true Britain soon cherished the benefits of deprecation as both trade and employment began to revive. Britain's role as a leading exporter and importer of goods (coupled with the fact that many of its import markets, such as New Zealand and Denmark, followed sterling off gold, ensuring a continued fall in import prices) meant currency depreciation had a particularly beneficial effect on the British economy. By 1934 production was higher than it had been in 1929. A housing boom, fed by reduced interest rates now sterling had left gold, saw three million dwellings built – the fastest ever rate of construction experienced to that date. Unemployment, too, fell from a peak of three million in 1933 to just over two million in 1938 (structural problems and the loss of export markets help to explain this lacklustre aspect of British recovery.) At the same time, the British government was also anxious that European countries committed to gold should remain there. It feared widespread currency chaos, with all the attendant danger it would bring to the already precarious condition of political life in central Europe.

Britain's abandonment of gold had wide-ranging international implications. Depreciation was an indirect form of protectionism for the British market – imports from nations still on gold were now more expensive – and legitimated the drive for protectionism by governments committed to gold. In the longer term, sterling's depreciation worked to increase the deflationary pressure faced by European countries still in the system and to undermine the credibility of the gold standard as a whole. Moreover, currencies that were once undervalued on gold, like the Belgian and French francs, became overvalued as the depression wore on. In the short term, too, dramatic consequences were readily apparent. Countries with large reserves of sterling in their bank vaults found it was worth considerably less after 20 September 1931 and that it could no longer be converted freely into gold. France, for example, was enraged that sterling reserves held in the Banque de France, totalling almost $62 million, or 8 billion francs, were now depreciated in value. Although French losses amounted to less than 2 per cent of the assets held by the Banque, it undoubtedly soured Anglo-French relations. The French government demanded compensation and promptly slapped a 15 per cent surtax on British goods entering France. Shortly afterwards, the French also began to sell their sterling holdings in favour of gold – a development which put increasing pressure on American gold reserves and Franco-American diplomacy.

Other countries holding sterling in their currency reserves were similarly affected, but their frustrations emerged in earnest at the World Economic Conference in June 1933. At present, there is no comparative record of these losses or of losses generated by subsequent devaluations. In the early 1970s historians and economists, led by Friedman and Schwartz, studied the role played by these foreign currency reserves to explain the speed and magnitude of the 1931 banking crises. More recent interest, however, has focused on the role played by foreign currency reserves and sterling's depreciation in the emergence of new currency blocs – the sterling bloc, the gold bloc and so on. These blocs frequently developed associated trading agreements, designed to give preference to trade with other members of the group over non-member countries. The blocs had important consequences both for economic recovery and diplomatic relations in the 1930s.

The 'sterling bloc', as it was called in the 1930s, was the first recognisable currency group to emerge in the international economy. (During the Second World War it shrank in size, became more focused in character and became known as the 'sterling area'.) With the value of sterling depreciating, countries whose central banks held large reserves of sterling and/or were highly dependent upon trade links with the United Kingdom, also opted to depreciate their currencies. Members of this informal group used sterling, instead of gold, as the monetary standard on which the international values of the various currencies were based. Unlike countries that adopted exchange controls, members of the sterling area could freely buy any currency or gold, but, of course, it was easier and more profitable to do business in sterling with other members of the group. The empire and the commonwealth were at the heart of this bloc. When Britain left gold it took with it empire currencies already pegged to sterling, namely India, Ceylon and Burma. Australia and New Zealand joined too. (Canada had already left gold in the winter of 1928/29 for domestic reasons.) Some European currencies also chose to peg their own currencies to the pound, including Norway, Sweden, Denmark and Portugal, with

Yugoslavia and Greece joining later. In the course of the 1930s, membership of the bloc came to include Egypt, Iraq, Iran, Japan, Argentina and Uruguay.

It was here that the regional portion of Britain's recovery strategy began. The British government relished the opportunity to reassert its power as a financial centre through the sterling bloc. The City of London and the Treasury now sought to make it 'as easy for as many as possible of the unstable currencies to base themselves on sterling so that we may become the leaders of a sterling block [which would] give sterling a new force in the world'.[10] At the same time, Britain did not control the bloc. Members of the group were free to adopt or give up the 'sterling standard' as and when they wished. There was no group organization or formal agreement amongst its members, but rather a common set of values and convictions. They shared a dissatisfaction with the operation and recent history of the gold standard and a determination to improve commodity prices. As an official history put it in 1951, the sterling bloc 'was a loose company of nations travelling down the same economic road in peace because general interests and objectives led them to adopt parallel monetary policies'.[11]

'Fortresses' within Europe

However informal the arrangements between members of the sterling bloc, the creation of this new monetary group also helped other groups to define themselves in relation to one another and to sterling. By the end of 1932 a 'gold bloc' had formed – its identity shaped by preparations for the World Economic Conference – centred on France and made up of countries still committed to the gold standard. This group was especially anxious that defectors like Britain be encouraged to return to the system. The very existence of the sterling bloc undermined the credibility of the gold standard and the system's claims to universality. Linked to the gold bloc, though in reality quite distinct from it, were a group of countries notionally committed to the gold standard, but which had introduced extensive exchange controls: the 'pseudo gold standard bloc' which included countries like Hungary, Germany, Poland and Austria.

The arrangements for cooperation within each of these groups were extremely informal. The tension between the blocs, however, was amplified by a new wave of protectionist measures that came in the wake of sterling's depreciation. In this respect, the flotation of sterling did little to improve Europe's economic prospects. Unlike the depreciation of the US dollar in 1933, Britain's action was not sufficient to reflate the world economy. Instead, it served to increase the resort to 'beggar-thy-neighbour' policies by countries still committed to gold. The latter were all too aware that the sterling bloc was a protectionist arrangement because the pound's depreciation in value made exports more competitive and imports into the sterling area from countries with fixed exchange rates much more expensive. As we have seen, France slapped a 15 per cent surtax on British goods entering France in the wake of sterling's flotation. In the summer of 1931 new and tougher quotas were also introduced by Belgium, Switzerland, the Netherlands, Czechoslovakia and France – all future members of the gold bloc. When it came to introducing quotas, the French government was widely considered to be the worst offender: by the end of the year, the French quota system covered over 1000 products; by 1934 it spanned 3000 different items. After 1931 quotas became commonplace in European trade. As in the 1920s, farmers' organizations played an important political role in securing protectionist measures, although increasingly such organizations were eclipsed, or fell under the influence of right-wing political groups with more extreme and ambitious agendas. In France, for example, the Société des Agriculteurs de France lost out to the Front Paysan, a rural movement with strong fascist tendencies. Equally worrying for the prospects of European peace and stability was the new nationalist rhetoric that accompanied trade restrictions.

A fiercely competitive climate came to characterize diplomatic relations in depression-bound Europe. It received an important boost from preferential trade arrangements concluded between particular groups of countries. Trade blocs now sprang up within Europe's boundaries, and between European countries and the rest of the world, intersecting with existing economic or political relationships. In May 1931 the Balkan countries of the 'Little Entente' concluded a preferential trade pact and by January 1932, France built on its political relationships with Hungary, Romania and Yugoslavia with economic agreements to give these countries special access to the French market. Franco-German rivalry in the region thereby continued. From 1932 onwards, political ambition and economic necessity (dictated by its system of exchange controls and blocked accounts) prompted Germany to conclude a series of preferential agreements with countries in southeastern Europe. In 1931 German plans for trade treaties with Romania and Hungary were scuppered by the objections of the United States and others under their MFN rights. By the end of 1932, however, a way around the problem had been found: plans were in place to break off treaties with France, Sweden, the Netherlands and Yugoslavia that had served as anchors for Germany's MFN treaties. Within months, Germany was free of these obligations and had also concluded preferential agreements with the Scandinavian dairy producers (Denmark and Finland). By 1933 the stage was set to enable the new Nazi government to establish a vigorous new course for German trade policy. In central and eastern Europe bilateralism and regionalism had firmly replaced multilateralism and MFN as the watchwords of trade relations. A similar trend was evident in northwestern Europe. In February 1933 Belgium, the Netherlands and Luxembourg signed the Ouchy Convention to guarantee one another exclusive tariff reductions. Although the plan was stalled for a year, by 1934 the Ouchy countries were joined by other members of the gold bloc – France and Switzerland – in the Brussels Protocol, which sought to expand their mutual trade and to discriminate against countries who had depreciated their currencies and deployed tariffs against them (like Britain).

Britain's transition to protectionism was arguably the most remarkable of all. Here, party politics, economics and a vision of historical destiny came together to shape Britain's break with the Free Trade ethos which had dominated its trade policy since 1846. The step had serious international ramifications because Britain continued to be the world's most important import market, taking in, for example, 63 per cent of all Danish exports, 21.4 per cent of Dutch produce, and 17.8 per cent and 10 per cent of French and German production respectively. Until 1931 over 80 per cent of imports entering Britain did so duty-free. Following the depreciation of sterling, a number of so-called 'emergency' measures to protect the British market were rushed through parliament by the National Government. As with Britain's departure from gold, at first, trade protection was presented as a short-term tactic taken to deal with the depression crisis. By November 1932, however, steps were under way to make British protectionism permanent. During the next six months the National Government, dominated by members of the Conservative party, moved to extend the Abnormal Importation Act to a full General Tariff. It raised duties on a long line of finished goods to 20 per cent, with levies of up to 33.3 per cent on products of what were considered to be key industries, such as motor vehicles (exceptionally, the tariff on steel imports was raised to 50 per cent to strengthen the hand of British officials negotiating with European cartels).

Historians have devoted considerable energy to determining how far Britain's move to protectionism was generated by longer-term trends in the British political economy – the decline of export industries, a preoccupation with the economics of empire, and growing frustration with the protectionist practices of continental Europe and the United States. As Garside's recent summary of the debate demonstrates, the budgetary crisis and deterioration in Britain's balance of trade also played a crucial role in persuading politicians and the public to move to protection. By 1931 it was accepted across the political spectrum that tariffs would generate much needed revenue for the government and reduce the volume of foreign imports entering Britain. Most businessmen, financiers and politicians believed the revenue generated by tariffs to be essential to forestall further budgetary crises and to keep the floating pound stable. The same rationale underpinned the move to protection in European countries still committed to gold. Some Liberals continued to provide a dissenting voice. They (rightly) argued that sterling's flotation negated the need for tariffs because depreciation had already increased import prices and cheapened exports. Indeed, protection actually threatened the benefits of the devalued pound to British export trade because countries might retaliate with new protectionist measures of their own.

History gave the protectionist debate in Britain a distinct dimension. Since the nineteenth century, calls to protect the British market had long been linked with demands for closer economic integration within the Empire and Commonwealth. In June and July 1932 these demands added the third and final layer of trade protectionism with agreements signed at the Imperial Economic Conference convened in Ottawa. The Imperial preference agreements reduced the tariffs levied on imperial primary producers by around 10 per cent, and thereby provided them with privileged access to the British market. The Ottawa agreements also enabled the National Government to appease working-class concerns that tariffs would increase food prices. Imperial preference, the public was told, meant cheaper food. Needless to say, these tariff arrangements reinforced the regional dimension to Britain's recovery strategy created by the sterling bloc, and enabled imperial debtors to earn sufficient sterling to pay off debts owed to British banks. It was the principal reason the City of London was in favour of protection.

Later on, similar imperial preference arrangements were also concluded between France and its overseas territories (p. 186). But while the promotion of, in Chancellor of the Exchequer Neville Chamberlain's words, 'historic links of kinship' improved economic and diplomatic relations between the co-signatories, others were pointedly excluded. The 'have-not' powers of Europe, countries like Germany and Italy, increasingly used imperial preference to justify their demands for empire.

When negotiating with other powers in 1931 and 1932, Britain did its best to conceal the implications of currency depreciation and protectionism for its relations with Europe. Historians now agree that Britain's departure from free trade and the gold standard marked a clear break with the internationalism that had informed its economic and monetary policies since the nineteenth century. But for the first 12 months, the implications of Britain's retreat into regionalism were far from clear to the other countries. The British government, particularly Prime Minister MacDonald, remained committed to maintaining peace in Europe by leading initiatives like the Lausanne debt negotiations in June 1932 and the Geneva Disarmament Conference, which opened for its first session in the autumn of 1932. Most countries, including Germany, France, Yugoslavia, Poland, Austria and the United States, took a pragmatic approach to the end of British Free Trade. They were reluctant to retaliate for fear of being isolated from the comparatively lucrative British import market. International concern was focused much more on the floating pound than the General Tariff, especially as every other European power had resorted to trade protection long ago, and recognized they were in no position to throw stones at Britain. Typical was the response of the German government, which regarded the tariff as 'part of the normal economic equipment of a country' and expressed its delight that Britain was 'abandoning its aloof attitude and was now ready to take part in the rough and tumble of tariff bargaining'.[12] This kind of economic bargaining would never reduce protectionism enough to promote a real revival of the world economy, but in the 1930s it became central to efforts to appease aggressor powers of Italy, Germany and Japan.

Policy Innovation

Aside from the renewed appetite for regionalism in Europe, by 1932 new approaches in the field of economics were making an impact on government policy. Governments had responded to mounting political pressure by acting to protect domestic production and, whenever possible, to maintain welfare payments. These steps were gradually reinforced by more interventionist government policies. Of course, in large parts of central and eastern Europe, governments had little choice but to become more involved in running the economy because of the problems experienced by banks, industry and agriculture during the banking collapse. But many European governments were specifically elected to take a more 'hands on' approach to the economy, motivated by the scale and persistence of the unemployment problem and the attendant social unrest, and informed by new ideas.

The Briton John Maynard Keynes is the economist credited with contributing the most to debates regarding the role of government policy in managing the economy. Although his ideas did not reach theoretical maturity, and a broader public, until the publication of his *General Theory of Employment, Interest and Money* in 1936, he was active as a member of the Economic Advisory Council set up by MacDonald in 1930, and an effective publicist for his ideas among elites, at home and abroad, long before then. While his policy proposals did not take hold in Britain until the Second World War, thanks to his high international profile and contacts overseas, his ideas informed and, in turn, were shaped by those of leading German economists, notably Wladimir Woytinsky, and the Swedes Bertil Ohlin, Gunnar Myrdal and E. R. Lindahl. Motivated by intellectual discovery and humanitarian concern for the unemployed, these economists challenged the established orthodoxy by demanding that government increase its spending by setting up programmes of large-scale public works to reduce unemployment and to stimulate demand, generating benefits that would grow and ripple ('multiply') out across the entire economy.

Discussion of the need for public work programmes became commonplace in Germany in 1932 and, unlike Britain, had exponents within the Economics Ministry like Günter Gereke and Wilhelm Lautenbach. By April 1932, encouraged in part by the findings of a commission set up by Brüning to study the problem of employment and the lobbying of ministers, the German government agreed to spend a modest 135 million Reichsmark on work creation. Under Chancellor Franz von Papen, the government spent an additional 167 million Reichsmarks to create 15 169 jobs in the textile industry and another 12 683 in mining. With over six million unemployed, it took time for the benefits of these programmes to be felt and to distinguish their effects from incentives granted to private industry to employ more workers. The benefits to the German economy, in the case of the Papen Plan and Schleicher's 'Sofortprogramme' (initiated by Weimar's final Chancellor, Kurt von Schleicher), came too late to profit Weimar's last Chancellors. However, Hitler quickly adopted public works into his political programme as a versatile means to generate recovery and later rearmament (p. 175).

It was Sweden, the most industrialized economy in Scandinavia, that appeared to adopt the most coherent approach. In 1932 a coalition government, dominated by the Social Democratic Party, took up the ideas of Ohlin and Myrdal in a series of initiatives that were presented as a radical break with the past. Finance Minister Ernst Wigforss took an innovative approach to the government budget (balancing it over a number of years rather than annually) to increase revenue available to the government. This money was then ploughed back into the economy in subsidized building schemes and public works programmes. The government also attempted to set wages for those employed on the schemes at market rates, rather than at the level of the lowest paid, in order to increase further the volume of demand in the Swedish economy. Contemporary estimates suggest that around 40 000 jobs were created between 1934 and 1935. To support agriculture, the government introduced new subsidies programmes, dubbed 'cow-swaps' by the general public. These measures undoubtedly played an important part in preventing even worse levels of unemployment and poverty. The Swedish 'experiment' was closely watched by many economists, including Americans who went on to shape Roosevelt's New Deal, but then, as now, its results remain controversial. Gustaffson has argued recently that in the Scandinavian context, the ideas underpinning the famous Swedish model were neither new nor particularly radical. There is evidence that public works and deficit financing had been employed already in Sweden before 1914 to combat unemployment, while in the 1930s state intervention in the Danish economy was not only much greater, but also more successful than in Sweden. (Comparatively little is known about Norway.)

Even in 'innovative' Sweden, the pressure for financial probity remained strong. As in Germany in 1932, the amounts spent by the Swedish government were not large – little more than one per cent of GNP from 1932 to 1934. Moreover, it now seems clear that Swedish recovery was strongly influenced by the benefits of a stable banking system (it experienced no defaults or problems meeting overseas payments), currency depreciation within the sterling bloc, low interest rates, price stability, and the recovery of both the British and German export markets. The role of Germany in Sweden's recovery grew particularly pronounced as German rearmament accelerated (p. 181).

Britain was the one major economic power that did not introduce large-scale public works in the 1930s. The apparent success of Italian public works certainly stirred the Labour leader Ramsay MacDonald's admiration: 'Italy today is violating the principles of the economically sound but her object is to increase national energy ... we must definitely bring national spirit into the catalogue of economic factors.'[13] But it was the Liberal Party which offered the British electorate the most innovative policies. Economists have estimated that if the Liberal Party's proposals, based on Keynesian ideas, for public works had been implemented some 300 000 unemployed Britons would have found work. But the traditional 'economic factors' were not easily sidestepped. Keynes's proposals were pooh-poohed as crackpot by the Treasury, in particular, where the determination to maintain a balanced budget remained very strong. It was also argued that government investment would discourage ('crowd-out') investment from the private sector, and many economists would now accept that, in economic terms, the effect of the 'multiplier' is not as strong as once thought. Political and psychological reasons also underpinned the 'Treasury view': if the government appeared extravagant, it might lose the support of business, currency stability would be threatened and the benefits of 'cheap money' lost. It was a view that gained credence following events in France after 1936 (p. 186). The prevailing culture of the political economy was, and is, not easily overturned. Until rearmament began in earnest in 1938, British deficits remained small.

Even the famed Italian public works schemes, initiated before the onset of the depression, were not an unqualified success. Piva and Toniolo estimate the total number of jobs created by public works to be some 60 000 – around 9 per cent of the total number of people unemployed. In the mid and late 1930s, large-scale public works were also initiated in eastern Europe, the 'Billion Pengö Plan' launched in Hungary in 1938, for example, but we know much less about their impact. Since the 1970s, however, historians and economists have become more sensitive to the economic shortcomings of such programmes – their social or political benefits are rarely measured – and to the danger of ascribing too much coherence to notions about the impact of public works in the depression, when fully formed ideas regarding government intervention developed only much later. Research into how nations collected statistics on economic performance has also made it clear that in the interwar period, most European governments lacked the detailed statistical data that was needed to implement Keynesian-style policies successfully.

Limits on Recovery

From 1930 until January 1933, the most significant steps toward the long-term recovery in the European economy had come with sterling's flotation. It marked the beginning of the end of the gold standard system. Freed from the budgetary constraints imposed by membership of the system, countries like Britain could have spent more public money than they did to offset the collapse in private spending and investment. But as we have seen, there were limits – real and perceived – about how far they could go, particularly when the national currency remained open to a collapse in confidence. (Countries with exchange controls were protected from this to a degree, but had different problems (p. 171)). The benefits of currency depreciation became more apparent with the flotation of the dollar in 1933. This is because in 1931 and 1932 the climate of international uncertainty continued to make countries, including those off the gold standard like Britain, anxious to hoard gold. In the immediate wake of sterling's flotation, the Bank of England began to rebuild its lost gold reserves, increasing the deflationary pressure of countries remaining in the system. The British were also very reluctant to let gold flow out as their economy revived. Given that British policy was supposed to have undergone a revolution, it was surprising to note how much it still had in common with countries that remained on gold. In 1932 France and the United States, the two countries who had enormous reserves of gold and could easily have afforded to take more fundamental expansionary measures than Britain's, for the time being remained psychologically and politically unprepared for such 'radical economics'.

Wage rates may also have acted as a drag on recovery. During the depression, many politicians repeated arguments made in the 1920s that wage rates were too high. Given the downturn in Europe's economic fortunes, these arguments carried more force than they did in the 1920s. Unemployment on the scale experienced by 1930s Europe should have encouraged wages to fall, especially given the slide in industrial and agricultural prices since 1929. But in all European countries for which there are figures, wage rates remained persistently higher than prices for much of the 1930s. (It has been calculated by Eichengreen that in 1933 wages were between 4 per cent and 19 per cent higher in relation to prices than they had been in 1929.) Some governments, notably those of Italy and France, did attempt to force rates down, but without much success. Germany, largely for political reasons, was the exception (p. 177). Economists and historians have struggled to explain why wage rates remained so stubborn and how far they acted as a drag on recovery. But when the social and political consequences of unemployment in interwar Europe are taken into account, it is hard to accept today's economists' criticisms that governments were wrong to adopt measures which encouraged workers to share available employment, by alternating three days of work with three days on the dole, for example, instead of making workers put in longer hours for less pay.

None the less, by the end of 1932, in some countries primary and industrial prices were at last beginning to rise, and levels of unemployment to fall, thanks to currency depreciation and state intervention. Protectionism, too, had helped farmers and primary producers. Conditions were improving in Britain, Scandinavia and central Europe. But the nationalism and regionalism which infused policy responses also put clear limits on economic recovery: levels of protectionism were too high and the structures too complex; prices were still very low; business and consumer confidence remained fragile.

Table 5.3 Constant Employment Budget Surplus, 1929–40 (per cent of GDP)

1929–30	+0.4	1935–36	+2.0
1930–31	+1.1	1936–37	+0.8
1931–32	+2.5	1937–38	0.0
1932–33	+3.0	1938–39	-1.6
1933–34	+4.2	1939–40	-12.2
1934–35	+3.2		

Source: R. Middleton, 'The Constant Employment Budget Balance and British Budgetary Policy, 1929–39', *Economic History Review*, 34 (1981).

The inability of democratic governments to cope with the onset of the depression also had brought authoritarian governments to power across Europe, some of whom explicitly challenged the diplomatic order established in 1919 and threatened international peace. The growing likelihood of war also shaped the manner of European recovery after 1932.

As Temin, Eichengreen and others have argued, the best way to effect national and international recovery from the depression was a strategy of internationally coordinated currency devaluations and reflationary measures. In this way, the deflationary pressures on the world economy would have been eased without any resort to 'beggar-thy-neighbour' gold sterilizations, currency depreciations or trade protectionism. International cooperation, then, was crucial to combating the depression, but, once again, interpretations of recent history, coupled with the nationalism which infused domestic recovery strategies since 1930, impeded cooperation. It is to the history of diplomacy, and its consequences for recovery and peace on the international and national level, that we now turn.

6

INTERNATIONALISM VERSUS NATIONALISM, 1931–34

The depression asked new questions of economic policy which European governments struggled to answer, and in 1931 the strain also began to show in international relations. In the Far East came Japan's dramatic incursion into Manchuria; the invasion's heady mix of imperialist aggression and economic nationalism was a worrying pointer to the future. Closer to home, the year also marked the first efforts to effect international cooperation to tackle the crisis with the Hoover Moratorium (p. 127). It came as the established channels of European and American international economic relations – trade negotiations and monetary cooperation through the gold standard – grew increasingly clogged with disputes over protectionism and, after September 1931, currency depreciation. Hoover's initiative did not mark the dawn of US leadership to goad other powers into new ways of thinking and dealing with the crisis. It did, however, have an important impact on shaping European expectations of US policy with regard to war debts and reparations. Conference diplomacy, so typical of international relations in the 1920s, continued to set the trend. The 1932 Lausanne Conference, for example, had important consequences for relations between Europe and the United States. It also set in train preparations for the Stresa Conference of 1932 to examine economic ties between eastern and western Europe, and established the principle and the parameters of the World Economic Conference held in the summer of 1933.

The year 1933 marks an excellent spot to stand and survey events:

147

there was a landmark policy shift with Roosevelt's momentous decision to float the dollar, although there were clear limits to his expansionism. The year also witnessed political developments on a national and international level – a National Socialist government in Germany, the collapse of the Geneva Disarmament conference – that set economic policies and diplomatic relations on paths from which it proved increasingly difficult to escape. The failure of international cooperation by the end of 1933 convinced Europe of the wisdom of nationally orientated recovery measures.

A large number of authors have emphasized the failure of the United States to provide the leadership vital to light the way out of the crisis. Regardless of whether others would follow, the United States was the only country in the 1930s with sufficient monetary power to make a big difference to the condition of the international economy. Slashing interest rates in 1929 or maintaining levels of loans overseas would have had a broadly beneficial impact on the international economy, as did the decision in April 1933 to abandon the gold standard. But the depression triggered the biggest economic crisis industrialized America had yet experienced and this, coupled with its 'exceptional' history and constitutional 'safeguards', meant that neither the American administration nor the American people were inclined to take the lead in economic diplomacy. Moreover, when it came to more political questions, like those embedded in trade protectionism or war debts and reparations, leading the way was only the first step in a complicated dance. The ability of other countries to demonstrate a genuine political will to cooperate was equally important. The rapid turnover in European governments since 1929, itself a consequence of the depression, introduced lots of new partners, some of whom were violently hostile to international cooperation, into the diplomatic mix. From the vantage point of the Cold War, it was all too easy for scholars to underestimate how difficult it was to achieve international agreement on an economic or monetary issue, even when countries shared similar liberal democratic values and capitalist economies. Leadership was not just about economic power, but also about diplomatic experience, political will, historical precedence and a perception of who was strong and who was weak in the context of the depression. The seesawing fortunes of the world's leading diplomatic actors further confused the picture. France, for example, entered the depression late; Russia seemed unaffected, while to its west, the smaller countries of eastern Europe and Germany were the most hard-hit in Europe. Britain was now too weak to provide assertive leadership to the world economy, but as the discussion of the World Economic Conference will show, its early recovery from depression, coupled with a long history of international involvement, led to misplaced expectations of British leadership in 1932 and 1933.

Conference Diplomacy

The first proposal for an international conference to revive European economic and political 'confidence' came in German-American talks in December 1930. The proposal resurfaced, championed by the British government, in the wake of the Hoover Moratorium in the summer of 1931. The development was not accidental. Domestic and international concerns combined with the legacy of history to trigger a short-lived British determination to, in Prime Minister MacDonald's words, take a 'big, bold lead in the world'.[1] The primary focus of British, and sub-sequently, conference diplomacy in 1931 and 1932 were reparation and war-debt payments. Britain's initiative, in part, grew out of the misleading signal to Europe in the Hoover Moratorium that the White House finally recognized the interconnection between reparations and war debts. This development, coupled with Republican urgings that the banking collapse was 'patently a European crisis' at meetings like that between French Premier Pierre Laval and President Hoover in October 1931, laid a trail that was to lead European policy on debts into direct confrontation with the interests of the United States in the summers of 1932, 1933 and, most dramatically, 1934.

Although British economic and monetary policy took on a strong regional perspective after 1931, the pragmatism which was a defining characteristic of British policy determined that an initiative in Europe to resolve the reparations and war-debts *imbroglio* would bring important economic and diplomatic benefits within, and beyond, European frontiers. The standstill agreements negotiated between Britain and its creditors in Europe were a significant force behind the development of policy too. These determined that the health of the British banking system was increasingly equated with the stability of German finance (p. 130). In the wake of the 1931 banking crisis, the British government noted with increasing alarm that many to the right of the German political spectrum increasingly blurred the distinction between reparations and Germany's commercial debts in demands that all

Germany's debts should be cancelled. With large amounts of commercial debts frozen inside Germany, Britain was anxious to nip the trend in the bud and increasingly advanced the view that the commercial credit extended to Germany would best be safeguarded by the complete abolition of political debts – in other words, reparations and war debts had to go. The British government believed the move would bring economic and political benefits, although the latter did not extend much beyond the vague presumption that abolishing reparations would shore up Germany's increasingly precarious democracy. Significant in the evolution of British diplomacy in the depression, and beyond, was the way Britain's strategy underlined the vital role Germany played in the heart of Europe, particularly, as the Treasury put it, after 'the freezing up of resources of Germany and other Central European debtor countries, financial embarrassments ... and the world-wide collapse in confidence'.[2] In some ways it is surprising that so much international attention was focused on reparations – the London conference of July 1931 was also devoted to the topic – given that they had not caused the economic slump. It is testimony to their potent role in the revisionist politics of central Europe and to the role of history in the way politicians and society viewed the economic collapse, notably the continued reference to the 1922–23 inflationary crisis. Reparations were also a means for powers to deflect international attention away from any detailed scrutiny of the evolution of domestic economic and monetary policy.

The Lausanne Conference, 1932

The central plank of British economic diplomacy in 1931 and 1932 was to pursue a European reparation settlement, primarily negotiated between Britain, France and Germany, before using the European deal as the basis to strike a bargain with the United States on war debts. (There was also talk of a concomitant settlement on non-German reparations.) While it was comparatively easy for Britain to secure Italian support for the plan, French acquiescence was a harder nut to crack. As France recognized all too well, Britain's was a risky strategy not least because it threatened to present the United States with a united front of European debtors – a move it had vehemently resisted since 1919 – at a time when US depression was more acute than that faced by any European country. France resisted British pressure to attend a conference on reparations – it became the Lausanne Conference – for almost a year, until the accession in May 1932 of a Radical-Socialist government, led by the Radical Edouard Herriot, changed the diplomatic landscape. A new government, a reassessment of Franco-German relations, and the determination to bring the French public on the side of reparation revision all contributed to the shift in French policy. (It is not yet fully appreciated how far French interests in eastern Europe also shaped its changing policy on the question of reparations.) As so often in the depression, however, changes in policy to tackle the crisis failed to keep pace with political developments. On 30 May Brüning resigned, to be replaced as German Chancellor by Franz von Papen who extended the Chancellor's extra-parliamentary powers yet further. Equally worrying, given the massive crisis of confidence that gripped Europe, was the fact that Papen's ultra-conservative cabinet, in common with its right-wing successors, now explicitly tied German demands for equality in armaments with a call for 'equality of economic rights'. It did not augur well for the disarmament conference due to open in Geneva that autumn, nor for the return of confidence in Europe's economy any time soon.

The deal negotiated at the Lausanne Conference in July 1932 enabled Germany to secure the benefits of Anglo-French diplomacy without any further responsibilities on the question of political debts. The final reparations settlement came on 7 July 1932 when, after a relaxed dinner together, Herriot and Chamberlain negotiated late into the night, sketching out the final settlement on Chamberlain's napkin. The issue of war guilt was resolved to the satisfaction of France, and Germany was to make one final, lump sum payment of 3 billion Reichsmarks (it never did) before the reparations slate was wiped clean. But before Britain could justly claim it had put an end to 13 unlucky years of international disputes over reparations and war debt payments, one sizeable obstacle remained: war debts due to the United States. In order to secure French agreement to the reparations settlement, Britain and France concluded a secret 'Gentleman's Agreement' that postponed ratification of the Lausanne deal until a 'satisfactory settlement' had been reached between Britain, France, Italy, Belgium (a further co-signatory) and 'their own creditors'. Should they fail, then in theory the arrangement with Germany would not be ratified, and the Young plan would be reinstated. In practice in the coming years, however, the problem of war debts became a running sore in European relations with the United States and, to a lesser extent, a source of tension between Britain, on the one hand, and France, Italy and Belgium, on the other. Only Germany was free from involvement in the disputes. It did not take long for the disagreements between the former allies in Europe and the United States to start. Within days news of the 'Gentleman's Agreement' leaked out and the deal was greeted with howls of dismay on the other side of the Atlantic. The White House and Congress were incensed at Europe's decision, in Hoover words, 'to gang up against the United States'.[3]

At the same time as slapping Uncle Sam in the face, the Europeans also sought to extend a hand of friendship and cooperation towards the United States by showing a renewed enthusiasm and commitment to calls for an international conference to tackle the depression. The fifth act of the Lausanne agreement called for the convocation of a World Economic Conference – a notable development was the emphasis that high-ranking politicians, as well as economic experts, should attend – to address issues like the collapse of economic confidence and prices, the operation of the gold standard, and international protectionism. From the British perspective, the World Conference was primarily designed to keep the United States involved in Europe's fortunes and to push for a new debt agreement; from the perspective of France, Belgium, Italy and the United States, amongst others, however, the conference offered the bonus of putting pressure on Britain and other members of the sterling group to rejoin the gold standard and to explore ways of improving the system. For all the participants there was also the opportunity to discuss obstacles to trade, although this issue generated little enthusiasm among the European powers.

The Stresa Conference

One way and another, the Lausanne Conference helped to set the agenda for international economic cooperation over the coming years. One of its less well known contributions was the creation of a special committee to consider the impact of indebtedness beyond German frontiers in central and eastern Europe. There was widespread and justified anxiety that, given the collapse in primary prices and international trade, this region, far more than any other, would have trouble making its debt payments. Although the depreciation first of, sterling in 1931 and then the dollar in 1933 should have helped to ease the problem – countries paying in currencies still linked to gold found their debts (if they were payable in sterling or dollars) were also devalued – the reality was rather different. In 1931 tariff barriers and exchange controls reached new highs, while international trade fell to its lowest point. Hungary's problems illustrate the dilemma in dramatic fashion: in 1932 the total amount earned from all Hungarian exports covered less than half the sum due in debt payments for that year! The committee's task was to submit proposals to help the region to the League of Nation's Commission of Enquiry for European Union. Indeed, it is striking how the League is central to the history of international cooperation to the east of Berlin, yet is rarely featured in accounts of the economic diplomacy of the west. The special committee's work resulted in the Stresa Conference of September 1932. Fourteen European countries took part: France, Germany, Italy, Austria, Belgium, the Netherlands, Switzerland, Bulgaria, Hungary, Romania, Poland, Yugoslavia, Czechoslovakia and Britain, the latter fresh from imperial negotiations in Ottawa. Extensive memoranda were prepared by both the participating nation states and the League of Nations on the inter-related problems of indebtedness and the crisis facing exporters.

But it was all in vain. The conference participants could agree on the symptoms of the collapse, but not on the remedy. Schemes to generate investment for central and eastern Europe were also discussed – Yugoslavia, for example, suffered enormously from the cessation of German reparation payments under first the Hoover Moratorium and then the Lausanne settlement, and had to secure a 300-million franc loan from France in October 1932. However, it proved impossible to agree on a plan of internationally sponsored loans. In the end, nothing concrete was decided, although the Stresa Conference did submit over two kilos worth of memoranda to the preparatory meetings of the World Economic Conference that were held in Geneva in November 1932 and January 1933. The failure of the Stresa Conference was a significant landmark in the growing frustration of Europe's smaller powers with the 'selfish' policy of their larger and wealthier neighbours to the west. The sentiment was underlined by their exclusion from preparations under way for the Economic Conference. They were not alone in their sense of frustration. Almost as soon as preparations for the World Conference began, many of the 65 countries invited to participate expressed private doubts as to whether it would achieve concrete results given the dismal history of similar, and smaller, gatherings and the complexity of the issues under discussion.

War Debts: The End?

American scepticism regarding the World Conference, however, came from a different source to that of eastern Europe. From the outset, and despite America's refusal to allow the issue onto the conference agenda, war debts were the primary focus of British, and to a lesser extent French, economic foreign policy. Unsurprisingly, the thrust of Anglo-French policy was to persuade the United States to accept a financial settlement similar to that made in July 1932 by scaling down war debts commensurate with the final lump sum owed by Germany. Britain marshalled strong economic arguments as to why payments should cease, most notably that the collapse of primary prices and international trade, coupled with the depreciation of sterling, had enormously increased the real value of the debts to be paid: the sum paid by Britain in 1923 represented the value of six months' worth of exports, whereas the payment due in 1932 equalled the value of four years' exports to the United States. As we shall see in Chapter Seven, the worst of the French depression was still to come.

Given the relative health and wealth of the French economy, Herriot's government took a different tack. It emphasized the political benefits to be had by freeing Europe from the burden of its political debts and the diplomatic value of the new concord in Franco-German economic and monetary relations; the latter reinforced by French overtures to the Weimar government to make joint policy preparations for the World Economic Conference. (The initiative died a rapid death with the advent of the National Socialist government in January 1933. The Italians made similar proposals to the NSDAP that were also turned down.) In the United States both the outgoing Republican administration and the incoming Democratic regime were unmoved by the Anglo-French case. They were unimpressed by the economic argument, especially given the apparent health of the French economy. Here, once again, the operation of the gold standard obscured reality. The Americans focused solely on the fact that France had 'withdrawn enough gold from the Federal Reserve to pay its entire war-debt obligation' until 1942, and ignored evidence of the French economy's growing malaise more generally.[4] Moreover, the political case was insufficient to sell the cancellation of debts to the American people, many of whom were struggling to meet debt payments – on their homes, their land, their cars – of their own. From 1932 to 1934 the administrations of both Hoover and Roosevelt shared the determination to secure concessions on a variety of issues, from tariffs to disarmament, to set against cuts in debt payments in order to sell any deal on war debts to the American people. None were forthcoming.

Instead, by December 1932 both Britain and France were threatening to default on their loans to the United States. At the eleventh hour Britain stepped back from the brink and made the payment due in full, frightened of the implications of default for its status as the world's most respected financial power (it feared the move would encourage debtors to default on loans owed to Britain). But payment was politically impossible for France. Despite an emotional appeal by Herriot to the French Chamber of Deputies to pay for the sake of Franco-American relations, France defaulted and the Herriot cabinet collapsed. The step had a damaging impact on French relations with the United States almost immediately. When Roosevelt extended invitations to foreign governments to come for talks in Washington in the spring of 1933, there was no invitation to the new French Premier Edouard Daladier. (When French representatives did arrive in Washington steps were taken to prevent photographs of a smiling President meeting them from appearing in the US press.) The President's advisers also warned him against visiting Europe or making any hasty agreements with European negotiators because any concession given in America's grave economic climate would be perceived by the American public as one 'which those clever devils in Europe had hornswoggled from you'.[5]

American suspicion as to how far European powers sought genuine cooperation with the United States was heightened by Britain's decision in June 1933 to stop full payments on its debts to America. Instead, in June and December 1933 Britain made only partial or 'token' payments, until the issue triggered a full-scale row, involving congress too, in 1934. In 1933 British and American negotiators conceded, in private, that war debts were a political question. The problem for the US administration lay in justifying a remission of European debts at a time of unprecedented crisis and, in the words of Assistant Secretary of State Dean Acheson, given the dangers of a backlash from 'an already hard-boiled Congress'.[6] (Upsetting Congress over Europe threatened Roosevelt's ability to secure Congressional support for his recovery measures.) The gulf between Europe and the United States widened further in 1934 when the Johnson Act was passed. Initiated in Congress by the isolationist Senator Hiram Johnson of California, the act aimed to stop further US loans being given to foreign governments who were already in default or behind on payments due to the United States. As a means of coercion, the act had long passed its use by date. In the 1920s the threat of withholding access to US credit was enough to persuade most European governments to pay up, but with little prospect of a revival of US lending in the 1930s, the act became more significant as a constraint on Roosevelt's abilities to help Britain and France when they went to war against Germany in 1939. A further, bitter irony was that while Britain, France, Belgium, Italy, Czechoslovakia, Estonia, Hungary, Latvia, Lithuania, Poland, Romania and Yugoslavia were now branded defaulters by the United States, countries which owed large amounts in commercial loans, like Germany, were not.

In 1933 and 1934 the showdown Britain had sought on political debts did not unfold as planned. It is important to recognize the central role played by the war-debt negotiations to the history of the World Economic Conference. Preparatory meetings and the conference itself were all timed by the British government, in their role as conference convenors and hosts, to coincide with payments due to the United States. Aside from the obvious intention of putting maximum political and public pressure on the Americans, from Britain's perspective it also offered the opportunity to divert international consideration of issues that threatened to isolate it, and not the United States, in international negotiations. During the extensive conference preparations, British monetary policy, alongside that of fellow members of the emerging sterling bloc, came under strong criticism from the remaining members of the gold standard, the charge led by France and the United States. Britain's role in the economic conferences of the 1920s as champion of the international gold standard and free trade increased the sense of frustration because of the gap between the expectations and the reality of British policy. History continued to influence the way other powers perceived Britain's role in the world economy. As a German delegate reflected, gone were the 'good old days when British leadership at international gatherings could be relied upon', now it was the 'United Kingdom that needed to be led'.[7]

By spring 1933 economic experts had produced an annotated conference agenda, but the second portion of their brief – to offer clear policies for recovery to which the politicians could accede – remained unfulfilled. Two months of international negotiations in Geneva only served to underline the way economic and monetary policies were now dominated by instruments of isolation not cooperation. The only concrete proposal to come out of eight months of talks was the Republican administration's call for a tariff truce:

participants would agree not to raise further protective tariffs prior to and during the conference. Protectionist Europe was surprised, if not appalled, when the tariff truce was taken up with great enthusiasm by the incoming Democratic administration. The new American Secretary of State, Cordell Hull, a longtime advocate of reduced tariffs, took every opportunity to publicize the administration's support for the truce and his resolve to secure Congressional authority to negotiate Reciprocal Tariff Agreements based on a flat-rate reduction of 10 per cent of existing barriers, a corresponding percentage enlargement of quotas, and bilateral agreements within unconditional MFN treatment. Central and eastern European powers, notably the German government, were horrified by the prospect of what they called an 'Anglo-Saxon' alliance bent on destroying the protectionist barriers that helped to insulate their economies from trade dumping and monetary pressures. European opposition was not the only obstacle that stood in Hull's way. So, too, did the increasingly nationalist bent of economic and monetary policy with the launch of Roosevelt's New Deal in the United States.

Roosevelt Floats the Dollar

Although elected by a landslide in November 1932, Roosevelt (FDR) did not assume the office of President until 4 March 1933. Throughout this long interregnum period, speculation continued to mount as to what precisely his promised 'new deal' for the American people meant in terms of policy. The prolonged uncertainty as to whether the United States would remain on gold, coupled with the already weak position of US banks, meant that on the day of his inauguration, the level of gold cover in the Federal Reserve System had fallen below its statutory 40 per cent requirement. Although the process took a further five weeks, step by step Roosevelt broke the US dollar's ties with the gold standard. The President faced strong political pressure from Congress to take steps to increase primary prices to help farmers, a position taken by other primary producers and a significant proportion of industry too. Equally influential was counsel from his special 'Brains Trust' advisors, who urged him to break free of the strict budgetary controls demanded by the gold standard to initiate domestic recovery policies and to strengthen US banks. In short, domestic considerations determined Roosevelt's momentous step to float the dollar on 19 April.

The action was unique for its time. The dollar, unlike the pound sterling, was not pushed from the system. The American government explicitly decided to leave for the sake of the domestic economy. By July 1933 domestic and foreign commentators were under no doubts that recovery was well under way. Within four months, the dollar had depreciated by around 40 per cent of its former value on gold and the US economy began to show signs of recovery. Taking the year 1929 as 100, factory employment had risen from 56.6 per cent in March 1933 to 70.1 per cent by July 1933, prices had risen from 59.8 per cent in February 1933 to 99 per cent by July of the same year, and department-store sales had risen from 57 per cent to 71 per cent – that these indicators had some way to go before reaching their 1929 levels also demonstrates that complete recovery was still some way off.[8]

Of course, given what we now know about the stranglehold gold standard membership had on the ability of countries to recover from the gold standard, Roosevelt's action begs important questions regarding America's failure to lead the rest of the world to recovery by effecting a coordinated devaluation or depreciation with countries still in the system. The dollar's flotation has been described by historians of the New Deal as the President's first nationalist act. Yet it could have been an internationalist act of tremendous import. There are, hidden among the documents of the period, memoranda that reflect what might have been. First, in late November 1932, came a proposal from Herbert Feis, international economic advisor to the State Department, for an American-led coordinated devaluation of all currencies within the gold standard system. His comment at the time, that the proposal belonged 'to the world of H. G. Wells', demonstrated quite how far the idea seemed beyond the pale.[9] Then, in April and May 1933, came widespread rumours in both the British Treasury and the Foreign Office – so far it has not been possible to trace their provenance – that Britain and other members of the sterling bloc were to join Roosevelt's new currency bloc of currencies off gold. And finally, there was a proposal from one of FDR's advisors, on the eve of the World Economic Conference, for the President to issue such a strongly worded attack on the gold standard as to push France and other members of the gold bloc out of the system. It was a call for America to take the lead and to force the world to be free of gold standard orthodoxy.

The failure of governments, of both western Europe and the United States, to take up these calls for a coordinated attempt to reflate the world economy lays bare may of the shortcomings of international cooperation in the depression. Firstly, it underlines the continued conservatism of monetary and economic policy, even when countries had abandoned gold. Neither Britain nor the United States, for example, went as far as they might have in efforts to reflate the domestic economy. To its credit, the British government considered the question of encouraging other countries off gold in the wake of sterling's depreciation in a more systematic way than America. But it was unprepared to promote a coordinated devaluation alone, or in tandem with the USA, and feared uncoordinated currency flotation would bring only uncertainty and chaos. There would also be a price to pay at home. As the Treasury put it: 'British competitive power would be greatly diminished if Austria and Czechoslovakia, for example, devalue their currencies. HMG would be severely criticized by traders if devaluation took place as result of pressure by us.'[10] Roosevelt's action had won warm praise in some quarters in Britain. The left-leaning *Daily Herald* newspaper, for instance, claimed 'Mr Roosevelt had the courage Mr MacDonald lacked. The government, the Treasury and the Bank of England remained obstinately timid' in their monetary policy.[11] But such views were not commonplace in Europe in 1933.

Even if America or Britain had attempted to give a lead on monetary policy, it was not necessarily enough to effect international collaboration in the fragmented world of the 1930s. Acting alone they had neither the political will nor the power to 'force' European nations to cooperate. As far as FDR was concerned, the European countries also had to demonstrate a political will to work with the United States. Indeed, America's ability to work with Europe was likely to have been reinforced by a clear European demonstration of a desire to cooperate with Washington. Instead, events in 1933 and 1934 appeared to confirm US suspicions that the major European powers were not interested in coordinating monetary or economic policy with the United States. So-called 'Anglo-Saxon' cooperation might have led the way, but the internationalists in Roosevelt's administration were discouraged and weakened by the direction of domestic economic policy and by Britain's determination to protect its national and imperial interests in preference to making friendly overtures to the United States.

The World Economic Conference Convenes, June–July 1933

On the 12 June 1933 delegates from 65 different countries and six international organizations squeezed into London's new Geological Museum for the opening of the World Conference. The gathering was unprecedented in both its scale and apparent ambition. The financial topics up for discussion were monetary and credit policy, exchange difficulties and the movement of capital. The economic questions for debate centred on the need to improve conditions of production and trade, with particular attention to the issues of tariff policy, prohibitions, restrictions and quotas, and producers' agreements. (In spite of American opposition, the British exploited their position as host to include a veiled reference to the problem of war debts.) Taken as a whole, the conference agenda was long on details of the symptoms of the monetary and economic crises, but was short on agreed proposals as to how these problems might be tackled. Moreover, despite the conference's pretensions to inclusiveness in international economic relations and to herald the dawn of renewed confidence in the world economy, the history of the World Conference demonstrated little had changed in the practise of economic diplomacy since 1918. As at the Brussels and Genoa conferences, the issue of currency stabilization soon dominated events.

From the outset, deliberations in the Geological Museum were overshadowed by confidential currency talks being held in the Bank of England between central bank officials from Britain, France and the United States to secure a *temporary* stabilization agreement. The idea for a stabilization agreement to cover the life-time of the conference had emerged first in October 1932, as a means to quell currency fluctuations between floating currencies and those on gold. Once agreed, the pact was intended to enable conference participants to get on with negotiating issues such as trade discrimination and international public works, free from the distraction of currency fluctuations. Instead, the negotiations for an agreement designed to facilitate deliberations at the World Economic Conference was to become the ostensible cause for the conference's acrimonious collapse.

By June 1933 much had changed, not least US monetary policy, since the second preparatory meeting held in January 1933. Although it had been the United States which first proposed the temporary agreement, and elaborated on it in March and April 1933, by late June American representatives at the stabilization talks were unable to retain Presidential acquiescence to the deal drawn up between British, French and American bankers in London. Roosevelt's growing frustration with, in particular, the nationalism of British and French economic and monetary policy, combined with the fact that the first two weeks of the World Conference had been hijacked by stabilization talks that were not officially part of the conference agenda, was made spectacularly clear in the President's infamous 'bombshell message', made public on 3 July 1933. This was a telegram sent to the conference from the President's yacht *Amberjack* – he was on holiday off the coast of New England at the time – which scuppered any hope for temporary currency stabilization between the floating currencies and the remaining gold currencies. The language of the 'bombshell' was undeniably strong. It condemned the 'old fetishes of so-called international bankers' for resurrecting talk of a revival of the gold standard and underlined Roosevelt's commitment to currency depreciation as a means of reinvigorating the American economy. It would be, he said, 'a catastrophe amounting to a world tragedy, if the great Conference of Nations ... should ... allow itself to be diverted by a proposal of a purely artificial and temporary experiment affecting the monetary exchanges of a few nations only.'[12] Roosevelt's monetary policy had not changed. He was still committed to raising prices in the United States and the ultimate reintroduction of the gold standard. New was his apparent hostility towards, and frustration with, proceedings in London.

The international economic and monetary discussions hosted by the President in Washington in the spring of 1933 had made it clear to the President that the European nations were not prepared to compromise their own national economic recovery strategies. Europe's economic nationalism had become all too apparent when negotiations in Washington turned to the possibility of international agreements to reduce tariffs or quotas – an issue close to the heart of the new administration. By 1932 many, both inside the Commerce and State Departments and without, began to argue that the United States should move away from the inconsistent, 'double-edged' Open Door and adopt a reciprocal trading policy. The State Department, in particular, was stung by repeated European criticism that US protectionism compromised its investments in Europe, that it had prompted Britain and France to abandon the collection of reparations, and was forcing countries like Germany from the international economy. The shift in official sentiment was supported by the increasingly free trade position of the largely capital intensive industries, like banking, and the oil and electricity companies which had fared rather better than most in the depression. Once Republican supporters, they were now increasingly drawn toward the professed low-tariff position of the Democratic party.[13]

In the new Democratic administration, Cordell Hull was the undoubted champion of such a strategy, intent on liberating world trade as 'the fundamental basis of all peace'.[14] From December 1932 (the initiative is more typically dated from 1934 or 1936), Hull's overtures for an agreement to halt the escalation of trade barriers were directed, in particular, at the British government. By January 1933, three months before he was fully installed as Secretary of State, Hull used the Republican sponsored tariff truce for the World Economic Conference in efforts to secure the first reciprocal tariff agreement (RTA) with the British government. The State and Commerce Departments even harboured hopes that an Anglo-American RTA would provide the basis for initiating multilateral tariff reductions throughout the world through the operation of unconditional most-favoured-nation treatment. American hopes were supported by the conviction that British power was founded on free trade and that Britain would, with American support, return to free trade. As one American official put it, 'the idea for a bilateral trade treaty with the British' arose because: 'they would probably be the easiest person [sic] to do it with ... and then see what kind of animal that would be and how wide its application would be to others.'[15]

The historian's privilege of hindsight makes the first two years of Roosevelt's presidency seem like a lost opportunity in Anglo-American economic relations. Back in 1933 the timing of Secretary Hull's tariff overture appeared particularly poor – Britain's Abnormal, General and Imperial tariffs had only just passed into law, and it remained unclear how far Hull enjoyed the support of a president apparently torn between the nationalist and internationalist elements in his administration. Equally unconvincing from the British perspective was the way that the State Department skirted over the sticky question of whether Congressional support for the RTA could be secured. On a more fundamental level, however, the problem was one of competition. Britain's £70 million trading deficit to the United States was a genuine obstacle to the conclusion of an Anglo-American trading agreement, as well as a source of great embarrassment; so, too, was British determination to strengthen its imperial power base and to meet promises to protect the national economy made to the electorate (p. 194).

In the same way that Roosevelt was not prepared to make any kind of monetary commitment that threatened his ambition to reflate the domestic economy, Britain also had refused to make any firm commitment to return to gold or to reduce its levels of domestic protection. Indeed, the President's suspicions about European nationalism appeared to be confirmed when the collapse of the stabilization talks after 3 July effectively killed-off the conference. The European powers, especially those still wedded to gold, argued that talks in the Geological Museum were now pointless given the fluctuating exchange values of many leading currencies. At the same time, the Americans were angry that FDR's rejection of the temporary stabilization agreement became the cause of the conference's collapse (especially as neither Britain nor any other members of the sterling bloc had any intention of returning to gold). As Congressman Sam McReynolds, a member of the US delegation in London and chairman of the House Committee on Foreign Affairs, protested: 'stabilization was made an excuse for some for wrecking the Conference and for throwing the blame on us … [it] was no more than a pretext as they, judging from all the signs, did not intend to make any material agreements relative to quotas, tariffs and embargoes.'[16]

A preoccupation with the shortcomings of US policy during the Great Depression led many scholars to lay the blame for the failure of internationally coordinated efforts to effect recovery at the door of the United States. Since the mid-1980s, however, new accounts of the failure of economic diplomacy in 1933 distribute the blame more widely. Firstly, it was now clear that FDR was right. As we have seen, returning to the gold standard orthodoxy implicit in the stabilization agreement, albeit a temporary one, was not the way to effect recovery. Secondly, while it is true that the American administration might have tried harder to demonstrate a clear lead by generating coordinated plans for currency depreciation, perhaps in tandem with the British government, there is little evidence to suggest members of the sterling or gold blocs would have supported it. Indeed, since his inauguration, Roosevelt had grown increasingly suspicious of the mismatch between European rhetoric, which emphasized the need for US-European cooperation, and the reality of European economic and monetary policy. There was Britain's relentless harping on the need for American concessions on war debt; MacDonald even mentioned them in his Presidential opening address to the World Conference. There was France, which first rejected the proposal for a temporary stabilization agreement but, when American monetary policy took on a more radical flavour in May 1933, exploited negotiations on the temporary agreement to demand that a new, *permanent* stabilization agreement should come out of the conference. Throughout the temporary negotiations, the French repeatedly argued it be of little value unless linked to a permanent stabilization agreement that would help to recreate the monetary world as it was before 1931. France was only interested in currency stabilization (theoretically an issue outside the remit of the conference) and demonstrated no real interest in the agenda proper. As Prime Minister Daladier put it: 'the maintenance of the gold standard was indispensable. Without permanent monetary stability, no economic agreement would be possible.'[17]

And then there was Germany. In meetings with President Roosevelt in May 1933, Schacht threatened German default on American commercial debts frozen in Germany under the standstill agreements. Reflecting on the talks, FDR later complained, 'I am in an awful mess with Europe ... European statesmen are a bunch of bastards.'[18] The reference to Europeans, as opposed to Germans, was not a slip of the tongue. Although Roosevelt was not all that sympathetic to the interest of American bondholders who would lose out if Germany defaulted on its debts, he was angered by reports from London that 'British banking authorities are working closely with German authorities to develop further plans satisfactory to themselves.'[19] While the World Conference was in session and the delicate stabilization talks were under way, Schacht and his old friend at the Bank of England, Sir Montagu Norman, renewed the Anglo-German standstill agreement that for the most part protected the interests of British bondholders and traders with Germany (p. 173). American annoyance at an Anglo-German commercial agreement, formalized into a long-term arrangement in 1934, was no accident. It was part of a deliberate German strategy to sow suspicion in Anglo-American relations to forestall a united 'Anglo-Saxon' front that might threaten Nazi ambitions at home and abroad at a time when the Reich was still vulnerable to international pressure.

With the benefit of hindsight, Germany's careful exploitation of its commercial debt negotiations to exploit tensions in Anglo-American relations should have sounded alarm bells in London, Washington and Paris. So, too, should the antics of Alfred Hugenberg, the leader of the German National People's Party (DNVP) who was a member of the German delegation in London. Hitler had issued instructions to the delegation to avoid controversial pronouncements or international commitments which would inhibit Nazi plans for recovery. But on 16 June Hugenberg, acting on his own initiative to counter what he saw as unfair criticism of Germany, issued an explosive memorandum to the world's press. In a direct challenge to the international tenor of the conference agenda, Hugenberg called for greater national self-sufficiency through the increase, not reduction, of trade barriers. He also demanded that Germany be granted both colonial possessions and, to the fury of Soviet Foreign Minister Maxim Litvinov who was also in London, settlement areas in eastern Europe. The episode was a warning of what lay ahead as Hugenberg's memorandum reflected the ultimate ambitions of German foreign policy. But in the summer of 1933, few took these demands seriously. The episode cost Hugenberg his job (enabling Hitler to consolidate NSDAP power in the cabinet), but did not lead to any fundamental reappraisal of German ambitions.

As it was, however, the spectacular bust-up over the stabilization agreement in London gave Germany, Italy and Japan front-row seats from which to assess the discord in diplomatic relations between the 'leading' democracies. The World Economic Conference did not fail for lack of viable proposals for cooperation, but for the dearth of the *political* will to cooperate. Already on 29 June, it was reported in Berlin that the conference had so enhanced Roosevelt's fears of isolation that he was now anxious to renew American economic links to Germany, China and the USSR. The Nazi government was delighted that the acrimonious collapse of the conference was 'not our fault' and believed that all Germany now needed to do was 'wait to heap the odium for the failure onto others, while ensuring that Germany reaped the benefits'.[20]

Equally troubling for Europe's prospects for peace and prosperity was the conference's failure to do much to help Europe's smaller powers. There were lengthy discussions, led by the International Labour Organization, to promote international public works schemes for the Danubian basin and the widespread introduction of the 40-hour working week. Here, too, progress was negligible. There were heated disagreements between Britain, America and France as to how such schemes would be funded, especially as the schemes called for the resumption of international lending. Britain and France offered proposals to create a common fund to supply central and eastern Europe with desperately needed foreign credit, but the plans received barely a mention in the proceedings of the Monetary Commission of the conference after the failure of the temporary stabilization agreement. As early as 19 June, Edvard Beneš, the Czech Prime Minister, complained to MacDonald, that the 'delegates of the smaller countries' were 'feeling left out'.[21] In a feeble attempt to make up for the lack of financial help, the British, German and US governments were in rare agreement that the countries of the Danubian region be encouraged to sign multilateral trading agreements with each other and to 'learn to speak with one voice' on economic issues.[22] The events in London left the 'lesser' powers of central and eastern Europe only more vulnerable to economic penetration by predators like Germany.

For most of the decade, policy-makers in London, Washington and Paris recognized their fundamental divergence on economic issues. Many of these differences originated in the national responses to the depression first taken in 1931 and 1932, and yet, for the most part, the sources of economic discord largely remained unresolved for the rest of the decade. Until 1936 the French commitment to the gold franc, America's determination to reflate its domestic economy, and Britain's dedication to war-debt revision with its economic independence intact, condemned efforts at economic diplomacy among the democracies to failure. This, perhaps, was only to be expected given that the move to economic nationalism was precipitated by the tremendous social and political pressures generated by the depression. However, the failure of, in particular, Britain and the United States and, to a lesser extent, France to employ energetically the lessons of their failed cooperative efforts between 1931 and 1934 generated sizeable obstacles to be overcome in the future. The war debts saga had ended with much of Europe branded in default to the United States; France led a band of hardy gold bloc members who were determined to cling to the gold standard; and Roosevelt, though the protagonist of last-ditch attempts to find an economic path off the road to war, offered only tariff agreements and limited cooperation on monetary issues, and remained resistant to any further economic commitment to the European democracies at the expense of American domestic public opinion. The failure of international diplomacy in 1933 reinforced and justified the recourse to nationalism that had dominated European economic and political life since 1931.

7

NATIONALIST ROADS TO RECOVERY, 1933–39

Rather than re-establish confidence that the world economy could revive and would profit through cooperative effort, the spectacular failure of the World Conference became the 'lesson of history' cited by many countries to eschew further efforts at cooperation for the remainder of the decade. When it came to promoting recovery, international agreements, whether pertaining to trade, debt or currency management, became narrow in focus, nationalist in ambition and of limited efficacy. Even the leading exponents of liberal capitalism, who professed to share a set of common political values – Britain, France and the United States – struggled to reach agreement on currency and trade questions. In the meantime, those engaged in overtly nationalist recovery strategies appeared to thrive.

The continued importance of monetary orthodoxy, combined in many, but not all, cases with an enthusiasm for public works also set the trend on Europe's periphery. One of the comparatively neglected, but fascinating, examples is that of Portugal under the leadership of Prime Minister António de Olivera Salazar. For much of the 1930s, this former Economics Professor sustained a budget surplus of some 2 million contos (then equivalent to some £20 million) on the national budget, which was spent on less orthodox initiatives to tackle Portugal's employment and development problems. The increased spending on public works schemes, social assistance programmes, rearmament, communications, electrification and education which were characteristic of Salazar's strategy were present, in varying degrees, in recovery policies across Europe. The tension between conservatism and innovation present in Portugal was also a notable feature of the national recoveries of Germany, eastern Europe, Scandinavia and Italy. Important, too, were the links between these countries, which helped to reinforce their steps to recovery.

The years after 1933, however, did not mark a period of improvement for all the countries of Europe. Aside from Spain's costly descent into civil war and its impact on the economies of interventionist Germany and Italy, the depression reached its height in Belgium in 1935 and France in 1936. Europe's economic depression was far from over. In 1937 the world economy turned down once more and, had it not been for war preparations, a new depression would have engulfed the European economy by the end of the decade.

Table 7.1   Industrial Output, 1934–39
1937=100

	1934	1935	1936	1937	1938	1939
Austria	66	75	81	100	101	
Belgium	76	83	90	100	81	86
Denmark	870	92	96	100	100	107
France	99	92	88	95	100	92
Germany	54	67	79	90	100	110
Italy	80	86	86	100	100	109
Sweden	73	81	89	100	101	110
UK	80.4	86.6	94.4	100	97.3	

Source: League of Nations, *Economic Survey* (Geneva, 1934–39).

The Context for Recovery

In part, of course, the drive for national recovery grew out of the economic and political consequences of the Great Depression in Europe. There were five principal features of the international political economy of 1930s Europe that helped to shape national recovery. The first was the condition of international trade. As we saw in Chapter 5, levels of international trade had collapsed and they failed to recover.

Protectionism was a serious impediment to economic revival for all European countries, even for nationalist governments which appeared to seek self-sufficiency and isolation. Secondly, the deterioration in prospects for trade was reinforced by the persistently depressed state of international lending. The movement of capital and investment in the international economy no longer lubricated the links between national economies to the good of the international system as a whole as it had in the 1920s. Instead, the most stable and apparently secure countries became sanctuaries for foreign capital. In the seven years from 1931, Britain absorbed some $4 billion, while the United States took in almost $5.5 billion between 1934 and 1937 (and ever larger amounts as war in Europe loomed), with Switzerland, the Netherlands and Scandinavia importing smaller amounts. Feinstein and Watson have not been able to determine quite where all the money was coming from, although gold bloc members France, the Netherlands and Belgium were undoubtedly important losers in this process as their continued membership of the gold standard came under pressure after 1931 (p. 186). With exchange controls and trade barriers continuing to rise, it is small wonder that investors remained cautious and preferred to squirrel their monies away in Britain and the United States (and other neutral, stable territories) rather than bearing the risk of putting it into countries, such as those in central and eastern Europe, where foreign investment was urgently required to effect recovery. There were a few exceptions, notably Romania, which secured foreign capital to develop its oil industries.

The international political context forms the third important determinant on the prospects for domestic recovery. The growing tension in international relations – with a major diplomatic incident erupting almost every year until the outbreak of war in 1939 – acted to depress confidence. Moreover, the proclaimed autarky of the nationalist aggressors in Europe, first Germany and then Italy, also sapped the political will of other countries to do anything about the spiralling levels of protectionism. Even some of the more positive political consequences of the depression, like the election of Franklin Roosevelt and the recovery of the US economy, had some negative consequences for international diplomacy. Financiers and bankers were in bad odour (export industries were also weakened), thereby silencing groups which had lobbied for American involvement in the wider world in the 1920s.

The fifth feature of the world economy in the 1930s was much more positive: the trends evident in the 1920s – of innovation, rationalization and modernization – once again began to make an impact (p. 70). Although it has become less fashionable in recent years to study the developmental role played by the new industries in Europe, their role remains significant. The production of motor vehicles, household appliances and new types of fabric all contributed to recovery and to an improved sense of well-being in Europe. (Bernstein also argues that in America's case, it is the failure of these consumer industries to forge ahead as they did later in the 1950s which explains why US recovery faltered by 1937.) Important advances also continued in the production of chemicals, while electricity became the principal source of light and heat; there were also new methods of communication, notably radio. But, as before, the processes of modernization and rationalization were implemented unevenly in the European economy. Increases in the levels of worker productivity, one of the basic indicators of modernization, were not impressive, especially when set against levels of over 4.0 per cent per annum achieved after 1945 in continental western Europe. In Germany productivity rose by only 1.3 per cent a year and by 2.5 per cent over the same period in Britain. The rise in British productivity in the 1930s was in many respects exceptional. Not only was the 2.5 per cent rise one of the highest in Europe, it was also higher than levels achieved by Britain in the 1920s (and close to the level achieved in the 1950s).

Table 7.2   Cost of Living Index
1929=100

	Czecho	France	Germany	Poland	Spain	UK
1930	98	101	96	92	103	96
1931	94	97	88	83	107	90
1932	92	88	78	75	103	88
1933	91	85	77	67	100	85
1934	90	82	79	63	102	86
1935	93	75	80	60	99	87
1936	94	80	81	58		90

Source: I. Svennilson, *Growth and Stagnation in the European Economy* (Geneva, 1954), p. 31.

Labour productivity remained a cause for concern in much of eastern Europe, Scandinavia and Italy. (Data on this has not yet been as comprehensively collated or assessed as for the 1920s.) The problem, alongside that of wage rates, is best examined on a national basis, but it is also worth bearing in mind that, throughout the 1930s, those in work found themselves relatively well-off. Prices continued to remain comparatively low when set against wages, so the hard-earned pound, franc or pengö went further at the shops. It is difficult to generalize about the reasons behind this. Historians have found it difficult to explain the relationship between the price level and wage level for even a single country: in France union power might have helped to keep wages high; in Britain lower prices may simply have been thanks to the coincidence of its high levels of imports and falling import prices In the interests of recovery, it would have been better if wages had fallen into line with price levels. Only Germany succeeded in pushing down wages. To flesh out why this was so, and to understand other forces underpinning Europe's shaky recovery from depression, we must turn to the national perspective.

The National Socialist Recovery

Unsurprisingly, once again, developments in Germany are among the best studied of the period. By 1936, with unemployment at 1.6 million (falling to 0.9 million in 1937) and industrial production rising for the first time above levels achieved in 1928, Germany appeared to have scored a genuine and sustained recovery. The history of recovery under National Socialism, however, begins where that of the Weimar Republic ended: with the impact of international capital on the German economy. After 1933 Germany experienced an outflow of over $1 billion. Of course, a proportion of these monies reflected the desperation of the victims of National Socialism to place their assets, if not themselves, abroad, and have been the focus of recent legal actions against Swiss and British banks. But Nazi Germany was also uniquely determined among members of the 'pseudo gold bloc' to reduce levels of its overseas debt in order to maximize its freedom to spend precious currency and gold reserves as it wished. (As we saw in the case of Hungary, when Britain and the United States floated their currencies, all countries still on gold found their sterling and dollar debts reduced automatically.) The exchange controls, first introduced by Reichsbank

President Hans Luther during the financial crises of 1931, evolved into a complex system of monetary and trade restrictions designed to manage Germany's foreign debt payments according to National Socialist economic and political priorities.

Table 7.3   Collapse of German External Trade, 1927–34 (in millions of marks)

	Imports	Exports
1927	14 114	10 801
1928	13 931	12 055
1929	13 359	13 486
1930	10 349	12 036
1931	6713	9592
1932	4653	5741
1933	4199	4872
1934	4448	4178

Source: B. Mitchell, *European Historical Statistics*, 1750–1975 (2nd Edn, London, 1978), F1.

The evolution of German trade and debt policy was both innovative and devious. The process began with the Law on Payments Due Abroad, announced on 1 July 1933, which partially blocked payments on German debts, and opened the way for special bilateral agreements that linked payments on debts to German trade. The system, of sorts, that emerged in the months that followed became explicit and systematized under the 'New Plan' announced by Schacht in September 1934. Once again, the German government continued to employ the rhetoric of the gold standard to emphasize the plan's primary goal: to safeguard Germany's scarce foreign currency reserves. But the New Plan also gave the regime much greater control over trade and debt payments. Imports could only be bought under license via commodity control boards, like the Reich Office for Eggs; capital could not be moved abroad freely; foreign earnings were deposited in blocked accounts and could only be spent on German goods and services. Whenever possible, Germany also negotiated barter agreements to swop German products for essential supplies of raw materials and food. The bilateralism present in German policy since the onset of depression, was now explicit and pronounced. Although the Reich's growing detachment from the international economy was cause for alarm, at the time many of the countries in western Europe that signed bilateral deals with Germany, like France and the Netherlands, drew comfort from the fact they had reached a 'practical method of dealing with their trade with Germany'.[1] At least, this way, payments due on French exports and loans to Germany were likely to be met, in the words of one French official, 'in contrast to the old experiences of promises being broken and minced words'.[2] The price of this greater state control was a lower level of German foreign trade when compared to the 1920s: in 1928 German exports were worth 12.3 billion Reichsmarks; during the 1930s, they never exceeded 5.6 billion Reichsmarks. By the mid–1930s, however, German trade had begun to recover some lost ground, especially in relation to other major economies. Overy calculates that by 1938 over 50 per cent of German trade was covered by bilateral agreement and these agreements also helped Germany to control its trade deficit. From 1935 to 1937, it even enjoyed a positive balance of trade.

In German foreign trade relations, countries which imported high levels of German goods were politically useful, and those which continued to lend money to the Reich were favoured over those who did not. The contrasting treatment administered to Britain and the United States, first seen in 1933, was illustrative of the trend and became conspicuous after the conclusion of an Anglo-German Clearing Agreement in July 1934 and the subsequent introduction of the New Plan. As we have seen, the standstill agreements of 1931 linked the health of banks in the City of London (and their pre-eminence in financing German trade) to that of the German economy and this, coupled with a balance of trade in Germany's favour, ensured a cooperative Anglo-German understanding on debts and trade. Germany paid fairly promptly for its imports from Britain (the Nazis were especially anxious to import rubber, tin and copper from the British Empire) and, more importantly, made the required repayments on its standstill agreements. This, in turn, secured continued British demand for German machinery and equipment and, more importantly, a continued supply of credit from Britain. Indeed, Britain became the pre-eminent source of credit to Germany. According to figures offered by Newton, in October 1931 around 28 per cent of all standstill credits were British, by September 1937 the figure stood at 52 per cent and peaked in 1939 at 56 per cent; it was only then that the Bank of England tried to reduce Germany's continued access to British credits. Switzerland, too, received special treatment from its Nazi debtors. The United States, on the other hand, exported more to Germany than it imported and this, coupled with its determination to remain aloof from Europe's diplomatic crises, meant that US creditors received short-shrift from their German debtors who, in all but name, defaulted on their obligations to the United States. That Britain and Switzerland benefited from German policy while America lost out also enabled the National Socialists to exploit suspicion established in Anglo-American relations in 1933. Research by McMurray has demonstrated that Soviet debts owed to Germany – its only noteworthy debtor, the USSR owed Germany one billion marks in 1933 – also played a central role in shaping economic and diplomatic relations between the two countries in the 1930s.

Spaulding has recently argued that, when it came to German trade, all the measures used by Hitler had been introduced by his predecessors as Chancellor since the onset of the depression. Together, they had successfully uncoupled German agricultural prices from world prices – in 1932 German farmers already earned an additional 2 billion marks of revenue on domestic sales over 1931 figures, thanks to state protection. With the farming lobby protected and increasingly content, it was much easier for the Reich to conclude bilateral agreements with primary producers elsewhere as Germany sought to exploit its productive power and capacity to consume as political and economic levers. (Britain, too, used its importing power as leverage in economic negotiations.) After 1933, the much trumpeted search for *Lebensraum* in the east motivated trade deals with Balkan countries, but these brought only limited economic gain for Germany, with exports to the region rising from only 6.9 per cent in 1935 to 11 per cent in 1938. Challenging earlier accounts of German penetration to the east, Kaiser has demonstrated how some countries in central and eastern Europe resisted the National Socialist ambition to draw them into a semi-colonial relationship because they were intent on industrialization and modernization. (Similar tensions surfaced in British imperial economics.) Bulgaria became the most dependent, taking all its imports from Germany and exporting over two-thirds of its produce to the Reich. Hungary, too, was drawn into an ever-closer trading relationship with Germany (p. 180). When strategy demanded it, however, Germany made considerable economic sacrifices for political gain. The most dramatic example was the Nazi-Soviet trade deal signed in August 1939.

The treaty committed Germany to massive exports of weapons and sophisticated equipment to the USSR – revising Hitler's 1936 decision that such exports be constrained – in order to secure Soviet 'support' for the invasion of Poland at a time when German industrial capacity was already under intense strain in the drive to rearm. But economic reality also intruded on the apparent primacy of politics in German trade policy. As before, German trade continued to be dominated by links to northern and western Europe, Latin America and the Middle East, especially as the pace of rearmament accelerated. However, the sharp rise in German exports to southern Europe, notably Spain and Italy, from 11 per cent to 21 per cent of total German exports between the years 1929 and 1938 was a novelty.

Recent research into the political economy of Nazi Germany makes it clear there are no clear cut answers to questions posed by the paradigms of 'continuity versus change' or 'the primacy of politics over economics' that dominated earlier accounts. James has sought to demonstrate that the Nazis benefited from the limited recovery under way in the German economy when they took power, thanks to interventionist measures already in place, a revival in consumption and restocking by German industry (inventories had been run to exceptionally low levels since the onset of depression). New research by Tooze has demonstrated how successive Weimar governments sponsored an unprecedented level of empirical research into the economy that formed an important legacy for National Socialist economic policy. But what distinguishes Nazi economics was the way that state intervention in the economy did not retreat as recovery took hold. Rather interventionist measures introduced by successive Weimar cabinets during the depression became the foundation for the command economy that emerged after 1936. Under the Nazis, state policy did not only come to control foreign trade, but also prices, wages, private investment banks and all other aspects of investment. It is this which, for Overy, explains both the speed and the scope of economic revival under the Nazis.

Temin, Overy and Abelshauser have all sought to tease out the features distinct to the recovery facilitated by the first years of National Socialist government: the clear political signal that the regime had broken with the past (akin to that given by Roosevelt in the Hundred Days); the centrality of recovery and a programme of government spending designed to stimulate demand and expand income (regardless of the actual sums of money involved); and the fact that much had still to be achieved by way of recovery in 1933. Indeed, during the first years of the Third Reich, officials in the US State and Treasury Departments and the White House all argued that German economic recovery was so fragile it was unlikely the Nazis would remain in office for long. Most historians agree that the revival of investment, much of it from the state, was central to the German recovery. Between 1933 and 1934 the level of public investment doubled as government funds went straight into employment schemes, industrial investment and construction plans. Government expenditure increased by a further 60 per cent during 1935. These figures were impressive when related to levels of direct state expenditure in the Weimar economy of the 1920s. Overy estimates that by 1938 state spending accounted for 33 per cent of GNP compared to 17 per cent of GNP spent in 1932. Levels of private investment grew much more slowly. Mefo bills have received a great deal of attention by scholars as the tool used by the German government to generate investment in heavy industry and to conceal rearmament. The bills, issued by the newly created Metallurgische Forschungsgesellschaft (Mefo), were used by government contractors to pay for what they needed. Mefo bills were then cashed in at the Reichsbank (or held by other banks or private investors) until the government was ready to repay them out of the increased revenue from taxation as the German economy grew. In effect, Mefo bills were used as an alternative currency and between the years 1934 and 1938 they achieved a circulation of around 12 billion Reichsmarks. The practice breached existing financial legislation in Germany and enabled the Nazis to circumvent a financial system which had been badly damaged by events in 1931 and 1932. At the same time, many of the tools used by the Reich to generate investment were also conventional, such as higher taxes, and designed in part to maintain the façade of orthodox monetary and fiscal policy, and to conceal rearmament. The Reich took considerable trouble to maintain an appearance of budgetary orthodoxy as befitted a nation that still claimed to be a member of the gold bloc.

What made the difference to Germany's recovery effort was the cumulative effect of National Socialist led investment and spending in the economy, although some Nazi programmes were more effective than others. It is estimated that public building and construction programmes, including tax concessions to renovate houses and to break up large units into smaller apartments and to repair and build new roads, were especially productive with employment in building industries up by 276 per cent between February 1933 and February 1934. (The famous autobahn-building programme began on a small scale in 1934.) It was the way the construction programmes interacted with other areas of government policy, including price rises in agriculture and the motorization policy (promoting the application of the motor vehicle to the German economy) that, taken together, explain German economic recovery. Small business, for example, benefited from government measure to ensure they received contracts to supply the new construction projects.

Spending policies also became a lever to extend National Socialist control over society. This is most clearly demonstrated in Nazi policies towards the working class. Temin emphasizes how personal freedom and autonomy were sacrificed to the government's determination to control wages and production by destroying labour unions (they were replaced by workers' courts) and making a government agent responsible for wage bargaining. They also introduced compulsory labour service in 1935. As a result, wages were kept low and failed to keep pace with rising national income, falling from 64 per cent to 57 per cent of national income between 1932 and 1938 – a policy that helped to earn Nazi economics the epithet 'capitalism with a cudgel'.[3] Here, Germany is the exception, for in every other European country in the 1930s for which calculations have been made, wage rates were higher than prices. Italy and France, two struggling members of the gold bloc by the mid-1930s, both tried and failed to introduce wage cuts. But recent research has been at great pains to demonstrate not all workers lost out financially – as Germany recovered, so demand for skilled workers soon outstripped supply and this group were able to secure wage increases. Nor were all German workers hostile to the regime, divided as they were by age, gender, occupation and 'race'. The point is illustrated clearly by the much vaunted scheme for marriage loans introduced in 1933. Newlyweds could apply to the Reich for a loan of up to 1000 Reichsmarks, in certificates, to buy furniture and household goods for the home. The loans were interest free and the sum owed was reduced for each child born to each new family (the loans, in effect, were transformed into family allowance). The certificates generated the desired demand for German small business, and proved very popular with over 183 000 loans taken up by the end of 1933. But there was also a sinister side. The loans were conditional on the woman giving up paid employment, a new attack on so-called 'double-earners', and were refused if one or both of the marriage partners were suffering from a hereditary, mental or physical illness as defined by the National Socialist state. The measure opened the way for racial registration of the population.

But Germany's economic recovery was not forged through a revival in consumer demand. Indeed, the manufacture of consumer goods came a poor second to the growth of producer goods that were to form the basis of future German rearmament. Consumers began to complain about the dearth of supplies, lack of choice and the poor quality of finished products like textiles. There were other scarcities that grew more pronounced as the economy revived. Towards the end of 1935, the Agriculture Minister, Walter Darré, identified a *Fettlücke* (gap in fats) that threatened the government's ability to feed the population properly. Equally, if not more important, given the regime's long-term intention to rearm the German economy, was the desperate shortage of raw materials needed for industrial production. Importing more food or more iron ore, for example, was one possible solution to the growing crisis, but it was not an easy one given the growing pressure on Germany's foreign exchange reserves. These had fallen from 2.8 billion Reichsmarks in 1930, hovered around 164 million in 1934, and fell to well below 100 million Reichsmarks in 1935 and 1936 – a sum sufficient to cover import requirements for only one week. In short, by 1935 the forces unleashed by Germany's recovery threatened to suck in more imports than Germany could afford, especially as levels of rearmament began to accelerate. Schacht's answer, supported by certain sections of German industry, was an 'export drive' that would seek to reintegrate Germany into the world economy, proved wanting in political and economic terms to leading members of the NSDAP. The usually persuasive Schacht lost the argument and in the wake of the ensuing political row, the spoils went to Hermann Göring: the Nazi minister, President of Prussia and Commander in Chief of the Luftwaffe was made Plenipotentiary of a Four-Year Plan. Through the plan, Göring intended to increase control over Germany's trade and international payments, increase self-sufficiency through a programme of import substitution, accelerate and intensify the drive for rearmament, and eliminate any room for independent manoeuvre that German businessmen still enjoyed. From 1935 onwards, public investment in rearmament replaced civilian job creation programmes as the basis for continued expansion. Levels of private investment had also revived, although it came increasingly under government control. Indeed, with some sectors of the old Weimar economy still lying idle, it was all the easier to direct the economy towards war production.

Despite the triumphalist propaganda which accompanied it, the plan did not achieve all of its aims. Volkmann estimates that in 1939 the Reich still imported over 90 per cent of its rubber requirements and despite increased domestic production, the targets set for the production of synthetic mineral oil in the Four-Year Plan were greatly exaggerated. While Germany was able to produce 55 per cent of its requirements for motor fuel in 1939, it produced only 19 per cent of the heating oil required by the navy. Thanks to rearmament, demand almost always exceeded production. Nor were all sectors of the economy brought under the coordination of the Nazi state, despite the changing pattern of industrial management that accompanied the plan's implementation: party hacks, soldiers, state officials and a new breed of industrial technocrats recruited from the private sector were all involved in managing the economy. Overy argues the plan's greatest significance was the regime's recognition that military capability and economic restructuring went hand in hand.

After 1936 economic recovery was well under way, exemplified by a growing shortage of skilled labour, as large-scale industrial investment and projects became commonplace in armaments related industries. The plan appeared to deliver the goods in military terms – aircraft production, for example, leapt from 3183 in 1935 to an annual average of 5317 between 1936 and 1938 – but volumes of trade and consumption remained depressed. Levels of productivity in German industry also remained low. The Four-Year Plan was intimately linked to Hitler's foreign policy ambitions. Although the economy was to serve these ambitions, Hitler exploited economic advantages wherever they were to be had in his foreign policy. For example, as a consequence of German intervention in the Spanish Civil War, the Reich set up two companies, Hisma and Rowak, to import, amongst other things, iron ore from northern Spain. By 1938 Germany's share of Spanish exports had risen, in terms of value, to 40.7 per cent from 13.1 per cent in 1935. The *Anschluß* also enabled Hitler to absorb both Austria's high foreign exchange reserves and its skilled workforce into the German economy.

Eastern Europe and Scandinavia

We have seen how the isolation of the smaller countries of central and eastern Europe drove some of them increasingly into Germany's orbit. But it is difficult to treat the recovery of eastern Europe in anything like the depth of Germany or Britain because we know much less about it. The efforts of these countries to develop a coordinated response to the depression – at meetings held in Warsaw in 1930 and at the Stresa and World Conferences – came to nothing (p. 148). Without new international loans or the revival of international trade (levels of foreign trade in the east were even lower than in the west), the efforts by Britain, France and Italy to help their particular 'friends' in the region brought little by way of economic benefits. As the League of Nations reported in 1934: 'it is hardly an exaggeration to say that foreign lending has ceased almost entirely!' Take the experience of Hungary and Bulgaria, for example. From 1929 to 1931 they were still able to import capital to the tune of $127 million and $27 million respectively, but by 1933 these levels had fallen close to zero. During the first four years of the depression here, as in Germany, the search to renew the confidence of investors, whether at home or abroad, reinforced membership of the gold standard. Financial orthodoxy helps to explain why Czechoslovakia and Poland, two of the most industrialized countries to the east, found it the hardest to combat the depression. Their failure, in large measure, was due to the strength of their continued commitment to the gold standard. Hungary was the first to abandon the system, albeit informally, while Albania alone remained on the gold standard until 1939, when it was occupied by Italy. However, Czechoslovakia resisted devaluation of the crown until 1934 (it had to devalue again in 1936, this time by 70 per cent), and Poland hung on until 1936 (p. 186). What was left of eastern Europe's export trade by 1933 was also damaged by the devaluation of sterling and the US dollar: countries in the region found their currencies overvalued by around 60 per cent by the end of the year, with all the disadvantages that brought. As a consequence, by 1933 the export receipts of Bulgaria, Hungary, Poland, Romania and Yugoslavia, when taken together, had fallen by around 62 per cent of the levels reached in 1929.

Given the international context, central and eastern Europe's recourse to protectionism, exchange controls and clearing agreements was largely a defensive act, despite the posturings of political nationalists in power at the time. With the notable exception of industrialized Czechoslovakia, it was peasant parties which made a distinct contribution to political and economic life, an unsurprising development, given the continued crisis in primary production.

Agricultural cooperatives grew increasingly popular, notably in Slovenia and Bulgaria, as the state attempted to encourage more modern methods of farming and finance into the countryside. Protectionist measures were sustained, and in many cases extended, while the search for markets overseas brought Yugoslavia and Hungary, in particular, into a closer economic relationship with Germany (p. 174). Politics and economics, taken together, explain why Poland and Czechoslovakia resisted the draw of the German empire. In March 1934 Hungary signed a new trade treaty in Rome with Italy and Austria in the hope of exporting more of its surplus wheat – there were persistent hopes that Italy would become more involved in the region. But by 1935 it was clear that neither Italy nor Austria were strong enough or large enough to take up the slack in Hungary's economy. The failure of this trilateral trade agreement, coupled with the Prime Minister Gömbös's admiration for Hitler, drew Hungary more closely into Germany's orbit. Indeed, by the following year, Germany also sought to dominate the industry by holding capital control of many Hungarian companies.

Germany's recovery also had important implications for Scandinavia, in general, and Sweden, in particular. As Germany revived so, too, did its appetite for raw materials. Swedish iron ore exports, for example, grew from three million tonnes in 1933 to 12.5 million tonnes in 1939, and over 70 per cent of this iron ore was shipped to Germany. At the same time, however, the general signs of the health and viability of the National Socialist idea – an empire based on the resources of central and eastern Europe – were not auspicious. The work of Abelshauser on the Nazi economy at war after 1939 underlines the primacy of western and northern Europe to Germany's war effort, especially when measured in financial terms, although Overy has demonstrated how the annexation of Austria, Czechoslovakia and Poland made large and essential contributions to Germany's heavy and engineering industry. The Reich, for example, not only exploited Czechoslovakia's armaments industry, but also harnessed iron and steel production and mining output.

Following a trend established before the First World war and continued in the 1920s, governments in central and eastern Europe also became increasingly involved in attempting to manage industry and employment (p. 77). Across the region, schemes for import substitution were introduced or extended in order to maintain the drive for industrialization and to secure improved levels of employment – both had been badly affected by the loss of foreign investment and trade opportunities. The rhetoric of war was not just reflected in talk of 'shock workers' and recovery 'campaigns', but also in state-directed industrial projects designed to enhance national security. Indeed, Poland's nationalism frequently obstructed western efforts to help it: in 1934, for example, the British government held over 100 meetings with Polish representatives in the hope of signing a trade deal, but Britain's efforts came to nothing.

After 1936, in Poland as in Italy, it was difficult to distinguish industrial recovery from war planning as government involvement in the economy was subsumed by preparations for national defence. Once off gold, Polish industrial output recovered pretty quickly, with the introduction of a 'Four-Year Investment Plan' for industry and a 'Six-Year Defence Expansion Plan' to run from 1936 to 1942. The Polish plans have been described by Ránki and Tomaszewski as: 'the first genuine attempt at central planning anywhere in Eastern Europe except the USSR.' Like Hungary's 'Billion Pengö Plan' of 1938, the Polish 'Central Industrial Region' (COP) was set up as part of the Investment Plan and was designed to build up industry in and around the capital city and away from vulnerable national frontiers. The COP contained around 15 per cent of Polish territory and a population of five million, but by 1937–38 it accounted for more than 25 per cent of all public investment and over 50 per cent the following year. (The scheme also benefited from a 2250 million franc loan from its ally France under the Treaty of Rambouillet – a generous act on the part of France given the upheavals under way in the French economy at the time.) By September 1939 the state owned over 100 industrial enterprises, including 80 per cent of the chemical industry, 40 per cent of iron and steel production, as well as 95 per cent of merchant shipping and all transportation networks. Poland had the highest level of state ownership of any country in Europe barring the USSR, and a number of authors have pointed to the strain this exerted on the Polish economy and society. Moreover, agriculture was largely neglected. In Bulgaria, where defence did not take such a high priority in government planning, there were even grandiose plans for 'electrified' peasant villages, connected by a network of railways, each with a 'hall of popular culture' and a silo store. The beginnings of recovery, however, did not solve the political problems of central and eastern Europe. The growing intolerance towards Jews, Gypsies, Communists and other so-called 'non-nationals' that permeated the nationalist 'war' for recovery was especially troubling. There were also widespread allegations of corruption against officials charged with administering the national recovery programmes.

There is still a good deal about the history of this region's political economy to be learned, but it has long been clear that strategies adopted to fight the depression neither helped secure the smaller countries of central and eastern Europe from their ambitious neighbours – Germany and the USSR – nor assisted the development of their economies in the long run. The gap between east and west widened during the 1930s, while the constraints of financial orthodoxy remained strong. Industry and agriculture were shielded from both market pressure and the technological expertise (not to mention capital) of the west that would have forced it to innovate. These shortcomings stored up trouble for the future.

Italy

The years 1935 and 1936 also proved a watershed in Italy. Since 1929 Mussolini had asserted, with characteristic bravado, that Italy was immune to the effects of the world crisis and claimed all the nations of the world were crying out in chorus, 'if only we had a Mussolini here'.[4] But, despite the grandiose boasts, by 1934 unemployment embraced at least 15 per cent of the industrial workforce. The regime's response to the ever tightening grip of deflation on its economy was to expand upon policies adopted in the 1920s: labour unions and factory councils remained outlawed, and there was continuous, if often unsuccessful, pressure to reduce workers' wages. Willson, among other historians, has demonstrated other limitations of fascist claims to have 'nationalized' the masses in the workplace. There were also hollow boasts that the process of corporatization – establishing institutions that, in theory, would link employers together with employees in shaping public policy and thereby avoid class conflict and market forces – would modernize the Italian economy and compensate for its fragmentary character. However, workers lost out because these corporate structures mostly strengthened the hand of big business. The cartelization of the Italian economy, under the guise of corporatism, that had been under way in the Italian economy since the mid-1920s was strengthened by a new law passed in 1932 (p. 73). Big business also profited from a variety of legislative and administrative changes, and from the deflationary pressures exerted by the return to gold, which helped to weed out small and weak firms. One of the most important developments came in 1933 with the creation of the Instituto per la Riconstruzione Industriale (IRI), which further strengthened the ties between government and industry. It was set up to manage the stocks and shares that had come under national control when the banks that had owned them collapsed, and still exists today. The IRI came to control all of Italy's steel production, 80 per cent of its shipping lines and most telephone companies. When it absorbed the Istituto Mobilare Italiano (IMI) in 1937, it then also controlled Italy's three largest banks (the Credito Italiano, the Banca Commerciale and the Banco di Roma) too. However, neither the IRI nor the corporations instituted by the fascists produced a redistribution of power in the economy away from the interests of business towards the workers or the state bureaucracy.

Table 7.4   Industrial Unemployment in the Three 'Great' Regions of Italy (estimated as a percentage of labour force)

	North-West	North-East and Central	South
1931	10.9	13.6	9.7
1932	13.0	17.7	13.6
1933	14.4	16.2	9.8
1934	14.2	17.4	12.1
1935	10.3	13.7	10.5

Source: F. Piva and G. Toniolo, 'Sulla disoccupazione in Italia negli anni '30', *Rivista Di Storia Economica*, 4 (Oct. 1987), 355.

Until 1936 the conservative character of fascist Italy's response to the depression resembled steps taken in Nazi Germany: big business profited over the interest of workers, producer goods won out over consumer goods, and every economic advance was shamelessly propagandized. (Of course, the administrative structures set up by the Nazis were also influenced by Mussolini's corporatist legislation of the 1920s.) The corporate framework also managed the distribution of resources, notably the allocation of raw materials and foreign exchange. There were strong echoes of the 'Schachtian' system established in Germany between 1931 and 1936. Indeed, in 1935 exchange controls, quotas and clearing agreements took on a renewed importance in Italy for two principal reasons. The first was the imposition of economic sanctions by the League of Nations in the wake of Italy's invasion of Abyssinia and the extensive economic pressures, and some opportunities, unleashed by colonial expansion into Africa. In 1936 Italian intervention in the Spanish Civil War only increased the shortfalls in foreign exchange and raw material supplies, as over the next three years the Italian War and Air Ministries spent some 6 billion lire (then around £64 million) on aid to Franco's forces. A series of new, extraordinary taxes – on property, share dividends and other sources of wealth – were introduced, but they were not enough to cover the considerable increase in government spending. (By 1938–39 the budget deficit was running at some 12 750 million lira.) To make matters worse, that year there were also poor harvests of olives and wheat that put even greater pressure on both farmers and the balance of trade. These were problems to which the government had no effective answer. Indeed, Mussolini's agricultural policies have been judged largely to have failed. Their only redeeming feature was a fall in the number of Italians employed as day labourers (a political irritant to the fascists), thanks, in part, to the opportunities to work on 'new' land generated by reclamation, one of Mussolini's pet public-work projects.

The war in Abyssinia and Spain brought benefits too. It soaked up Italy's remaining surplus labour – unemployment now fell to pre-depression levels – as government spending increased, notably on military equipment. The demands of the war absorbed the surplus capacity in the Italian economy that had lain idle since the onset of depression; it also generated new capacities, notably in the north of Italy. Yet despite further state intervention, notably Mussolini's claim in 1937 that autarky was now the primary goal of national economic policy, the fascist state never really challenged the autonomy of big business and, unlike Nazi Germany after 1936, its economic policies retained their essentially conservative character. Indeed, it remains an uncomfortable fact that some of Italy's impressive industrial growth after 1945 was thanks to fascist policies.

The second reason why exchange controls took on a renewed significance in 1935 was the pressure recovery and war exerted on Italy's foreign exchange reserves – the same pressures that were at work in the German economy in 1935. One of the government's more colourful responses to the problem was the 'day of the wedding ring', launched in 1936, when the government managed to collect some 400 million lira in gold from its people, carried along by a wave of popular enthusiasm for the invasion of Abyssinia. But taken together, these steps were not enough to shore up Italy's dwindling reserves. Now it was the turn of the Italian central bank to override the rule which insisted gold reserves be maintained at 40 per cent of the currency in circulation. While shamelessly continuing to exploit Italy's membership of the gold bloc for propaganda reasons, the façade of gold standard membership had begun to slip. Unlike Germany, however, fascist Italy opted to devalue the lira officially in October 1936. The timing makes it difficult to assess the impact of devaluation, rising government spending or war in isolation. Zamagni has calculated that by the end of the year the Italian government had resorted to printing money to cover its burgeoning budget deficit – she estimates that by 1937 over 30 per cent of the national budget was paid for this way. By 1938 inflation was on an upward trend. Interestingly, despite the breakdown in Franco-Italian relations over events in Spain, the Italian government opted to peg the devalued lira to the French franc, a currency that was also devalued in 1936.

The End of the Gold Bloc: Recovery in Belgium and France

External pressures, notably the beggar-thy-neighbour effects of US dollar policy, and to a lesser extent sterling's depreciation, also took their toll on members of the gold bloc. The strain was greatest on Belgium and France which, unlike Germany and other members in central and southern Europe, had not acted to constrain the impact of currency flows through exchange controls. The pressure intensified when, on 31 January 1934, Roosevelt opted to stabilize the dollar at a gold price of $35 per ounce (the pound settled at a $5.10 rate). This brought uncertainty regarding the dollar's exchange rate to an end, although FDR refused to rule out further dollar depreciation in the future. Exporters once more began to ship goods held back in the climate of monetary uncertainty and speculators began to buy dollars sponsoring a tremendous capital inflow into the United States. By December 1934 the American monetary base had risen by 14 per cent of its December 1933 level. While all these developments were good news for the American economy, they marked the beginning of the end for the gold bloc.

   Throughout 1934 France rigorously continued to employ deflationary measures, cutting domestic expenditure further and adopting more

Table 7.5   Gold Reserves of the Bank of France, 1928–32 (in millions of francs)

Date	Gold Reserve	Notes in circulation	Reserve Ratio (in percent)
June 1928	28 935	58 772	40.45
January 1929	33 995	62 153	41.28
June 1929	36 625	64 921	44.11
January 1930	42 921	70 399	48.76
June 1930	44 052	72 594	50.19
January 1931	55 510	78 559	53.34
June 1931	56 426	78 927	56.07
January 1932	71 625	84 723	63.39
June 1932	82 100	80 667	75.90
December 1932	83 017	85 028	77.29

Source: K. Mouré, *Managing the Franc Poincaré* (Cambridge, 1991), p. 55–6.

quotas to restrict the inflow of cheap imports, particularly from the United States. Already by February of that year, the competitive and speculative pressures on the gold bloc were too great for Czechoslovakia and it was forced to abandon gold. Next came Belgium. In 1932 the impact of deflation on the economy triggered a series of protracted and bitter strikes across the country, and banks and businesses began to fail. By 1934 unemployment reached 247 698, an interwar high that represented 20.5 per cent of the working population. It was a rude shock for Belgians, who had enjoyed full employment in 1929. By March 1935 devaluation had become irresistible. With scarcely a backward glance, the government of Paul van Zeeland devalued the Belgian franc by 28 per cent. Recovery followed almost immediately. By the summer, not only were many banks and businesses back in the clear, but workers, in the wake of renewed agitation, were able to negotiate wage rises, an improvement in working conditions and a week's paid holiday a year. Measures were also under way to reorganize the financial sector.

Belgium's successful devaluation appeared to strengthen the case put by those who argued that France, too, should devalue. In 1935 in public, at least, France appeared as committed as ever to the gold standard. It was not that, as Sauvy alleged, Frenchmen were ignorant of economics or misunderstood the implications of Britain and America's departure from the gold standard. We have seen how the perception of history shaped the elite, and popular commitment to gold produced a coherent, if misguided, interpretation of the origins of the depression centred on British and US irresponsibility. The result was a redoubling of French determination to make Britain, America and others return to gold, and to play by the rules of the system. (Ignoring, of course, that French authority to press this case had been undermined by France's failure to play by the rules in the 1920s (p. 62).) The international dimension of this policy failed in 1933. Moreover, claiming the moral high ground on gold made it impossible for France to introduce exchange controls. As a consequence, capital continued to leave France for safer havens and bank deposits declined. The trend made life difficult for industry and agriculture. By 1934 government was also having trouble borrowing money, a development that only heightened the pressure for budget cuts to reverse the growing proclivity of domestic investors to hoard capital, and to attract foreign investment back into France. (The same dynamic had shaped Brüning's policies.)

Until the election of the Popular Front in May 1936, successive French cabinets continued to follow the two lines of policy laid down since 1931: trade protectionism and budget cuts. In 1934 and 1935 the right-wing governments of Pierre-Etienne Flandin and Pierre Laval found it easy to get new bilateral tariffs, marketing boards and the like through the Chamber of Deputies and the Senate. However, cutting the rising deficit in the national budget – up from one per cent of national income to 3 per cent in 1933 and 4 per cent in 1935 – was another matter. The strain of pushing legislation to secure renewed cuts in public expenditure took a heavy political toll, prompting 11 changes of cabinet from 1932 to 1936. As Jackson has demonstrated, the constitutional arrangements of the Third Republic and bitter party-political rivalries did not help. Nor did the stance of important interest groups. Although the full story of how interest groups shaped the political economy of interwar France remains to be told, Vinen has shown how history and politics combined to generate a culture where big business pulled in its horns, by restricting output to maintain prices rather than innovate or invest. Big business also lost out in government policy which favoured the interests of small business and agriculture – it did not stop colourful conspiracy theories regarding the former's political power circulating throughout the country. Flandin and Laval increasingly resorted to extraordinary measures to raise additional revenues for the government by borrowing monies from government agencies like post-offices and railways, and setting up new funds to try to entice members of the public with capital to invest it in France (as opposed to hoarding or exporting). Caron's account of the period brings out how, as in 1931 in central Europe, financial pressures induced these right-wing cabinets to increase state-ownership in the economy by coming to the rescue of companies too important to be allowed to collapse. An involvement in transportation featured strongly. Government became the most important shareholder in the Société Air-France (founded in 1933), the Société Nationale des Chemins de Fer (SNCF, set up in 1937), and the Compagnie Générale Transatlantique. Some authors have also identified corporatist tendencies in the French economy.

The government also rescued several banks, notably the Banque Nationale de Crédit. Although the problems for French commercial banks were never to become as severe as they had been for Germany, Austria or Hungary in 1931, their condition did not compare favourably with commercial banks in Britain. As Lescure demonstrates, French citizens, like their counterparts in Germany, continued to lack confidence in the banks after the inflation of the early 1920s. French savers remained timorous. In 1936, for example, the deposits of the Crédit Lyonnais equalled 19 per cent of those held by the Midland Bank in Britain (in 1911 the figure was 89 per cent). France had experienced fewer commercial bank failures in 1931 than many other countries in continental Europe. But after 1934 pressure began to build as the economic and monetary health of the country deteriorated, and by the end of 1935 the government was having trouble paying the bills because it had reached the legal limit of its floating debt. Here Germany's remilitarization of the Rhineland actually worked in favour of the French economy by prompting the Chamber of Deputies to increase the level set on the government's floating debt from 15 billion to 22.5 billion, largely to be spent on rearmament.

In the meantime, however, the domestic political struggle over deflation continued to rage, levels of unemployment spiralled and gold continued to bleed from the coffers of the Bank of France (it lost 3 billion francs in April 1936 and 2.7 billion francs in the first week of May). The timing could not have been more unfortunate. France faced its deepest financial crisis at a time when Germany was moving its economy onto a war footing. By the beginning of 1936, French Treasury officials admitted, albeit in private, that devaluation of the franc was inevitable if the political and economic paralysis over the budget deficit was to be broken. Their preference was for an international agreement in which the franc might be devalued, and then restabilized to make the step palatable to French political and public opinion. France's search for an international agreement to cushion the shock of devaluation was also born of international considerations as the French Treasury believed the franc's devaluation, far more than that of sterling or the US dollar, would trigger further competitive devaluations. Without the restabilization of sterling, there was every reason to fear that the Bank of England would allow the pound to fall to offset the franc's decline, in the same way that the sterling bloc had depreciated by 8 per cent in 1933 to offset the dollar's flotation. The French also wanted to demonstrate their political alignment with the western democracies and there was the other members of the gold bloc to consider. If and when the franc left gold, it was very likely that Switzerland, the Netherlands and Poland, too, would succumb to competitive depreciation.

However, neither Britain nor the United States offered much in the way of constructive cooperation to help France. Britain did provide a loan to help support the gold franc, but like the French loan to Britain in the summer of 1931, it was quickly washed away as pressure on the franc mounted in 1936. Cooperation was hampered for the first six months of 1936 by British reluctance to discuss the restabilization of sterling and American unwillingness to take the lead given the tension in Anglo-American monetary relations. The French expected better of British and US politicians and advisors who, for most of 1935, had chorused as one that France inevitably was being propelled towards devaluation by its ever-weakening economy. The British and US Treasuries calculated that a controlled French devaluation would bring more benefits than trouble to the international economy, but, once again, this recognition did not translate into clear cooperative initiatives. With breathtaking short-sightedness, the British Treasury argued there was no need for Britain or America 'to make any bargain about stabilization in order to induce France to do what was in her own interests'.[5]

The Popular Front marked an important, though by no means clean, break with the past governments in both its composition and its policies. It was not only the cooperation of socialist, communist and radical parties that demonstrated the French Left had learned the lessons of socialism's failure to defeat the menace of fascism in the Weimar Republic; the Popular Front also had a economic strategy designed to exploit the resources of France that currently lay idle, notably its workforce. Prime Minister Léon Blum introduced paid vacations, to working-class acclaim, and promised a 40-hour week without a cut in pay. The measures marked not, as some authors have alleged, the subordination of recovery to the demands of the working class, but the government's determination to soak up excess capacity and to increase demand within the French economy. So, too, were the plans drawn up for public works, government bonds designed to attract the small investor and subsidies for agriculture. However, for all the apparent innovation, historians are broadly critical of the Popular Front's recovery policies, in general, and the introduction of the 40-hour week, in particular. Blum and his advisors underestimated the costs to industry of the measure – it calculated production costs would rise by 20 per cent, Asselain argues the figure was closer to 35 per cent – or to facilitate the redeployment of workers from areas and industries with high unemployment to sectors experiencing labour shortages.

The ideal of the Popular Front had been to reflate the French economy without devaluing the currency. But the results of its first four months in office made it clear devaluation was imperative: levels of production and investment fell yet further, unemployment rose and pressure mounted on the franc. Unlike Roosevelt's New Deal, policy innovation in France preceded currency devaluation, but France could not escape it. It came in September 1936, when the franc was devalued by between 25 to 33 per cent, but not immediately returned to gold. A recovery of sorts followed almost immediately. By January 1937 the value of shares on the stock market was double that of July 1936 and the number of workers needing financial assistance fell by 70 000. But devaluation was not enough to save Blum's recovery programme. By February 1937 innovation in policy was in abeyance, and by May the economy was once more in a tail spin. Historians, for the most part, continue to be highly critical of Blum's failure to achieve a lasting improvement in French living standards or levels of productivity (in the coal industry it fell by 8.5 per cent), although debate has been reinvigorated recently by the econometric analyses of Villa who argues that the Popular Front did help real wages, consumption and even levels of investment in some industries to rise. France's retreat into imperial trade is an often neglected dimension of its policy response to the depression. In the 1930s one-third of all French exports went to its empire, set against levels of under one-fifth before 1929. But the development, like imperial preference for Britain, proved a mixed blessing (p. 195). France's trade balances were consistently in deficit: taking the empire as a whole, French exports in the late 1930s covered only two-thirds of imports, leaving France with a colonial deficit of around £20 million a year.

Schwartz has also drawn attention to the continued financial pressure faced by the Popular Front. Unlike Britain or the United States, devaluation did not bring an end to the withdrawal of capital from France. Indeed, in early 1937 the pressure for financial orthodoxy grew only more acute as the focus of government economic strategy shifted from a preoccupation with recovery to rearmament. Without resorting to exchange controls, government policy had to reflect the mindset of its investors if it wished to attract and maintain investment in France that was vital in the drive for rearmament. (As Parker has demonstrated, speculative pressure against sterling in 1939 exerted a similar burden on British rearmament and opened up questions of how far liberal capitalism was compatible with war preparations.) The policies of Daladier's new government, inaugurated in March 1938, provided the necessary, conservative context. Daladier had proved himself the champion of monetary conservatism in 1933 and was able to divert attention away from the budget deficit with policies designed to appease the middle classes and stimulate private investment. The 40-hour week was quietly dropped, wage and price controls were introduced to prevent inflation and the government mounted a vigorous attack on tax evasion and fraud. The French state also became much more involved in directing production, although we still lack a comprehensive picture of the French economy in the final stages of its war preparations. Daladier's government's anti-communism and union bashing may also have played a role in the return of economic confidence to France – it deployed troops and military discipline to break up an attempted general strike in 1938. There are many bemusing features about life in Europe on the eve of the Second World War. One of them is the way that investors, who had withdrawn their capital from France during 1934 to 1936, returned it in 1938 and 1939 – at a time when war was imminent and the government was engaged in the biggest programme of expenditure and deficit financing since the end of the First World War!

The International Dimension, 1936–39

Aside from the consequences for domestic recovery, the devaluation of the French franc also had important international ramifications. It marked the end of the gold bloc: Italy devalued its currency while the Netherlands and Switzerland abandoned the system, and economic recovery soon followed. As one monetary bloc appeared to dissolve, so another was formed with the announcement of a tripartite stabilization agreement between France, Britain and the United States on 25 September 1936. An agreement between the leading democracies had been reached only at the eleventh hour, when it was clear the franc could no longer withstand the speculative pressures and Britain had come round to the view that while it was not prepared to restabilize sterling, it would, in effect, offer to 'prestabilize' the pound (hold it steady) to facilitate a moderate devaluation of the franc and to prevent a further disruptive wave of currency instability. It was not quite the tripartite stabilization agreement the Popular Front had wanted to sell the franc's devaluation to a largely sceptical public, but it would have to do. So would the fact that, in spite of the deteriorating diplomatic climate, dramatically confirmed by the outbreak of the Spanish Civil War, a prickly Chamberlain refused to endorse Franco-American claims that the agreement was an important step in trans-Atlantic cooperation.

Clarke's claim that the agreement was a success has been challenged by a new generation of historians. The stabilization pact's most obvious shortcoming was that it was not a genuinely joint agreement at all, but rather a set of simultaneous declarations in which each nation pledged cooperation to minimize exchange rate instability and welcomed the adjustment of the franc. In Drummond's words, each government made 'its declaration for different reasons, and each had its own reservations and hidden assumptions'.[6] There was neither the commitment nor the means, by way of a common fund or mutual credit system, to support currency rates, although the agreement did moderate the initial depreciation of the franc and served to solidify the dollar's gold price, providing a nominal anchor for the international system. These considerable shortcomings make it easy to ignore the political achievement. The declarations proved that agreement was possible between the world's leading democracies after years of rancour on monetary and economic issues. Moreover, for the first time, negotiations for an international monetary agreement were dominated from the beginning by Treasury, not central bank officials, a development which marked a new phase in international economic diplomacy. In an effort to present the Axis powers with the spectacle of democratic solidarity, the White House welcomed the agreement as a 'masterpiece of diplomacy and a happy ending to the economic warfare which has been waged by nations which have everything in common'.[7] There was also talk of America initiating a new 'World Recovery Programme', a proposal that re-emerged with the economic missions in Europe of the former Belgian President Paul Van Zeeland in 1939 and US Assistant Secretary of State Sumner Welles in 1940. Of course, US rhetoric surrounding the agreement was overblown, but it did mark a concrete beginning to more fruitful economic cooperation between nations soon to become allies, particularly as the Americans began to demonstrate a political will for cooperation so miserably absent since 1931. Interestingly, it was Britain and France, the weaker economic powers with more to lose and with their security increasingly under threat, which proved to be the more reluctant partners.

British Recovery and the Anglo-American Tariff Agreement

A further, albeit weak, sign that economic relations between the West's 'leading' democracies were improving came in 1938 with the conclusion of the Anglo-American Reciprocal Tariff Agreement. The road to the agreement, from America's first intimations in 1933 that it desired a trade agreement with Britain, through negotiations that opened in 1936 to their successful conclusion in November 1938, was paved with mutual suspicion and recrimination. What had changed to cause Britain to accept the American proposal it had so firmly rejected in 1933? (p. 162). The answer lies, in part, in the strains that began to appear in Britain's, hitherto apparently successful, policy response to the depression after 1936. Since 1931 unemployment had fallen, levels of output and trade revived, and its political system remained intact. Indeed, the structure of the British political economy remained largely unchanged from the 1920s. British industry, unlike its German counterpart, retained its independence, the contribution and needs of organized Labour were recognized by government (witness concerns about wage rates and union activity in planning British rearmament), and the City of London, if anything, found its role in policy formulation reinforced in the wake of sterling's departure from gold. Cheap money and investment from the City formed the backbone of Britain's domestic recovery, while the sterling bloc played a vital role in sustaining trading and financial interests overseas. By 1937 British exports to the sterling bloc had risen to £308.4 million, overtaking its exports to the rest of the world by some £95.5 million. More impressive was the growth in sterling bloc imports into Britain. By 1937 Britain imported over £491.4 million of sterling bloc produce (including 79 per cent of all South African exports and 76 per cent of goods exported by New Zealand).

But by 1936 Britain's persistent trading deficit with other members of the sterling bloc, notably those nations covered by imperial preference, had become something of a worry. As Cain and Hopkins have demonstrated, until then the trading deficit was tolerated by the government, and even welcomed by the City of London, because high levels of imports into Britain enabled bloc members to earn sufficient sterling to purchase financial services such as insurance, pay off their loans to the City and build up reserves of sterling – outcomes that bolstered the power and prestige of sterling abroad. Indeed, this strategy also helps to explain why the City and the Treasury remained anxious that British budgets remained balanced: members in the bloc had to believe sterling was a stable currency and a stable currency demanded financial discipline (p. 133). The most obvious signs of frustration were found among British exporters who were angry that members of the empire bought less from Britain than they sold (enthusiasts of imperial preference had underestimated, in particular, the Dominions' determination to strengthen their own manufacturing industries), and with the decision of members like New Zealand and Australia to link their currencies to sterling at a new, devalued rate.

The sterling bloc also faced new political threats. Aside from the established problems within imperial relations, like Britain's healthy level of food imports from 'foreign' countries like Argentina and Denmark, confidence in sterling began to evaporate as war with Germany loomed. At the same time, developments in Europe, notably the Czech crisis and the failure of appeasement, also forced Britain to face its growing dependence on the United States for imports vital to rearmament and, to a lesser extent, the need for political unity among the world's leading democracies. Politics dictated that Anglo-American relations had to be improved and given the limits on Roosevelt's ability to make foreign policy as he would have wished, a trade deal was the best way to go about it. Secretary of State Cordell Hull took the political lead in trying to secure terms agreeable on both sides of the Atlantic, with Canada playing a pivotal role in negotiations. (Canada also signed a trade agreement with the United States in 1938.)

The Anglo-American trade deal was a bitter pill for Neville Chamberlain to swallow. As one official put it, whatever the value of a friendly America, 'a friendly empire is of greater importance still.'[8] Although hard-bargaining had left British protective tariffs, including the Ottawa agreements, largely intact, few doubted that in the longer term, the price of Anglo-American cooperation would inevitably lead to weakening of imperial preference and British power along with it. The scale of Britain's trading deficit to the Unites States (it imported goods worth £114 million while earning only £31 million) further complicated negotiations, as did the cumbersome structure of the American Reciprocal Tariff Agreement Act, and personal animosities, notably between Chamberlain and Roosevelt, that had festered since 1933. It took a full 28 months for an agreement to be reached. By November 1938, any hope of restraining Hitler with a spectacle of Anglo-American solidarity was long lost. Indeed, in October 1938 the British government's chief economic advisor told a visiting German trade delegation that the European economy 'would be in serious danger if the European Great Powers worked against one another instead of cooperating' because they were 'faced with the ever-growing strength of the American economy'.[9] From Britain's perspective, Germany continued to be the key log in the global economic and diplomatic jam. In 1938 the National Government's position was underlined by the renewal of the Anglo-German payments agreement in July 1938 and its new enthusiasm to conclude cartel agreements with German industrialists to neutralize the threat of revitalized German competition to hard-pressed British manufacturers.

For Britain, economic appeasement was not just about resolving the 'German question', but also maintaining British power in the face of keen competition from the United States. But despite Britain's best efforts, the strategy failed. By early 1939, the likelihood of war and the pressures of rearmament had caused Britain to lose more than half its foreign exchange reserves. The sterling crisis began to bite as levels of inflation rose at home, and international political solidarity counted for little as members of the sterling bloc and Americans, too, tried to sell their pounds. The growing monetary crisis increased British determination to go to war with Germany sooner rather than later. It also forced leading figures in Britain and the United States to recognize that if, and when, war broke out, British survival, and with it any hopes for its ally France and the resurrection of democratic politics across

Europe, depended on Britain's future ability to borrow from the United States. Improving British relations with the American executive and the American people fast became one of the primary objectives of British foreign policy. However, the economic legacies of the First World War and the Great Depression, notably the history of war debts, were not easily overcome. When polled in 1945, after the war in Europe had been won, the American public revealed its belief that both the USSR and China were far more likely to pay back wartime loans than Britain.

Economic historians have long been critical of the Anglo-American Reciprocal Tariff Agreement's (RTA) economic achievements. Diplomatic historians have taken a more generous view, highlighting its value in educating the American public as to the benefit of international trade, in general, and productive relations with Britain, in particular. Scholars of international relations have also identified the Anglo-American RTA as a landmark in the evolution of US economic diplomacy. When taken together with the Export-Import Bank and the Foreign Bondholders' Protective Council, the RTA helped lay the foundations for US leadership of the international economy that dominated the successful reconstruction of the world economy after 1945. Some scholars continue to be puzzled, if not downright hostile, to US determination to barter lend-lease aid in 1941 for a British commitment to abandon imperial preference and the sterling area at war's end. But America's persistent overvaluation of British wealth– what Kimball has called the 'temptation of British Opulence' – too, can best be understood through the lessons of history.[10] While the depression had confirmed the worst fears of British policy-makers who believed they were managing a world-power in decline, to many people, whether American, French or German, it seemed that Britain had secured the best of all worlds in the way it recovered from depression: an economic recovery which preceded that of all other nations; economic isolation with a ready market for its manufactures; and continued dominance of the world stage. The lessons of the history of the Great Depression also dominated Anglo-American talks regarding the reconstruction of the world economy that began in 1939. Despite the grumbling of British officials who claimed they had more pressing matters to worry about, the need for postwar planning, international cooperation and leadership were lessons taken to heart by both sides.

CONCLUSION

TWO POSTWAR ERAS IN COMPARISON: THE LESSONS OF HISTORY APPLIED?

The contrast between the two postwar eras was striking. In the 20 years that followed the First World War, Europe was bedevilled by crises – economic, political and diplomatic – yet the 20 years that followed the Second World War were the most prosperous and stable of the twentieth century. While it had taken until 1928 to recapture the degree of currency stability and levels of international trade enjoyed in 1913, by 1952 not only had western Europe recovered from the war, but national economies continued to grow at an average rate of 7 per cent a year for the next ten years. This contrast between the two postwar eras is all the more surprising given that the economic costs of fighting the Second World War were even greater than the First. Much more was spent on waging war, far more property and infrastructure lay in ruins, and, on a global scale, many more people lost their lives through warfare than in the First World War. Across the world around 60 million people died, a figure which includes six million Jews murdered by the Nazi state.

Once again, the physical and human losses were not distributed evenly. Among the 'great' powers, around whom the conflict revolved, the poorest 'great' power in Europe, the USSR, suffered the greatest loss of life and the highest levels of physical destruction: over 25 million lives, with 25 per cent of its national assets destroyed. In Britain, around 271 000 soldiers and 60 000 civilians died, Yugoslavia sustained between

1.5 and 2 million dead, Germany lost around six million (although this figure is not entirely reliable), and Poland, which was at war longer than any other European power, also lost close to six million of its citizens. As after the First World War, however, and in statistical terms, the loss of physical assets – factories, railroads, bridges, roads and the like – outweighed the cost in human life and, once again, replacing these physical loses was an early stimulus to economic recovery.

Only the United States suffered negligible human and physical losses. Indeed, America was now, in absolute and relative terms, wealthier and stronger than it had ever been before. During the war its gross national product had more than doubled and, in sharp contrast to 1919, by 1945 it enjoyed the military muscle, diplomatic expertise and political will for intervention in international affairs. After its entry into the war in 1941, the United States attempted to provide the leadership and policies to shape the reconstruction of Europe that had been so desperately absent in 1919. Reconstructing and recasting national and international economies was central to American planning for the postwar order. There were new organizations designed to facilitate reconstruction and to create and maintain an open world economy: the International Bank for Reconstruction and Development (IBRD), otherwise known as the World Bank; the International Monetary Fund; and a proposed International Trade Organization. America encouraged revised forms of regional cooperation in Europe too. But some European cooperation emerged independently of state influence between western European businessmen – who, in many cases, also demonstrated a new enthusiasm for the process of Americanization begun in the first half of the twentieth century.

Equally central to the successful reconstruction of the European economy was the attitude of governments which demonstrated a new confidence and determination to manage the domestic economy, and a political will to balance the needs of the national economy with that of the international economy as a whole. The two decades following the Second World War were not to be shaped by a dramatic swing towards internationalism and currency stability as in the 1920s, to be followed by an equally pronounced swing towards currency instability and the virulent nationalism that had characterized the 1930s. Rather, the second postwar era was distinguished by a new balance between the national and the international. Indeed, developments on the domestic front were even more important than international ones in explaining the unprecedented levels of economic growth in Europe after 1948. Not only did the Second World War bequeath beneficial economic legacies for the largest economies in Europe, governments had tested new tools with which to stabilize and facilitate growth in the domestic economy. There were also favourable domestic economic conditions that had nothing to do with government policy.

It is important to recognize two important caveats in the discussion to follow. The first is that – despite the plans drawn on a national and international scale, designed to cope with the chaos at war's end – for the first two years, European economic recovery was precarious. It was only after 1947 that the European economy began a steady, upward trend that was to herald an era of unprecedented economic growth and political stability. The second caveat may seem obvious, but is often omitted from assessments of recovery after 1945: the economic success of the West was built in a divided Europe. By the end of 1947, the Cold War separated the economies of Western and Eastern Europe (central Europe effectively had disappeared). Although Communist-controlled Eastern Europe enjoyed a strong spurt of recovery and growth, this dissipated by the early 1960s. One consequence is that when authors write of two postwar eras in comparison, they are not comparing like with like given that after 1945, some of the most economically and politically troubled countries of the interwar period were no longer intimately tied to the capitalist system of the West.

A New Internationalism

American planning for the postwar economic order began two years before the United States had even entered the Second World War. Britain was America's main partner in this process. From the outset, US policy-makers and advisors, like their British counterparts, were determined to learn the lessons of the interwar period. The point was underlined when President Roosevelt reflected on the significance of the Atlantic Charter, the blueprint of principles for postwar cooperation, announced in August 1941: 'the well-intentioned but ill-fated experiments of former years did not work ... It is my intention to do all that I humanly can as President and Commander-in-Chief to see that these tragic mistakes shall not be made again.'[1] This preoccupation with the lessons of history, unsurprising given the spectacular failure of the international cooperation after 1931, helped to generate a sustained determination on the part of the American government to set up institutions to safeguard not only international peace, but monetary stability and economic cooperation.

Roosevelt, like Woodrow Wilson in 1918, thought in global terms. He argued that both economic stability and national security could only be achieved on a world-wide scale, and that the United States now had to demonstrate clear 'leadership' and 'responsibility' – the new watchwords of US foreign policy – in its economic policies. Europe's repeated criticisms of US 'irresponsibility' on economic and diplomatic issues in the interwar period appeared to have struck home. But plain, old-fashioned self-interest also shaped America's new enthusiasm for internationalism. American efforts to supply Allies overseas, coupled with economic mobilization, had reunited the interests of the US economy with the international economy as a whole. There was a new, powerful constellation of interest groups whose well-being now was dependent on the continued export of US goods and money overseas. In other words, the forces of economic history unleashed by the war also shaped America's postwar economic policy.

In 1944, the systematic examination of the world economy, undertaken primarily by economists from the United States and Britain, culminated in Bretton Woods. This small town in the American state of New Hampshire gave its name to the international agreements signed there between the non-Axis powers that set up the International Monetary Fund (IMF) and the International Bank for Reconstruction and Development (IBRD) or World Bank; an International Trade Organization (ITO) was proposed, but was not established. It proved much easier to reach agreement on monetary questions than on trade because British and American experts held similar views as to how best to 'manage' the international economy. They agreed a new monetary system to be based on fixed, but flexible exchange rates (currencies were permitted to move within a specified range) with the dollar as the anchor currency linked to gold, although it did not work as intended until the late 1950s. The World Bank was given a treasury of $7.6 billion (mostly American) to help rebuild war-torn Europe and to promote economic development in Africa, Asia and Latin America. The IMF's mission was to help countries by offering stabilization loans to control the currency crises that, otherwise unchecked, would destabilize the entire international economy. America's intention was also that these institutions would encourage governments to pursue expansionary economic policies in concert, to prevent another Great Depression. (Its motto could have been '1931: Never Again!')

The issue of trade dominated the early Anglo-American negotiations. Roosevelt returned to a theme first raised in preparation for the World Economic Conference in 1933: the regime's ambition to liberalize international trade. America's commitment to economic international-ism was also influenced by the strategic advantages Germany had accrued through economic nationalism in its preparations for war. As Herbert Feis, the administration's International Economic Advisor, wrote, it was easier 'for the dictators to handle the [diplomatic] crisis than for liberal capitalistic governments whose free market economies leave them open in times of international tension'.[2] American policy was also informed by its conviction that the strengthening of British and French imperial economic links in the 1930s had fuelled the drive for similar advantages by the 'have not' powers. In theory, many individuals in the British government were sympathetic to Roosevelt's and Hull's determination to promote freer trade – they liked the idea of a *Pax Americana* based on the model of the free-trading *Pax Britannica* of the nineteenth century. But, as usual, the British were suspicious of the mismatch between US rhetoric and the reality of its trade policy. The vehemence of America's professed anti-imperialism also made the British government nervous, and the issue was further complicated by British calculations that it would need discriminatory trading practices and currency controls to rebuild its economy after the war. Yet for all the time and effort devoted to the planning for an International Trade Organization to implement tariff reductions on a multilateral basis, the ITO failed, not because of European imperialism, but because American farmers and industrialists would not accept the end to their protection. Congress destroyed the ITO at birth in 1946. Not for the first time, US diplomatic rhetoric failed to reflect domestic constraints and political circumstances. None the less, the proposed ITO was quickly replaced by the General Agreement on Tariff and Trade (GATT) which worked to promote tariff reductions on the basis of bilateral agreements and unconditional MFN.

Although assured of greater political support on both sides of the Atlantic than the ITO could command, the IMF and the World Bank also got off to a shaky start. When they first opened their doors, these institutions found themselves overwhelmed by European demands for reconstruction funds. In 1947, when recovery faltered, the World Bank lent some $753 to Europe as a whole. The loan to France, for example, financed the construction of two steel mills and helped to buy 113 locomotives, 36 cargo vessels, 18 tankers and around 180 smaller craft.

But, for the most part, historians have assessed the World Bank's contribution to European postwar recovery as insignificant. The sums lent to Europe amounted to less than one-twentieth of Marshall aid and the bank found it was unable to navigate its way through the political tensions that surrounded the debate about Europe's future in the early Cold War years. It came to prefer its developmental role in Africa, Asia and Latin America. The early historical record of the IMF is little better. Plans for leading currencies to have pegged exchange rates (rates were fixed but could be moved up or down within an agreed band) and a return to full convertibility came to nothing in the early years. The continued monetary bond between Britain and its sterling area partners, in particular, stymied the American aspirations for western European countries to secure full convertibility with the dollar any time soon. (Echoing the re-evaluation of British power in the 1930s, recent accounts of the sterling area have highlighted how, until the mid-1950s, sterling, not the US dollar, was the most widely used of all international currencies.) In the battle for recovery, foreign exchange rationing remained widespread in Europe and currency crises fairly commonplace as countries struggled to pay for desperately needed overseas imports of food, seeds and machinery, while domestic industries had yet to return fully to a peacetime footing. This tension pushed balance of payments into the red and triggered currency crises: the year 1949 saw countries in the sterling area and Scandinavia, alongside France, Germany, Belgium and Portugal, all devalue their currencies.

The early accounts of postwar European history made great play of the role of Bretton Woods and Marshall aid in facilitating economic reconstruction, in large part because many of the authors were the very government advisors during the Second World War who studied the failure of the interwar economy and helped to set up these institutions in the first place: the accounts by Raymond Mikesell, William L. Langer and S. Everett Gleason and William Adams Brown are all good examples. It was not mere vanity that prompted these authors to place these international institutions and the contribution made by American leadership of the system at the heart of their explanations of the success of the postwar era. These institutions were a genuine improvement on the *ad hoc*, informal and very private cooperation between bankers and governments in the interwar period. Moreover, it is possible, given the tone and content of these early accounts, to view them as *prescriptive* rather than *descriptive* histories which highlight the dangers of what might happen if formal institutions to safeguard cooperation in times of crisis did not exist. When these books appeared the United States government was engaged in 'information' programmes designed to sell the benefits of economic internationalism to the American people.

Indeed, James's recent work underlines the important role played by the Bretton Woods institutions in the growth of the international economy after 1958. Once the task of reconstruction and recovery in Europe was complete and new institutions of western European economic cooperation were inaugurated, the IMF, the World Bank and GATT came into their own. They established a code of conduct, and institutions to safeguard and to promote that code, which facilitated an orderly interaction between nation-states when it came to international economics. It was a far cry from the chaos of gatherings like the World Economic Conference of 1933 intended to facilitate economic cooperation in the interwar period. Although the economic and monetary contribution of the IMF and the World Bank to the international economy did not meet the lofty plans and expectations of its architects, in the first 20 years after the war, these institutions played an important role in smoothing relations between states and in providing a focus for domestic political education. The Bretton Woods institutions also promoted stringent codes of conduct to liberalize international monetary and commercial relations which, when state policy fell short (and it often did), acted as a yardstick against which national performance could be measured and compared.

The early history of GATT was equally unimpressive when set against the more spectacular tariff cuts achieved after 1962, when President Kennedy responded to the creation of the European Common Market by agreeing to across-the-board tariff reductions in order to further liberalize world trade. But when compared to the bitter and frustrated history of negotiations in the interwar period, the achievements of the first set of negotiations held in Geneva in 1947 were considerable. Twenty-three countries, led by the United States but including most of western Europe, agreed to reduce tariff among themselves, to adhere to unconditional MFN and to prohibit quantitative restrictions. In practice, however, imperial preference was not outlawed immediately; neither were quotas. It was recognized among GATT members that quotas were essential, in the short term, at least, to safeguard the fragile balance of payments. Import restrictions were also permitted on politically sensitive commodities, such as fish and agricultural products.

Nevertheless, in 1947, 123 agreements covering over 45 000 tariff items were signed. Significantly, the United States also agreed to deeper tariff cuts than any other GATT member. This seemed only right to the other members given their dependence on US imports and US capital with which to buy them. To western Europe it seemed the United States had, at last, heeded complaints about American protectionism and access to US dollars that bedevilled their relations in the interwar period.

The GATT process faltered in the 1950s, with western European attention diverted by new structures for regional cooperation and the US administration facing fierce lobbying from its domestic producers. After 1962 the path-breaking Kennedy Round kick-started the process again. Industrialized countries reduced tariffs on over 70 per cent of their dutiable imports, and more than two-thirds of these cuts were by 50 per cent or more. Whatever its shortcomings, GATT established a stable and clear set of rules that facilitated negotiations and helped to ensure there was no way back to the divisive trade protectionism of the 1930s.

Even the Marshall Plan, the American aid programme announced in June 1947, is no longer regarded by historians as central to Europe's economic recovery after the Second World War. To meet Europe's urgent need for supplies, its yawning trade deficit and a desperate shortage of dollars, the United States provided western Europe with $12.4 billion. The step was remarkable when compared with the character and the damaging impact of war debts on European and American relations in the interwar period. It was testimony to the United States administration's new appetite for internationalism after the Second World War, although the simmering Cold War also helped to sell Marshall aid, or the European Recovery Program as it was officially known, to the American public. Whereas in the 1930s 'freedom' meant the freedom of the administration to pursue US economic interests as it saw fit; now the White House presented 'freedom' to the American people as one where the United States needed to exercise 'responsible', liberalizing policies in the world economy that would not only safeguard economic growth, but also protect political 'freedom' in countries where it appeared threatened by communism.

Instead, recent assessments of Marshall aid have come to highlight its political contribution to western European growth. Milward took the lead in challenging early economic assessments that Marshall aid was vital to western European reconstruction by demonstrating that reconstruction and investment in western Europe was well under way before the aid was given. However, the generosity of Marshall aid eased European fears of financial chaos and commodity shortages, thereby greatly reducing the chances of new political instability. The flow of US funds into European coffers, in the short-term also enabled certain states to sidestep bitter political conflicts over the distribution of scarce resources that had proved so damaging in the early 1920s.

Marshall aid had important political consequences. The timing of the plan was crucial and not just for the escalation of the Cold War: the US imposed terms on the acceptance of Marshall aid that reflected its own proclivity for free market economics, and strengthened the hand of politicians in continental western Europe who shared the American view against opponents who wanted to extend state intervention in the economy. The economic historian Nick Crafts has also become intrigued by some of Marshall aid's less conspicuous features, notably the scheme providing Technical Assistance that offered technical expertise to European manufacturers and had a powerful impact on the productivity of recipient countries.

The final contribution of Marshall aid to European recovery was also its most durable: President Truman's administration made the coordination of national recovery programmes a precondition for aid. This provision, alongside the European Payments Union (EPU), set up to administer payments under the plan, also helped to foster European integration. New forms of regional cooperation within Europe, very different to those of the interwar period, made an important contribution to European recovery and growth after 1945. The new regional structures also acted as an important stepping stone from the nationalism of the 1930s – reinforced by the need to wage war – to the global, integrated economy championed by the United States.

Domestic Sources of Recovery

Following the Second World War, the rejuvenation of Europe, after the first unsteady splutters in 1945–48, came quickly and durably, in a way that it had not done after 1919. By 1952 postwar reconstruction had largely been achieved, yet once property and goods lost through war had been restored, this did not mark the end of European industry's resurgent growth, as it had done after the First World War. It was rather the beginning. The most important reasons for Europe's recovery and sustained levels of growth in the first years after war's end were neither international nor regional, but domestic. Despite the unprecedented scale of destruction caused by the Second World War, the war also brought benefits which helped to facilitate recovery in the first five years afterwards. In particular, the conflict, far more than the First World War, triggered significant levels of industrial investment, especially in countries that had not been highly industrialized when war broke out. Britain, France, Italy, the USSR and Germany all finished the war with higher stocks of machine tools than before the war had begun. (In Germany industrial investment effectively countered the impact of Allied bombing on the economy.) Moreover, these increased levels of domestic investment were sustained after war's end and were substantially higher than in the interwar period. As the leading American economist of the period, Alvin Hansen, reflected: 'Our capacity to produce $90 billions for war purposes in the calendar year 1943, and at the same time maintain so high a level of consumption, is an amazing demonstration of the extent to which we failed to use our resources prior to the war.'[3]

Levels of research and development in European industry, increased during the war, were also sustained in the post-Second World War period. There were regional variations, however, none more so than in Eastern Europe, where scholars have struggled to measure the nature and extent of postwar recovery because the process was so heavily interwoven with the collectivization of agriculture and industrialization imposed by the forced Stalinization in the 1950s. Indeed, it is worth noting here that of all the 'great' powers engaged in the Second World War, the USSR enjoyed the dubious distinction of being the only nation whose economic performance was not permanently enhanced by the war effort.

Whether on the winning or losing side, the war effort also gave an important boost to the process of 'Americanization' under way in the European economy (p. 70). Indeed, the superior production power of the United States during the Second World War was impressive testimony as to the benefits to be had from centralized, large-scale mass production. The Allied powers were able to out-produce the Axis, in part, because their weaponry was based on standardized products with interchangeable parts, specialized factories and conveyor-belt production. But Germany and Italy only made a concerted attempt to abandon their dependence on small firms of artisans, who took pride in the careful honing of each product, when the war was well under way. Once the war was over, however, the legacy of craft production stood Germany and Italy in good stead. In the civilian economy, it was precisely the mixture of mass production and skilled, flexible production patterns that were needed. (The same was true of Japan.) In the years to come, this advantage was accentuated by advances in information technology. The war also triggered an expansion in the amount and reliability of statistical information available on the performance of the economy. There were many more trained economists in government, and outside it, during and after the Second World War than before 1939.

Perhaps the most obvious contrast between war's end in 1918 and 1945 was the comparative absence of financial uncertainty. The financial institutions in capitalist Europe proved robust and wherever signs of financial chaos appeared, domestic governments, sometimes with US help, acted quickly to stamp it out. In Belgium, for example, the Finance Minister, Camille Gutt, implemented a drastic currency stabilization programme in October 1944, even before the country had been liberated. In September 1945 the Netherlands emulated the Belgian measure by introducing the Lieftinck Reform, supplemented by a policy of price control and continued rationing. As noted above, currencies were not stable, however, new tools of domestic economic management and the regional and international context established by Bretton Woods, organizations for European economic cooperation and the Cold War, ensured that inflation did not spiral out of control, as it had done after the First World War. Where essential, exchange controls were maintained without triggering the rivalry and retaliation that had soured economic relations in the 1930s, and US loans, such as that advanced to Britain in 1949 to help stabilize the pound, were secured.

After 1952 growth was faster in western Europe (as in Japan) than in the United States, with unprecedented rates of growth, sometimes averaging more than 7 per cent a year. In West Germany the transformation became known as the *Wirtschaftswunder* (Economic Miracle), and saw a redefined Germany increase its gross national product from 98 to 162 points between 1949 and 1954. Italy, too, enjoyed its own *miracolo economico* from 1951 to 1965. The process was aided by market developments, including a significant growth in population, and the emergence of a mass-consumer market which created higher living standards and prosperity for all those in work.

There was also a move towards bigger units as the great corporations began to flourish, often as an international force. Of the recovering nations in western Europe, Britain's recovery was the most sluggish, with annual growth rates of around 2.7 per cent a year (approximately the same as that of the USA).

Meanwhile, other trends established during the first half of the century continued: the numbers of farmers continued to dwindle – in Italy the proportion of workers employed in agriculture and fisheries fell from 43 per cent to 14 per cent. The numbers of workers in the tertiary (service) sector began to expand rapidly. In western Europe's boom years, the fastest growing and most prosperous social category were the executive or middle-manager class – in France they were known as *cadres*. Regional differences persisted too. While the wage and standard of living in northern Italy, for example, comfortably equalled those of Europe's wealthiest regions, the poor agricultural communities became progressively more impoverished, with substantial numbers migrating to West Germany to work as *Gastarbeiter* (guestworkers).

When it came to governmental economic policy, there were also strong contrasts with the first postwar period of the twentieth century. Whereas in 1918 the dominant impulse had been to try to recreate the economic world before 1914, in 1945 there was a determination to learn from, but break with, the past. The Second World War helped western European governments to draw new conclusions regarding the importance of educating and training the workforce, and the network of social and political relationships which sustained this process. In short, a social consensus, sometimes also known as the 'postwar settlement', had emerged across Europe. Although its terms differed across countries, it usually involved the acceptance of social reform and a recognition of workers' rights in return for higher labour productivity and wage restraint. In Germany, for example, government investment in its population was directed towards improving workers' skills by way of labour training and apprenticeship schemes. In Britain, by contrast, the determination to distribute 'fair shares' to a people that had sacrificed so much in war was expressed in schemes for universal health care and education.

The postwar settlement undoubtedly contributed to economic growth, notably in Italy, France and Germany. There remain significant disputes in the literature regarding the role of government policy in securing unprecedented growth and very high levels of employment in the first 20 years after war's end. Some authors argue that market failure was not always met by government success. Recent studies of domestic economic policy in western Europe after 1945 underline the constraints on government action, and the importance of finding a balance between market force and administrative policy in their social context. The implementation of Keynesian economic policies in some western European countries, for example, was effective so long as government efforts to stimulate demand affected output and not wages or prices. But once full employment gave workers the power to push up wages and prices, then economic growth began to slow down.

In international politics, the postwar policy consensus in western Europe (usually) also involved support for alliance with the United States. Indeed, the creation of the North Atlantic Treaty Organization (NATO) in 1949, in sharp contrast to the failure of collective security arrangements in 1919, provided a comparatively secure international context in which economic investment could take place. The Cold War did not adversely affect Europe's economic recovery. Indeed, it triggered hot wars outside, beyond Europe's frontiers, notably in Korea in 1950, that generated demand for European produced goods: the State Department placed large Offshore Procurement Contracts in western Europe to strengthen NATO and boost European recovery. The Cold War also produced a system of sorts that helped to stabilize relations within Europe for over 40 years.

A New Regionalism

The new regional institutions that mushroomed in Europe after 1948 provided an important bridge between the full-blown integrated international economy sought by the planners at Bretton Woods and the continued primacy of the domestic economy, especially strong in the first years after the war. The idea of a European Union had emerged long before 1945, but it was only after the First World War – which had exposed the reality of European relations as one of bitter, bloody conflict – that the campaign for a European Union had begun in earnest. In interwar Europe, as we have seen, some steps were taken towards regional cooperation, be it through reparations, like the links between German and French businessmen, or by development of ideas for European union by men like Hungarian intellectual Count Coudenhouve-Kalergi, the French Foreign Minister Aristide Briand and the Belgian socialist Hendrik de Man. But the impulse to cooperate took on a definitive and divisive character thanks to the competitive pressures unleashed by the Great Depression.

The postwar debate over European cooperation was opened by the former British Prime Minister, Winston Churchill, in a speech in Zürich in 1946. However, the real impetus to European cooperation came with the arrival of Marshall aid and the acceleration of the Cold War in 1948. The Marshall Plan prompted a radical shift in US economic foreign policy. Although the United States remained committed to the drive for a global, integrated economy championed by the Bretton Woods institutions, Washington, for economic and political reasons, now advocated economic integration in capitalist Europe. In sharp contrast to the regional structures of the 1930s, which were seen to replace the need for internationalism, regionalism after the Second World War was conceived as a means to ease Europe's re-entry into a liberal world economy.

As noted above, the contribution of the European Payments Union (EPU) to this process has been the recent focus of much scrutiny by scholars. By 1948, the volume of trade between the 16 western European nations and the western zones of Germany which made up the OEEC (Organization for European Economic Cooperation), the administrative body set up to implement the US aid programme, meant they were in debt to one another to the tune of $762 million. At first countries attempted to make payments bilaterally, with the same damaging consequences to trade as those wrought by bilateral agreements in the 1930s (p. 122). An important step forward came with the creation of the EPU by the OEEC in September 1950. The EPU helped western Europe to break from bilateralism by establishing a multilateral clearing system. At the end of every month, each member of the EPU reported its net balances to the Bank of International Settlements, and the EPU ensured that each member country was left with debts and/or credits, not to individual countries, but to the Union as a whole. The system brought a large number of benefits. By ensuring that western European countries could pay one another for their imports and exports on a broader basis, the EPU led to a rapid expansion of intra-European trade and investment, and underlined that western European industrial economies were complementary rather than competitive in their economic structures. Over its lifetime, the EPU settled over $47 billion in debts and credits, banished bilateralism and greatly liberalized western European trade. Indeed, the revival of German trade, as Buchheim has demonstrated, was especially important to western and northern European growth as a whole.[4]

The EPU also served to reinforce cooperative links between the OEEC and other organizations, notably the Bank of International Settlements. Although it appeared paradoxical, the EPU, alongside other regional organizations in Europe, helped to reinforce the drive to internationalism because it established a clear code of conduct (it set strict limits on trade quotas for example) and enabled its members to manage the needs of the domestic economy in tandem with the drive for greater trade liberalization. The very fact the EPU worked so well encouraged its members to believe that the move towards a global, integrated economy was there to stay and that the commitment of fellow members to greater liberalization was genuine.

There were other, positive movements in intra-European economic cooperation, most notably in the creation of a Benelux customs union in January 1948. Although negotiations were difficult, this regional cooperation between Belgium, Luxembourg and the Netherlands removed controls on 90 per cent of trade between the three countries. It was soon mirrored by similar groupings amongst other European nations: Sweden, Norway and Denmark formed a group to the North; in the Mediterranean there were rumours that Greece and Turkey were planning to form a customs union. These associations were intended to promote domestic recovery and afford these traditionally smaller European nations a stronger voice in shaping their future than they had enjoyed in the interwar period. In sharp contrast to the 1930s, regionalism did not triumph over globalism, it now acted as a stepping-stone towards it. Geiger has argued that without the creation of the Common Market, western Europeans might have resisted further trade liberalization through GATT.[5] At the same time, it was the very effectiveness of these regional institutions, that encouraged President Kennedy to initiate one of the most successful GATT rounds in the agreement's history.

From the outset, almost all states in western Europe, as now defined by the 'East-West' conflict of the Cold War, favoured 'functional cooperation' over plans for political federation. This was a pragmatic, evolutionary approach to European cooperation by which collaboration could be pursued in areas of common economic interest. The best example of functional cooperation was also one of the first, the European Coal and Steel Community (ECSC), created in Paris in 1951.

The ECSC managed the production and exchange of commodities crucial for western European recovery and located in Europe's industrial heartland – the French province of Lorraine and the German Ruhr valley. Whereas in 1923 the Ruhr region was a battlefield for Franco-German rivalry whose outcome severely damaged the Weimar's economy, after 1951 Ruhr coal formed the basis of the Franco-German cooperation that was to become the backbone of the European Common Market. The ECSC was supported by the six European powers most committed to greater European cooperation: the Benelux countries, France, Germany and Italy, and helped steel output to increased by 50 per cent. (Britain joined in 1954.)

The institution was also a landmark in European history, for the ECSC established the principle of supranational cooperation under which participating states had to cede authority to a European agency, restricted though it was to the production and sale of iron, coal and steel. A court to settle disputes amongst members was also set up along with an assembly which convened in the European Council's Chamber in Strasbourg. The ECSC, like the EPU, created the right context and framework for future western European multilateral agreements, notably the creation of the European Economic Community (EEC) with the Treaty of Rome in 1957. In the ten years that followed, economic resurgence was particularly impressive within the EEC and this success helped persuade countries of the community's potential benefits. Britain, alongside Denmark, Norway, Sweden, Switzerland, Austria, Portugal, and later Finland and Iceland, had opted for looser cooperation afforded by the European Free Trade Association (EFTA), set up in 1960. But, in time, as the economic benefits of EEC membership were proven, many of these countries reconsidered their attitude toward a common market, .

At the same time as intra-European links were forged, Europe's former 'great powers' were dissolving long-held imperial ties. Germany and Italy, of course, were forced to give up their claims to empire in the wake of unconditional defeat. Indeed, the importance of occupied western Europe to the Nazi war economy had already demonstrated the hollow economic logic of *Lebensraum*, a notion which encapsulated Nazi Germany's conviction that its economy was best served by expanding to the east. For Britain and, to a lesser extent, France, the process of decolonization was more painful and protracted. As we have seen, the economic retreat into empire was an important outcome of the Great Depression. But British dependence on the sterling area had grown markedly during the war, in large part because Britain borrowed extensively from its commonwealth and imperial partners. The accumulation of large sterling balances by the commonwealth members, in particular, (so large they had the power to bankrupt Britain) limited the British government's room for manoeuvre in economic foreign policy. At the same time, the Second World War had proved the worth of empire and at war's end, the maintenance of Empire remained central to plans for Britain's postwar reconstruction for at least a decade after 1945.

By the mid-1950s, however, it was clear the empire was falling apart, evidenced by the loss of political control in territories like India, the growing weakness of sterling (there were three major sterling crises in four years) matched by the faltering performance of the British economy, and the gradual erosion of intra-imperial trading links. In the late 1940s Britain conducted around half of its foreign trade with the commonwealth and other members of the sterling area, and around one-quarter with Europe. By the time Britain joined the EEC in 1973, this position had been reversed, although British trade with western Europe was rising so rapidly in the 1950s that it had already applied for membership in 1961. (This application was rejected.) The political and economic challenges presented by Britain's recoupling with continental Europe, and the demand for new products and new standards of productivity – echoing the tasks before Britain in the 1920s – continued to dominate British history for the remainder of the 1950s and 1960s.

Economic reconstruction and recovery after the Second World War was both flexible and multifaceted in its constitution. There was a new balance between the priorities governing the management of the domestic economy and increasingly enthusiastic participation in the international economy. There was also a greater appreciation of the value of regional cooperation as a bridge between the national and international political economy, and of the benefits to be had from educating public opinion as to the need for cooperation. In all this the Cold War undoubtedly played an important part. Comparing the postwar period to the interwar period as a whole, economic historians are agreed that growth and stability came readily after 1945 thanks to the benefits of regulated exchange rate flexibility, the huge expansion of multilateral trade and institutionalized international cooperation on finance and trade. In Europe the economic lessons of the interwar period were repeated again with the end of the Cold War in 1990. In sharp contrast to 1918, it was striking how nationalist leaders who emerged in post-Cold War Europe, even the most virulent, pledged their unwavering belief in the open, capitalist global economy championed by the United States.[6]

NOTES

Introduction

1. Report of the Preparatory Commission for the World Economic Conference, November 1932, reprinted in *The Economist*, 10 June 1933, p. 6.
2. The Cold War has led to considerable confusion in the literature as to the boundaries of Europe. The term 'central' Europe is now rarely seen, while Eastern Europe begins at Germany's eastern border. This text attempts to be sensitive to this problem without explicitly addressing it.
3. One further point of definition may be helpful here regarding the term 'devaluation'. Today, 'devaluation' is taken to mean the decrease in the value of a currency relative to other currencies, then its restabilizing at a new, fixed level. The failure to refix the currency price on gold is called currency depreciation or flotation. Back in the interwar period, however, any diminution of the legal foreign value of a currency was called 'devaluation', while the process as a whole was called 'depreciation. For the sake of clarity, I have adopted the modern usage throughout.
4. The role played by financial considerations in Britain's appeasement of Nazi Germany is a classic example.
5. See P. Temin's 1989 call, *Lessons from the Great Depression* (Cambridge, MA, 1989), p. 17.

1 Frustrated Expectations, 1919–24

1. J. A. Salter, *Recovery: The Second Effort* (London, 1933), p. xiii.
2. Revised figures taken from N. Ferguson, *The Pity of War* (London, 1998), pp. 294–303.
3. J. G. Williamson, *Karl Helfferich, 1872–1924* (Princeton, NJ, 1971), p. 129.
4. This appears in C. P. Kindleberger, *The World In Depression, 1929–39* (Harmondsworth, 1974, 1987), p. 24, although with a typographical error in the 1987 edition that turns millions into billions. B. Eichengreen's more recent calculations in *Golden Fetters: The Gold Standard and the Great Depression, 1919–39* (Oxford, 1992), p. 85, are based on the 1938 estimates

of Cleona Lewis, which broadly match Sauvy's estimates.

5. J. M. Keynes, *The Economic Consequences of the Peace* (London and Cambridge, 1984), p. 146.
6. F. Nitti, *Peaceless Europe* (London, 1920), p. 21.
7. Keynes, *The Economic Consequences of the Peace*, p. 34.
8. F. Simonds, *How Europe Made Peace Without America* (William Heinemann, London, 1927), pp. 83–4.
9. Keynes, *Economic Consequences of the Peace*, p. 280.
10. S. Schuker, *American 'Reparations' to Germany, 1919–1933; Implications for the Third-World Debt Crisis*, Princeton Studies in International Finance, 61 (Princeton, NJ, 1988), p. 21.
11. C. S. Maier, *In Search of Stability: Explorations in Historical Political Economy* (Cambridge, 1987), p. 191.
12. Cuno's confession cited in Schuker, *American 'Reparations'*, p. 22.
13. F. Costigliola, 'The United States and the Reconstruction of Germany in the 1920s', *Business History Review*, 4 (1976), p. 481.
14. Ibid., p. 478.
15. Lamont quoted in A. Orde, *British Policy and European Reconstruction* after the First World War (Cambridge, 1990), p. 258.
16. W. Guttman and P. Meehan, *The Great Inflation. Germany, 1919–1923* (London, 1976), p. 209.
17. Owen Young quoted in Schuker, *American 'Reparations'*, p. 37.

2 The Price of Stability, 1924–29

1. C. P. Kindleberger, *The World In Depression, 1929–39* (Harmondsworth, 1974, 1987), p. 290.
2. M. Flandreau, 'Central bank cooperation in historical perspective: a sceptical view', *Economic History Review*, 50:4 (1997), p. 735.
3. Sir Charles Addis quoted in R. W. D. Boyce, *British Capitalism at the Crossroads, 1919–32* (Cambridge, 1987), p. 58.
4. Sir Frederick Leith-Ross quoted in D. E. Moggridge, *The Return to Gold, 1925: The Formulation of Economic Policy and its Critics* (Cambridge, 1969), p. 67.
5. Quoted in ibid., p.88.
6. R. Sarti, 'Mussolini and the Italian Industrial leadership in the battle for the lira', *Past and Present*, 47 (May 1970), p. 98.
7. Quoted in R. T. Berend and G. Ránki, *Economic Development in East-Central Europe in the 19th and 20th Centuries* (Columbia University Press, New York and London, 1974), p. 218.
8. I. M. Drummond, *The Gold Standard and the International Monetary System, 1900–1939* (Basingstoke, 1987), p. 38.
9. Moreau's diary extract, 29 July 1926, quoted in A. Boyle, *Montagu Norman: A Biography* (London, 1967), pp. 198–9.

3　A European Revival? 1925–28

1. Some scholars now argue that unemployment levels were larger than perceived, see P. Fearon, *War, Prosperity and Depression: The US Economy, 1917–1945* (Deddington, 1987), pp. 62–4.
2. The German figures relate only to unemployed workers who were members of trade unions.
3. Quoted in J. Noakes and G. Pridham, *Nazism: A History in Documents and Eyewitness Accounts 1919–1945* (Exeter, 1983), vol. 1, p. 17.
4. C.-L. Holtfrerich, 'Comments on Harold James' paper', in I. Kershaw (ed.), *Weimar: Why did German Democracy Fail?* (London, 1990), p. 156–7.

4　Into the Whirlwind, 1927–31

1. Letter from Moritz Bonn to David Lloyd-George, November 1929, Private papers of Moritz Bonn, box 51, Bundesarchiv, Koblenz.
2. H. James, *The German Slump* (Oxford, 1986), p. 161.
3. See, for example, B. Lieberman, *From Stabilization to Catastrophe: Municipal Stabilization and Political Crisis in Weimar Germany* (New York, 1998), *passim*.
4. M. Leffler, 'The New Era and American Foreign Policy', in E. W. Hawley (ed.), *Herbert Hoover as Secretary of Commerce: Studies in New Era Thought and Practice* (Iowa, 1981), p. 169.
5. W. C. McNeil, *American Money and the Weimar Republic: Economics and Politics on the Eve of the Great Depression* (New York, 1986), p. 243.
6. From *Nouvelle Fortune*, quoted E. Weber, *France: The Hollow Years* (New York, 1994), p. 104.
7. Views expressed on 20 Oct. 1927 to Heinrich Köhler, Reichsfinanzminister, and quoted in B. Kent, *The Spoils of War: The Politics, Economics and Diplomacy of Reparations, 1918–32* (Oxford, 1989).
8. Ogilvie to Keynes, 29 June 1932, Papers of John Maynard Keynes, Modern Archives, King's College, Cambridge, A/32/1.
9. Quoted in H. van der Wee and J. Blomme (eds), *The Economic Development of Belgium Since 1879* (Aldershot, 1997), p. 241.
10. Quoted in D. E. Moggridge, *The Return to Gold, 1925: The Formulation of Economic Policy and its Critics* (Cambridge, 1969), p. 88.

5　In the Depths of Depression, 1931–32

1. Speech by Brüning, July 1931, in W. Steilz (ed.), *Quellen zur Deutschen Wirtschafts- und Sozialgeschichte vom Ersten Weltkrieg bis zum Ende der Weimarer Republik* (Darmstadt, 1993), p. 458.
2. L. Magyar, 'The World Economic Crisis', in *International Press Conferences*, 13:26 (1933), p. 559.
3. Aguado has recently discovered important new evidence on the role of

cross deposits in the Creditanstalt collapse. See I. Aguado, 'The failed Austro-German Customs Union of 1931', unpubl. M.Phil. thesis, University of Cambridge, 1999.

4. E. W. Bennett, *Germany and the Diplomacy of the Financial Crisis, 1931* (Cambridge, MA, 1962), p. 126.
5. M. J. Bonn, *Wandering Scholar* (London, 1949), p. 317.
6. *The Economist*, 14 May 1932, p. 1058.
7. Bonn, *Wandering Scholar*, p. 317.
8. The policy of cheap money was reinforced by the June 1932 conversion of the 5 per cent War Loan.
9. Private papers of William Borah, Manuscripts division of the Library of Congress, Washington DC, Borah: 782, speech by Borah, 29 April 1933.
10. The Treasury view cited in I. M. Drummond, *The Floating Pound and the Sterling Area, 1931–39* (Cambridge, 1981), p. 10.
11. Economic Cooperation Administration Special Mission to the UK, *The Sterling Area: An American Analysis* (Washington DC, and London, 1951), p. 26.
12. PRO Cab 27/475, memorandum by Rumbold, 18 March 1932.
13. PRO PRO30/69/679, MacDonald to Runciman, 21 Aug. 1933.

6 Internationalism versus Nationalism, 1931–34

1. Private papers of John Simon, Bodleian Library, Oxford, box 70, MacDonald to Simon, 17 Dec. 1931, 27 Dec. 1931 and 31 Dec. 1931; Private papers of Ramsay MacDonald, Public Record Office, Kew, London, PRO 30/69/677, MacDonald to Simon 14 Nov. 1931.
2. Private papers of Robert Brand, Bodleian Library, Oxford, box 112–3, Brand to Arthur Henderson, 28 Oct. 1931.
3. Quoted in the private papers of Thomas Lamont, Baker Library, Harvard University, Boston, MA, box 107, file 8, Lamont to MacDonald, 13 May 1932.
4. Private papers of Frederick Leith-Ross, Public Record Office, Kew, London (hereafter T188), T188/47, meeting to discuss war debts, 21 November 1932.
5. Private papers of Norman Davis, Manuscripts Division, Library of Congress, Washington DC, box 51, Davis to Roosevelt, 15 October 1932.
6. T188/74, conversation between Acheson and Leith-Ross, 16 Oct. 1933.
7. Private papers of Moritz Bonn, Bundesarchiv, Koblenz, Germany, box 18, memorandum by Bonn, 3 Nov. 1932.
8. Churchill College Cambridge, Hawtrey papers, HTRY: 1/1/6, memorandum by Hawtrey, August 1933.
9. Records of the State Department, National Archives II, Washington DC, SD 550.S1/9, memorandum by Feis, 9 Sept. 1932.
10. T188/55, DPC 11, memorandum by the Treasury, 6 September 1932.
11. Quoted in J. Dizikes, *Britain, Roosevelt and the New Deal: British Opinion* (New York, 1964), p. 65.

12. Roosevelt to Hull, 2 January 1933, *Papers relating to the Foreign Relations of the United States*, 1933, vol. 1, pp. 673–4. The telegram arrived at 8.00p.m. and was made public the next day.

13. T. Ferguson, 'Industrial Conflict and the Coming of the New Deal: The Triumph of Multinational Liberalism in America', in G. Gerstle and S. Fraser (eds), *The Rise and Fall of the New Deal Order, 1930–1980* (Princeton, NJ, 1989), pp. 17–18.

14. Hull's speech to the World Economic Conference, 13 June, 1933, *Papers relating to the Foreign Relations of the United States*, 1933, vol.1, pp. 636–40.

15. *Diaries and Papers of James Warburg*, Butler Library, Columbia University, New York, James Warburg, vol. 3, diary entry of 7 April 1933.

16. Private papers of Cordell Hull, Library of Congress, Manuscripts Division, Washington DC, reel 46, memorandum by Reynolds, 5 August 1933.

17. Quoted in *The Times*, 10 June 1933.

18. Diary of Henry Morgenthau Jnr, 9 May 1933, *Farm Credit Diary*, Book 9, Franklin D. Roosevelt Presidential Library, Hyde Park, New York.

19. Records of the State Department, National Archives II, Washington DC, SD 862.51/3168, communiqué from Hull to Phillips, 11 June 1933.

20. Secretary Lammers quoted in P. Clavin, *Failure of Economic Diplomacy: Britain, Germany, France and the United States, 1931–36* (London, 1996), p. 141.

21. Papers relating to the Ministerial Committee of the World Economic Conference, Public Record Office, Kew, Cab. 29/142, meeting between MacDonald, Beneš and Hymans, 19 June 1933.

22. Ibid.

7 Nationalist Roads to Recovery, 1933–39

1. Quoted in report to Leith-Ross on German clearing agreements, PRO T188/102, August 1934.

2. Ibid.

3. C. S. Maier, *In Search of Stability: Explorations in Historical Political Economy* (Cambridge, 1987), p. 87.

4. D. Mack Smith, *Mussolini* (London, 1981, 1993), p. 171.

5. PRO T188/116, memorandum by Leith-Ross, 11 March 1935.

6. I. M. Drummond, *London, Washington and the Management of the Franc*, Princeton Studies in International Finance, vol. 45 (Princeton, NJ, 1979), p. 2.

7. Papers of Franklin Roosevelt, Hyde Park, New York, FDR:OF 229, Leon to McIntyre, 28 Sept. 1936.

8. Troutbeck quoted in I. M. Drummond and W. Hillmer, *Negotiating Freer Trade: The United Kingdom, the United States, Canada and the free Trade Agreements of 1938* (Waterloo, Ontario, 1989), p. 75.

9. Frederick Leith-Ross quoted in B.-J. Wendt, *Economic Appeasement: Handel und Finanz in der britischen Deutschland-Politik, 1933–39* (Düsseldorf, 1971), p. 526.

10. W. Kimball, 'Lend-Lease and the Open Door: The Temptation of British Opulence, 1937–42', *Political Science Quarterly*, vol. 86, (June 1971), p. 232–59

Conclusion: Two Postwar Eras in Comparison: The Lessons of History Applied?

1. 'Christmas Eve Fireside Chat on Tehran and Cairo Conferences, 24 December 1943' in S. I. Rosenman (ed.), *The Public Papers and Addresses of Franklin D. Roosevelt* (New York, 1950), p. 559.
2. Library of Congress, Manuscripts Division, Private papers of Herbert Feis, box 125, memorandum by Feis, 3 March 1937.
3. A. Hansen, *After the War – Full Employment and Postwar Planning* (Washington DC, 1943), p. 12.
4. C. Buchheim, *Die Wiedereingliederung Westdeutschlands in die Weltwirtschaft, 1945–58* (Munich, 1990), pp. 109–66.
5. T. Geiger, 'Multilateralism, *Pax Americana* and European Integration, 1945–58', in T. Geiger and D. Kennedy (eds), *Regional Trade Blocs, Multilateralism and the Gatt* (London, 1996), pp. 56–78.
6. J. Mayall, 'Nationalism', in A. Danchev (ed.), *Fin de Siècle. The Meaning of the Twentieth Century* (London, 1996), pp. 153–7.

BIBLIOGRAPHY

1 General Histories of the Interwar Economy

The best available general survey of the interwar economy is C. H. Feinstein, P. Temin and G. Toniolo, *The European Economy Between the Wars* (Oxford, 1997). Also useful is R. Munting and B. A. Holderness, *Crisis, Recovery and War: An Economic History of Continental Europe, 1918–1945* (Hemel Hempstead, 1991), although this study omits Britain. F. B. Tipton and R. Aldrich, *An Economic and Social History of Europe, 1890–1939* (London, 1987) brings out the social dimension; while M. Kitchen, *Europe between the Wars* (London, 1992) is probably the best concise survey of the political history of the period. For an introduction into the international economy of the period, J. Foreman-Peck, *A History of the World Economy: International Economic Relations Since 1850* (London, 1983, 1986) is always reliable, although a little dated. For a more up-to-date survey, see A. G. Kenwood and A. L. Lougheed, *The Growth of the International Economy, 1820–1990*, (3rd edn, London, 1992).

2 Studies of the Great Depression

There is no study which focuses exclusively on the history of the Great Depression in Europe. Nor does any single account bring out the political, economic and social history of the crisis in equal measure; the total history of the Great Depression in Europe remains to be written. The dominant perspective is, quite rightly, global. Here, the work of B. Eichengreen is essential. See B. Eichengreen, *Golden Fetters: The Gold Standard and the Great Depression, 1919–1939* (Oxford, 1992), and his summary of current work on the depression, entitled 'The Origins and Nature of the Great Slump Revisited', *Economic History Review*, 45:2 (1992). D. Rothermund, *The Global Impact of the Great Depression, 1929–*

1939 is an excellent summary of its impact on Africa, Asia and Latin America. On the technicalities, I. M. Drummond's short book, *The Gold Standard and the International Monetary System, 1900–1939* (Basingstoke, 1987), remains a useful introduction to the topic. While the central thesis of C. P. Kindleberger's magisterial, *The World in Depression, 1929– 39* (Harmondsworth, 1974, 1987) has been challenged, this remains the most readable account of the crisis. The most recently published study is T. E. Hall and J. D. Ferguson, *The Great Depression: An International Disaster of Perverse Economic Policies* (Ann Arbor, MI, 1998). Paul Krugman offers a spirited defence of 'managed inflation' and relates the crisis of 1929–33 to Asia's Crash in the 1990s in *The Return of Depression Economics* (London, 1999). Studies of trading patterns in the period are in shorter supply. Still useful is P. L. Yates, *Forty Years of Foreign Trade: A Statistical Handbook with Special Reference to Primary Products and Underdeveloped Countries* (London, 1959); and M. Tracy's work on agriculture. See M. Tracy, *Government and Agriculture in Western Europe, 1888–1999* (3rd edn, London, 1989). Important contributions to our understanding of the timing of the crisis have been made P. Temin and T. Balderston, 'The Beginning of the Depression in Germany, 1927– 30: Investment and the Capital Market', *Economic History Review*, 36 (1983). Important, too, are H. James, 'Financial Flows Across Frontiers in the Great Depression', *Economic History Review*, 45:3 (1992); and W. C. McNeil, *American Money and the Weimar Republic: Economics and Politics on the Eve of the Great Depression* (New York, 1986). For a study that assesses the impact of debt and the depression, see H. Fleisig, 'War Related Debts and the Great Depression', *American Economic Review*, 66 (1976); while the liveliest study of the Wall Street Crash remains J. K. Galbraith, *The Great Crash, 1929* (Harmondsworth, 1987).

For further details on the impact and character of the financial crisis of 1931, see H. James, 'The Causes of the German Banking Crisis, 1931', *Economic History Review*, 37 (1984); and R. Glenn Hubbard (ed.), *Financial Markets and Financial Crises* (Chicago, IL, 1991). H. James, H. Lindgren and A. Teichova (eds), *The Role of Banks in the Interwar Economy* (Cambridge, 1991); and C. H. Feinstein and K. Watson (eds), *Banking, Currency and Finance in Europe between the Wars* (Oxford, 1995) are also relevant. For an account of the diplomacy, see R. Bassett, *Nineteen-Thirty-One* (2nd edn, Aldershot, 1969); and E. W. Bennett, *Germany and the Diplomacy of Financial Crisis, 1931* (Cambridge, MA, 1962). Although the Creditanstalt's records remain off limits to researchers, the best study in English is A. Schubert, *The Credit-Anstalt Crisis of 1931*

(Cambridge, 1990). For the sterling crisis, see D. Kunz *The Battle for Britain's Gold Standard in 1931* (London, 1987). For the perspective of the Bank of France on the crisis, see E. Moreau, *Souvenirs d'un Gouverneur de la Banque de France* (Paris, 1954). An important book on the American depression that moves the focus away from the gold standard is E. Wicker, *Banking Panics and the Great Depression* (Cambridge, 1996). Also relevant is M. Bordon, C. Goldin and E. White, *The Defining Moment: The Great Depression and the American Economy in the Twentieth Century* (Chicago, IL, 1998). For a discussion of how the history of the Great Depression shapes current policy debates, see, P. Temin, *Lessons of the Great Depression* (Cambridge, MA, 1989). Also relevant are B. Eichengreen and P. Lindert, (eds), *The International Crisis in Historical Perspective* (Cambridge, IL, MA, 1989); and H. James (ed.), *The Interwar Depression in an International Context* (Munich, 2000). For an example of contemporary analysis which helped to shape the economic order established after 1945, see H. V. Hodson, *Slump and Recovery: A Survey of World Economic Affairs* (London, 1938). Of the older studies, I. Svennilson, *Growth and Stagnation in the European Economy* (Geneva, 1954) is the most interesting and contains a wealth of useful information.

3   The 1920s

N. Ferguson, *The Pity of War* (London, 1998) contains new assessments of the price paid by Europe in the First World War. A. Offer, *The Agrarian Origins of the First World War* (Oxford, 1989) underlines the role of agriculture in the conflict; while G. Hardach, *The First World War, 1914–1918* (London, 1977); and D. H. Aldcroft, *From Versailles to Wall Street, 1919–1929* remain useful surveys of the period. For a study of the diplomatic implications of the financial changes generated by the war, see K. Burk, *Britain, America and the Sinews of War, 1914–18* (London, 1985). For studies on British policy towards European reconstruction at war's end, see A. Orde, *British Policy and European Reconstruction after the First World War* (Cambridge, 1990); and D. Newton, *British Policy and the Weimar Republic, 1918–1919* (Oxford, 1997). G. D. Feldman has underlined the link between the war and the inflation that swept Europe in its wake in, *inter alia*, G. D. Feldman, *The Great Disorder: Politics, Economics and Society in the German Inflation* (Oxford, 1993). G. D. Feldman (ed.), *Die Nachwirkungen der Inflation auf die deutsche Gesichichte* (Munich, 1985) contains a number of very useful essays in English. C.-L. Holtfrerich, *The German Inflation, 1914–1923* (New York, 1986) is another important study. So, too, is E. Boross, *Inflation and Industry in Hungary, 1918–1929* (Berlin, 1994), although there remains considerable scope for additional national studies. For a stimulating, comparative study of the challenge of generating stability in postwar Europe, see two contributions by C. S. Maier, *Recasting Bourgeois Europe: Stabilisation In France, Germany and Italy in the Decade after World War* (Princeton, NJ, 1975, 2nd edn 1988), and 'The Two Post-war Eras and the Conditions for Stability in Twentieth-Century Western Europe', *American Historical Review*, 86:2 (1981). Maier also makes an important contribution to literature on the relationship between the state, the economy and interest groups. See C. S. Maier: *In Search of Stability: Explorations in Historical Political Economy* (Cambridge, 1987), and ed. C. S. Maier, *Changing Boundaries of the Political: Essays on the Evolving Balance between State and Society* (Cambridge, 1987). Also helpful is P. Evans, D. Rueschemeyer and T. Skocpol, *Bringing the State Back In* (Cambridge, 1985); and M. Furner and B. Supple (eds), *The State and Economic Knowledge: The American and British Experience* (Cambridge, 1990).

For an overview of the role played by reparations in European diplomatic and economic relations in the 1920s, see B. Kent, *The Spoils of War: The Politics, Economics and Diplomacy of Reparations, 1918–32* (Oxford, 1989); S. Marks, 'The Myth of Reparations', *Central European History*, 11 (December 1978) and S. Shuker, *American 'Reparations' to Germany, 1919–1933; Implications for the Third-World Debt Crisis*, Princeton Studies in International Finance, vol. 61 (Princeton, NJ, 1988). Important studies of French policy include: S. Schuker, *The End of French Predominance in Europe* (Chapel Hill, NC, 1976); M. Trachtenberg, *Reparation in World Politics* (New York, 1980); and S. Jeannesson, *Poincaré, la France et la Ruhr (1922–24): Historie d'une Occupation* (Strasbourg, 1998). Conan Fischer's forthcoming book on the Ruhr crisis will take a different tack by highlighting the heavy social and economic cost paid by the Weimar Republic. See also his article, 'Heavy Industry, Society and Aspects of Foreign Policy in the Weimar Republic', *Revue d'Allemagne*, 230:1 (Jan.–March 1998). For American policy, see W. G. Pullen, *World War Debts and the Foreign Policy of the United States, 1919–1929* (New York, 1987).

More general studies of America's role in European economic and diplomatic relations are F. Costigliola, *Awkward Dominion: American Political, Economic and Cultural Relations with Europe, 1919–33* (Cornell,

NY, 1984); M. Leffler, *The Elusive Quest: America's Pursuit of European Stability and French Security, 1919–33* (Chapel Hill, NC, 1979); and M. J. Hogan, *Informal Entente: The Private Structure of Cooperation in Anglo-American Diplomacy, 1918–1928* (Columbia, NY, 1977). For a new appreciation of American protectionism, see E. W. Hawley (ed.) *Herbert Hoover as Secretary of Commerce: Studies in New Era Thought and Practice* (Iowa, 1981); while C. Fink *The Genoa Conference: European Diplomacy, 1921–1922* (Chapel Hill, NJ, 1984); and H.-J. Schröder (ed.), *Confrontation and Cooperation: Germany and the United States in the Era of World War One, 1900–1924* (Oxford, 1993) offer details of the first international efforts to stabilize the European economy in the 1920s. The latter, alongside the work of B. J. C. McKercher also questions how far American foreign and economic policy can be blamed for the shortcomings of international relations in the 1920s. See B. J. C. McKercher (ed.), *Anglo-American Relations in the 1920s: The Struggle for Supremacy* (Basingstoke, 1990), and 'Wealth, Power and the International Order: Britain and the American Challenge', *Diplomatic History*, 12 (1988). For an introduction into how research into the interwar period has shaped the appreciation of interstate relations by international relations theorists, see I. Clark, *Globalization and Fragmentation: International Relations in the Twentieth Century* (Oxford, 1997); and J. A. Frieden and D. A. Lake (eds), *International Political Economy: Perspectives on Global Power and Wealth* (3rd edn, London, 1995). Private bankers played a large role in the 'informal' diplomacy of the 1920s. For an introduction to the main personalities and issues involved, see S. V. O. Clarke, *Central Bank Cooperation, 1924–1931* (New York, 1967); S. V. O. Clarke, 'The Reconstruction of the International Monetary System: The Attempts of 1922 and 1933', *Princeton Studies in International Finance*, 33 (1973); and R. H. Meyer, *Bankers' Diplomacy: Monetary Stabilisation in the Twenties* (New York, 1970). R. S. Sayers *The Bank of England, 1891–1944* (Cambridge, 1986) is also helpful. For the other side of Anglo-American cooperation, see F. Costigliola, 'Anglo-American Financial Rivalry in the 1920s', *Journal of Economic History*, 37 (1977). There are fascinating biographies of many of the leading figures, including two of the most intriguing: H. Pentzlin, *Hjalmar Schacht* (Berlin, 1980); and A. Boyle, *Montagu Norman: A Biography* (London, 1967). We still lack a full history of the Bank of International Settlements, set up as part of the Young Plan in 1930. R. Auboin, 'The Bank of International Settlements, 1930–1933', *Princeton Studies in International Finance*, 22 (1955) is the best survey in English. Also valuable is F. Costigliola, 'The Other

Side of Isolationism: The Establishment of the First World Bank, 1929–
30', *Journal of American History*, 59 (1972).

4 Unemployment

British unemployment: the political and social dimensions are discussed
in N. Whiteside, *Bad Times: Unemployment in British Social and Political
History* (London, 1991); and J. Stevenson and C. Cook, *Politicians and
the Slump: The Labour Government of 1929–31* (2nd edn, London, 1994).
R. W. Garside offers an interesting analysis of the evolution of government policy towards the problem in *British Unemployment, 1919–1939*
(Cambridge, 1990); A. Booth and M. Pack, *Employment, Capital and
Economic Policy: Great Britain, 1918–1939* (Oxford, 1985); and S. Glynn
and A. Booth, *The Road to Full Employment* (London, 1987) are also
important studies. On Germany see R. J. Evans and R. Geary, *The German Unemployed: Experiences and Consequences of Mass Unemployment from
the Weimar Republic to the Third Reich* (London, 1987), H. Kramer's es-
say on 'Frankfurt's Working Women: Scapegoats or Winners of the Great
Depression' in that volume highlights the mixed fortunes of women in
the depression, although there is more to be uncovered about the gender history of Europe in the Great Depression. Also invaluable is P. D.
Stachura (ed.), *Unemployment and the Great Depression in Weimar Germany* (New York, 1986). B. Eichengreen and T. J. Hatton (eds), *Interwar
Unemployment in International Perspective* (Dordrecht, 1988) adopts a comparative approach. The literature on the role played by economists in
both the evolution of government economic policy, and the contribution of the Great Depression to the history of economic thought, is
enormous. For an introduction to German developments, see A. Barkai,
Nazi Economics: Ideology, Theory, and Policy (Oxford, 1990); and J. Back-
haus, 'Economic Theories and Political Interests: Scholarly Economics
in Pre-Hitler Germany', *Journal for Economic History*, 12 (1983). An important, recent contribution is N. Tooze, 'Weimar's Statistical
Economics: Ernst Wagemann, the Reich's Statistical Office and the
Institute for Business-Cycle Research, 1925–1933', *Economic History Review*, 52:3 (1999). For Britain, see A. Booth, *British Economic Policy,
1931–49: Was there a Keynesian Revolution?* (London, 1989); and G.
Peden, *Keynes, the Treasury and British Economic Policy* (London, 1988).
R. Skidelsky, *Politicians and the Slump* (Harmondsworth, 1970) remains
relevant, alongside his more recent biography of *John Maynard Keynes*,

2 vols (London, 1983 and 1992), with volume 3 forthcoming in 2000. For a wide-ranging study of the role played by economists acting as government advisors in the depression, see S. Howson and D. Winch, *The Economic Advisory Council* (Cambridge, 1977). C. Uhr, 'Economists and Policymaking, 1930–36: Sweden's Experience', *History of the Political Economy*, 9 (1977) offers details of Sweden, while P. Hall, *The Political Power of Economic Ideas: Keynesianism Across Nations* (Princeton, NJ, 1989) takes a broad, comparative approach. To compare European developments with America, two books by W. Barber are essential starting points: *From New Era to New Deal: Herbert Hoover, the Economists, and the American Economic Policy, 1921–33* (Cambridge, 1985), and *Designs within Disorder: Franklin D. Roosevelt, the Economists, and the Shaping of American Economic Policy, 1933–1945* (Cambridge, 1996).

5 International Economic Relations in the 1930s

In the last ten years, interest in the failure of international cooperation in the 1930s has undergone a considerable revival. For an example of the older studies which emphasise the shortcomings of American policy alone, see L. C. Gardner *Economic Aspects of the New Deal* (New York, 1964); and C. P. Kindleberger, *The World in Depression, 1929–1939* (London, 1974, 1987). For a study which underlines European unwillingness to cooperate with the United States, see P. Clavin, *The Failure of Economic Diplomacy: Britain Germany, France and the United States, 1931–1936* (London, 1996). For details on the World Economic Conference see P. Clavin, 'The World Economic Conference, 1933: The Failure of British Internationalism', *Journal of European Economic History*, 20:3 (1991), and P. Clavin '"The Fetishes of So-Called International Bankers": Central Cooperation for the World Economic Conference, 1932–3', *Contemporary European History*, 1:3 (1992). Also relevant is B. Eichengreen and M. Uzan, 'The World Economic Conference as an Instance of Failed International Cooperation', *Berkeley Department of Economics: Working Paper*, 90–149 (1990). For a contemporary view, see P. Einzig, *The Sterling-Dollar-Franc Triangle* (New York, 1933); while H. Feis, *Characters in Crisis: 1933* (Boston, MA, 1966), although overly critical of American shortcomings, is a lively account of events in 1933, written by one of the Conference's participants. An additional, failed effort at cooperation is detailed in R. W. D. Boyce, 'Britain's First "No" to Europe: Britain and the Briand Plan, 1929–1930', *European Studies*

Review, 10 (1980).

For an insight into how the events and policies adopted in the Great Depression shaped international relations in the run up to the Second World War, see J. Becker and K. Hildebrand (eds), *Internationale Beziehungen in der Weltwirtschaftskrise, 1929–1933* (München, 1980) – some of the essays are in English – and I. M. Drummond, 'London, Washington, and the Management of the Franc, 1936–9', *Princeton Studies in International Finance*, 45 (1979). For further suggestions, see national studies detailed below. Also relevant are I. M. Drummond and N. Hillmer, *Negotiating Freer Trade: The United Kingdom, the United States, Canada and the Free Trade Agreements of 1938* (Waterloo, Ontario, 1989); and R. A. C. Parker, 'The Pound Sterling, the American Treasury and British Preparations of War, 1938–39', *English Historical Review*, 98 (1983). For the French perspective, see S. Bernstein, 'Les Conceptions du parti en Matière de Politiqiué Economiqué Extérieure', *Relations Internationales*, 13 (1978); M. Thomas, *Britain, France and Appeasement: Anglo-French Relations in the Popular Front Era* (Oxford, 1996); and J.-B. Duroselle, 'Notes de lecture: Inspecteurs des Finances et politiqué étrangere dans les années trente', *Relations Internationales*, 13 (1978). On the Van Zeeland mission, see M. Dumolin, 'La mission van Zeeland: Essai de clearing diplomatique de l'appeasement, 1937–1939', *Relations Internationales*, 19 (1984). P. M. R. Stirk (ed.) treats the 1930s as the prelude for cooperation, not war, in *European Unity in the Context of the Interwar Period* (London, 1989). B. Simons offers a comparative, theoretical approach to the failure of international cooperation in *Who Adjusts? Domestic Sources of Foreign Economic Policy during the Interwar Years* (Princeton, NJ, 1994).

6 National Studies

6.1 Britain

Now in its fourth edition, S. Pollard, *The Development of the British Economy, 1914–1950* (London, 1992) remains one of the best introductions to the British economy. Also useful is S. Glynn and A. Booth, *Modern Britain: An Economic and Social History* (London, 1996). S. N. Broadberry, *The British Economy Between the Wars: A Macroeconomic Survey* (Oxford, 1986) is a pathbreaking, macroeconomic survey of the British economy's performance. D. N. Moggridge, *British Monetary Policy, 1914–1931:*

The Norman Conquest of $4.86 (Cambridge, 1972) is the best study of Britain's return to gold, while Britain's mounting disillusionment with internationalism is detailed in R. W. D. Boyce, *British Capitalism at the Crossroads, 1919–32* (Cambridge, 1987). P. Williamson, *National Crisis and National Government: British Politics, the Economy and the Empire, 1926–1932* (Cambridge, 1992); R. Middleton, *Towards the Managed Economy: Keynes, the Treasury and the Fiscal Policy Debate of the 1930s* (London, 1985); and P. Clarke, *Keynesian Revolution in the Making, 1924–36* (Oxford, 1988) offer details of the political, economic and intellectual history of the British depression. (See, also, studies listed under 'Unemployment'.) For an examination of Britain's decision to move to protectionism see F. Capie, *Depression and Protectionism: Britain between the Wars* (London, 1983); and the more recent, *Tariffs and Growth: Some Insights from the World Economy* (Manchester, 1994). Also useful is W. R. Garside, 'Party Politics, Political Economy and British Protectionism, 1919–1932', *History*, 83 (1998). A. Marrison offers a richly detailed study of *British Business and Protection* (Oxford, 1996). Also relevant is T. Rooth, *British Protectionism and the International Economy: Overseas Commercial Policy in the 1930s* (Cambridge, 1993). For details of Britain's new appetite for empire, P. J. Cain and A. G. Hopkins, *British Imperialism: Crisis and Deconstruction, 1914–1990* (London, 1993). The debate has been recently taken forward in, R. E. Dumett (ed.), *Gentlemanly Capitalism and British Imperialism: The New Debate on Empire* (London, 1999); see, in particular, the essay by Angela Redish on the sterling bloc. More details on the economics can be found in I. M. Drummond, *British Economic Policy and the Empire, 1919–1939* (London, 1972), and *The Floating Pound and the Sterling Area, 1931–1939* (Cambridge, 1981). For a taste of how Britain's response to the depression shaped its foreign policy, see R. A. C. Parker, *Chamberlain and Appeasement: British Policy and the Coming of the Second World War* (London, 1993); and A. Trotter, *Britain and East Asia, 1933–7* (Cambridge, 1975).

6.2 Germany

Germany is the best studied of European nations in the Great Depression. Seminal articles by Knut Borchardt on the late Weimar economy have been reproduced in K. Borchardt, *Perspectives on Modern German Economic History and Policy* (Cambridge, 1991). Among the most influential are 'Could and Should Germany have followed Great Britain in leaving the Gold Standard?', *Journal of European Economic History*, 13 (1984). Borchardt's pathbreaking 'Noch Einmal: Alternativen zu Brünings Wirtschaftspolitik?, *Historische Zeitschrift*, 237 (1983) has been reproduced in English and debated by experts in the field, in I. Kershaw (ed.), *Why did Weimar Fail* (London, 1990). The best book on the German depression is H. James, *The German Slump* (Oxford, 1986). See also J. B. von Kruedener (ed.), *Economic Crisis and Political Collapse: The Weimar Republic, 1924–1933* (Oxford, 1990). Balderston has made important contributions to our understanding of the condition of the late Weimar economy and the onset of the Great Depression in Germany. See T. Balderston, 'The Origins of Economic Instability in Germany, 1924–30: Market Forces versus Economic Policy', *Vierteljahrsschrift für Sozial- und Wirtschaftsgeschichte*, 69 (1982), and T. Balderston, *The Origins and Course of the German Banking Crisis, 1923–1932* (Berlin, 1993). Debate regarding the failure of the Weimar Republic recently has returned to a preoccupation with the political reasons for its collapse. See G. D. Feldman, 'Hitler's Assumption of Power and the Political Culture of the Weimar Republic', *German Politics and Society*, 14: 1 (1996).

For an insight into both German economic recovery and its implications for German foreign policy, the work of R. J. Overy is essential. See, *inter alia*, R. J. Overy, *The Nazi Economic Recovery, 1932–38* (2nd edn, Cambridge, 1995), and *War and Economy in the Third Reich* (Oxford, 1994). W. Abelshauser provides a lucid appreciation of both how Germany recovered from depression and the contribution of the German war economy to the postwar *Wirtschaftswunder* in 'Germany: guns, butter and economic miracles', in M. Harrison (ed.), *The Economics of World War II: Six Great Powers in International Comparison* (Cambridge, 1998), pp. 122–76. The contribution by H. E. Volkmann, in W. Deist, *Germany and the Second World War* (Oxford, 1990), contains a wealth of statistical detail. One of the best works on the relationship between industry and the National Socialists' rise to power remains, J. Turner, *German Big Business and the Rise of Hitler* (Oxford, 1987). However, the last ten years has seen a large number of more detailed studies come to light, including P. Hayes, *Industry and Ideology: IG Farben in the Nazi Era* (Cambridge, 1987); and B. P. Bellon, *Mercedes in Peace and War: German Automobile Workers, 1903–1945* (New York, 1990). J. Garraty, 'The New Deal, National Socialism and the Great Depression', *American Historical Review*, 78:4 (1973) is one of the few studies to compare National Socialist recovery with Roosevelt's New Deal. For details of the relationship between Anglo-German economic relations and 'appease-ment', see S. Newton, *Profits of Peace: The Political Economy of Anglo-German Appeasement* (Oxford, 1996); and, still important, B.-J. Wendt, *Economic Appeasement: Handel und Finanz in der britischen Deutschland-Politik, 1933–39* (Düsseldorf, 1971). On Nazi-Soviet relations in the depression, see D. S. McMurray, *Deutschland und die Sowjetunion, 1933–36* (Cologne, 1979). Two contemporary studies of German penetration of central and eastern Europe are A. Basch, *The Danube Basin and the German Economic Sphere* (London, 1944); and A. T. Bonnell, *German Control over International Economic Relations, 1930–1940* (Urbana, IL, 1940). More recent studies include D. E. Kaiser, *Economic Diplomacy and the Origins of the Second World War: Britain, Germany, France and Eastern Europe, 1930–9* (Princeton, NJ, 1980); V. Berghahn (ed.), *Quest for Economic Empire: European Strategies of German Big Business in the Twentieth Century* (Oxford, 1996); and R. M. Spaulding *Osthandel and Ostpolitik: German Foreign Trade Policies in Eastern Europe from Bismarck to Adenauer* (Oxford, 1997).

6.3 France and the Benelux Countries

The best study of the economics of the French depression is K. Mouré, *Managing the Franc Poincaré* (Cambridge, 1991); while H. Clark Johnson, *Gold, France and the Great Depression, 1919–1932* (New Haven, CT, 1997) is a recent addition to the field. J. Jackson offers two excellent accounts of the depression's political consequences: *The Politics of Depression in France, 1932–6* (Cambridge, 1985), and *The Popular Front in France: Defending Democracy, 1934–38* (Cambridge, 1988). J. Asselain's study of the period, *La France en Mouvement, 1934–38* (Paris, 1986), too, is of interest; while P. Villa offers a more positive assessment of Popular Front economic policy in 'Une Explication des Enchaîne-ments Macroéconomiques sur l'Entre-Deux-Guerres', *Le Mouvement Social*, 154 (1991), 213–43. Also helpful is R. Boyce, 'Business as Usual: The Limits of French Economic Diplomacy, 1926–33', in R. Boyce (ed.), *French Foreign and Defence Policy, 1918–1940: The Decline and Fall of a Great Power* (London, 1998) and R. Vinen, *The Politics of French Business, 1936–1945* (Cambridge, 1991). For a more general survey, see E. Weber, *France: The Hollow Years* (New York, 1994). Although dated, the following accounts offer useful details on the broad performance of the French economy: A. Sauvy, *Histoire Économie de la France entre les Deux Guerres* (Paris, 1967); and F. Caron, *An Economic History of Mod-*

ern France (London, 1979). For an insight into how the depression affects French foreign policy, see also J. C. Cairns, 'A Nation of Shopkeepers in Search of a Suitable France, 1919–1940', *American Historical Review*, 79 (1974); and the work of R. Young, including, *France and the Origins of the Second World War* (London, 1996). For the Netherlands, see R. T. Griffiths (ed.), *The Netherlands and the Gold Standard* (Amsterdam, 1988); while H. van der Wee and J. Blomme (eds) offer details of Belgium in *The Economic History of Belgium Since 1870* (Aldershot, 1997).

7 Mediterranean Europe

Here the range of material available in English on economic history, in general, is dwarfed easily by studies on the political, military and social history. For Italy, see V. Zamagni's excellent, *The Economic History of Italy* (Oxford, 1993); and G. Federico (ed.), *The Economic Development of Italy Since 1870* (Aldershot, 1994). D. J. Forsyth offers details of the financial crisis that engulfed Italy after the First World War in *The Crisis of Liberal Italy: Monetary and Financial Policy, 1914–1922* (Cambridge, 1993); while the best study of Italian unemployment remains F. Piva and G. Toniolo, 'Sulla disoccupazione in Italia negli anni '30', *Rivista Di Storia Economica*, 4:3 (1987). For details of Italy's return to gold, see R. Sarti, 'Mussolini and the Italian industrial leadership in the battle for the lira', *Past and Present*, 47 (May 1970). G. Toniolo, *L'economia dell'Italia fascista* (Rome, 1980) is the best study of the fascist economy. For a recent study of the interaction between politics and economics in fascist policy, see P. Morgan, 'The Party is Everywhere: The Fascist Party in Economic Life, 1926–40', *The English Historical Review*, 114:455 (1999). P. Willson offers an interesting insight into gender politics in the period in question in *The Clockwork Factory: Women and Work in Fascist Italy* (Oxford, 1993). Although there is only one study of the Greek depression in English, it is fortunately a very good one, M. Mazower, *Greece and the Interwar Economic Crisis* (Oxford, 1991). For Spain and Portugal, see N. Sanchez-Albornoz, *The Economic Modernisation of Spain* (New York, 1987); while C. Leitz offers a fascinating account of *Economic Relations between Nazi Germany and Franco's Spain, 1936–1945* (Oxford, 1996).

8 Central and Eastern Europe

In the literature on central and eastern Europe (excluding Germany),
the focus is less on the impact of the Great Depression than on questions of agricultural and industrial development in the interwar period
as a whole. Again, the literature in English is limited. The work of I. T.
Berend and G. Ránki dominates the field. See their: 'Economic Problems of the Danube Region after the Break-Up of the Austro-Hungarian
Monarchy', *Journal of Contemporary History*, 4 (1969); *Economic Development in East Central Europe in the 19th and 20th Centuries* (New York,
1974); *The Hungarian Economy in the Twentieth Century* (London, 1985);
and G. Ranki, *Economic and Foreign Policy: The Struggle of the Great Powers
for the Hegemony of the Danubian Valley* (New York, 1983). They also make
a large contribution in the seminal, two-volume study, *The Economic
History of Eastern Europe, 1919–1975*, 2 vols (Oxford, 1986). The following are also useful studies: D. H. Aldcroft, 'Destabilising Influences in
the European Economy in the 1920s', in C. Holmes and A. Booth (eds),
*Economy and Society: European Industrialisation and Its Social Consequenc-
es: Essays Presented to Sidney Pollard* (Leicester, 1991); Z. Landau and J.
Tomaszewski, *The Polish Economy in the Twentieth Century* (London, 1985);
M. R. Jackson and J. R. Lampe, 'The Evidence of Industrial Growth in
South Eastern Europe before the Second World War', *East European
Quarterly*, 16 (1982); J. R. Lampe, *The Bulgarian Economy in the Twenti-
eth Century* (London, 1986); F. Singleton, and B. Carter, *The Economy of
Yugoslavia* (London, 1982); A. Teichova, *The Czechoslovak Economy, 1918–
1980* (London, 1988); A. Teichova and P. Cottrell (eds), *International
Business and Central Europe, 1918–1939* (London, 1983); and D. Turnock,
The Romanian Economy in the Twentieth Century (London, 1986). The
League of Nations produced a large number of studies on the eco-
nomic and social conditions in central and eastern Europe. For a sample
of their work, see League of Nations, *Conference for the Economic Restora-
tion of Central and Eastern Europe* (Stresa, 1933), League of Nations,
*European Conference on Rural Life: Population and Agriculture with Special
Reference to Agricultural Overpopulation* (Geneva, 1939), and League of
Nations, *European Conference on Rural Life: The Capital and Income of Farms
in Europe as They Appear From Farm Accounts for the Years 1927–28, 1934–
35* (Geneva, 1938). Other contemporary materials in English include,
Royal Institute of International Affairs, *The Balkan States: A Review of
the Economic and Financial Development of Albania, Bulgaria, Greece, Romania and Yugoslavia since 1919* (Oxford, 1939). (There is also a survey

for 1940.) See under Germany for details of sources on German economic penetration of the region.

9 Scandinavia

Again, the range of literature available in English is limited. When not
focused on the specific question of how far Scandinavia adopted original policies to deal with the crisis, the predominant approach is a
general one. Of relevance are: B. Gusttafsson, 'A Perennial of Doctri-
nal History: Keynes and the Stockholm School', *Economy and History*,
16 (1973); F. Hodne, *The Norwegian Economy in the Twentieth Century*
(London, 1983); H. Johansen, *The Danish Economy in the Twentieth Century* (London, 1987); L. Jonung and R. Ohlsson (eds), *The Economic
Development of Sweden Since 1870* (London, 1997); A. Lindbeck, *Swedish
Economic Policy* (London, 1975); and D. Winch, 'The Keynsians Revolution in Sweden', *Journal of Political Economy*, 74:2 (1966).

10 Postwar Recovery

Here the literature is enormous. M. Harrison (ed.), *The Economics of
World War II: Six Great Powers in International Comparison* (Cambridge,
1998) examines the economic impact of the war and its consequences
for postwar stability. C. Maier, 'The Two Post-war Eras and the Conditions for Stability in Twentieth-Century Western Europe', *American
Historical Review*, 86 (1981) is a stimulating comparison of the inter-
and post-Second World War periods. The most important, recent accounts of economic stabilization and growth in the postwar period are:
B. Eichengreen (ed.), *Europe's Postwar Recovery* (Cambridge, 1995); N.
Crafts, 'The Golden Age of Economic Growth in Western Europe, 1950–
73', *Economic History Review*, 48:3, (Aug. 1995); A. Milward, *The
Reconstruction of Western Europe, 1945–51* (London, 1984); and H. James,
International Monetary Cooperation Since Bretton Woods (Washington DC,
1996). H. Van Der Wee, *Prosperity and Upheaval: The World Economy,
1945–1980*, (Harmondsworth, 1987) continues to be one of the most
readable surveys that, in part, explores the relationship between postwar Europe and the rest of the world. Older studies, which reveal as
much about the mindset of American policy-makers in the early 1950s
as they do the history of the interwar period, include: R. Mikesell, *United*

States Economic Policy and International Relations (New York, 1952); W. L. Langer and S. Everett Gleason, *The Challenge to Isolation: The World Crisis of 1937–40 and American Foreign Policy* (New York, 1964); and W. A. Brown, *The United States and the Restoration of World Trade* (Washington DC, 1950).

INDEX